ONLY IN
PARIS

Duncan J. D. Smith

ONLY IN
PARIS

A Guide to Unique Locations,
Hidden Corners and Unusual Objects

Photographs by
Duncan J. D. Smith

The
Urban
Explorer

For those who love Paris

Above: Fragrant roses at the Musée de la Vie Romantique off Rue Chaptal (see no. 51)

Page 2: The glorious stained glass cupola of Au Printemps on Boulevard Haussmann (see no. 91)

Contents

Introduction   9

CITY CENTRE (Right Bank)
1st Arrondissement Louvre, 2nd Arrondissement Bourse,
3rd Arrondissement Temple, 4th Arrondissement Hôtel-de-Ville

1	These Shops are Different!	11
2	Living Art and Artists	13
3	The Duluc Detectives	15
4	Paris by Covered Passage	17
5	Da Vinci's Other Masterpiece	20
6	A Haven for Book Lovers	22
7	Egypt on the Seine	24
8	The Original Statue of Liberty	26
9	Little Wenzhou and Chinatown	28
10	The Oldest House in Paris	31
11	A Market for Everyone	33
12	The Most Extraordinary Museum in Paris	35
13	From the Parisii to Proust	37
14	In Paris Pletzl	39
15	Through Quiet Cloisters	41
16	On the Way of Saint James	44
17	Descent into a Gothic Underworld	46
18	A Truly Magical Museum	48
19	What Remains of the Bastille?	50
20	Where the Hashish Club Met	53
21	The Seven Walls of Paris	55
22	The Real Hunchback of Notre-Dame	59
23	Saint Vincent and the Crown of Thorns	61

CITY CENTRE (Left Bank)
5th Arrondissement Panthéon, 6th Arrondissement Luxembourg,
7th Arrondissement Palais-Bourbon

24	An Historic Jazz Cellar	64
25	House Signs and Street Names	66

26 The Lady and the Unicorn 68
27 Journey to the Centre of the Earth 70
28 An Englishman and his Fountains 72
29 Mint Tea Beneath a Minaret 74
30 The Ruins of Roman Lutetia 77
31 Extraordinary Events in the Panthéon 80
32 Illustrated Histories of Medicine 82
33 The Beat Hotel and Other Accommodations 84
34 Zinc Bars and Philocafés 86
35 At Home with Natalie Barney 88
36 The Best Bistro in Paris? 91
37 A Revolutionary Form of Measurement 94
38 Some Not So Famous Addresses 96
39 A School for Beekeepers 98
40 A Rich, Restless, Magnificent Life 100
41 The Angel of Nagasaki 102
42 Some Towering Statistics 104
43 A Curious Crystal Skull 107
44 Tout à l'Égout! 110

NORTHWEST SUBURBS
8th Arrondissement Élysée, 9th Arrondissement Opéra,
16th Arrondissement Passy, 17th Arrondissement Batignolles-Monceau,
18th Arrondissement Butte-Montmartre

45 Passionate about Plants 112
46 An Arch and its Secrets 114
47 Mysterious World of the Freemasons 116
48 The Bones of Louis XVI 118
49 The Lair of the Phantom 120
50 A Discreet Armenian Community 122
51 George Smoked her Cigars Here! 125
52 Wonders from the East 127
53 The Home of Art Nouveau 129
54 Monsieur Hulot and Modernism 132
55 Monet's Impression of Sunrise 135
56 Two Thousand Years of Fakery 137
57 Along Flower-Filled Lanes 139

58	Cabaret at Gill's Rabbit	141
59	New Vines for Old Montmartre	143
60	Paris on the Big Screen	146
61	On the Mount of Martyrs	149
62	A Visit to a Hindu Temple	151
63	A Litany of Liturgies	153

NORTHEAST SUBURBS

10th Arrondissement L'Entrepôt,

11th Arrondissement Popincourt, 12th Arrondissement Reuilly,

19th Arrondissement Buttes-Chaumont,

20th Arrondissement Ménilmontant

64	Concealed Courtyards and Secret Squares	155
65	Illuminating the City of Light	158
66	In the Sparrow's Nest	160
67	Like an Army of Shadows	162
68	Paris at Work	164
69	Peace amongst the Gravestones	167
70	Hagia Sophia in Miniature	169
71	All the Fun of the Fair	171
72	On Colonialism and Immigration	173
73	The Curse of Vincennes	175
74	Navigating Saint Martin's Canal	177
75	The Little Hills of Paris	179
76	Remembering Georges Brassens	181
77	The Waters of Belleville	183
78	"To Live, to Die, to Be Reborn"	185
79	Exploring Urban Jungles	188

SOUTHERN SUBURBS

13th Arrondissement Gobelins, 14th Arrondissement Observatoire,

15th Arrondissement Vaugirard

80	Tapestries for the Sun King	190
81	Looking for a Lost River	192
82	An Experiment in International Living	194
83	Dinner Chez Jim	196
84	Entering the Empire of Death	198

85   The Last Prison in Paris   201
86   Paris at your Convenience   203
87   Descent into the Capuchin Quarries   206
88   Putting Paris on the Map   208
89   Heroes of the Polar Seas   210
90   Some Hidden Church Treasures   212
91   Paris for the Bon Viveur   215
92   The Spirit of Montparnasse   217
93   The French Art of Communication   219
94   A Mausoleum for Louis Pasteur   221
95   Russians in Paris   223
96   A Very French Ball Game   226
97   The First 'Lost and Found'   228
98   The Story of a Forgotten Railway   230

APPENDICES

Opening Times   232
Bibliography   237
Acknowledgments   239
Imprint   240

Introduction

> "Paris est un véritable océan. Jetez-y la sonde,
> vous n'en connaîtrez jamais la profondeur."
> (Paris is truly an ocean. Cast the sounding-line,
> but you will never fathom its depth.)
> *Le Père Goriot*, Honoré de Balzac (1799–1850)*

Straddling the River Seine, Paris, *La Ville-Lumière*, is one of the world's most visited cities. It is also one of the most written about. Romantic, revolutionary, and achingly beautiful, it contains myriad places to discover. It is good to know that the famous sights, reflecting the city's 2,000-year-long history, still retain a few secrets. Away from the tourist hotspots, however, there are many less well-known locations, each providing a hidden history of the place. Devotees of the city will agree with the novelist Balzac: the deeper one delves, the more Paris unfurls like the petals of a rose.

This book has been written for the explorer, the *Flâneur*, and for all those who wish to discover Paris anew. A few minutes of planning and a glance at a street map** will get the reader quickly off the beaten track, where they can experience a different city. This is the Paris of ancient ruins and underground worlds, of eccentric museums and idiosyncratic shops, of hidden communities and unusual places of worship.

Some of these journeys are self-contained itineraries, the result of the author's urban odysseys through the city's 20 *Arrondissements Municipaux*, which unwind clockwise inside the *Périphérique*. Others act merely as an *entrée* to broader themes, starting points from where the reader can embark on their own voyages of discovery. It was the poet Baudelaire who opined that old Paris was no more, and that a town changes more swiftly than the human heart. Whilst this may be true it is hoped that the locations described in the following pages will enable the reader to reacquaint themselves with the old Paris, whilst also encouraging them to sample the delights of the new.

Many of the locations are to be found in the city centre either side of the Seine *(Arrondissements 1–7)*. Encompassing both the Marais on the *Rive Droite* and the Quartier Latin on the *Rive Gauche*, these are the city's oldest neighbourhoods, as well as its geographical centre. A similar number, however, lie outside these areas, in both the leafy bourgeois northwest *(Arr. 8 & 9, 16–18)* (notably in Montmartre) and the former industrial northeast *(Arr. 10–12, 19 & 20)* (along the Canal Saint-Martin and around the Cimetière du Père Lachaise). Yet more are to be found in the densely populated south *(Arr. 13–15)* centred on Montparnasse.

Whilst walking is undeniably the best mode when exploring Paris, those with less time available will find the citywide *Métro* network invaluable. Others might opt for an eco-friendly *Vélib'* bicycle – or even a chauffeured Citroën 2CV***! Whatever the mode, all directions have been kept to a minimum, leaving the explorer free to find their own particular path.

So whether searching for the city's best *Bistro*, celebrating with Tamils in a Hindu temple, marvelling at Louis Pasteur's mausoleum, or exploring limestone quarries beneath the Left Bank, it is the author's intention that the reader will experience some sense of personal discovery, and thereby take away a more indelible memory.

Happy Exploring!

Duncan J. D. Smith
Paris – Vienna

---

* Dates given after the names of French rulers are regnal years; those after other personalities relate to their birth and death.

** Most street maps of Paris cover all twenty of the city's administrative districts (Arrondissements) and include Métro routes. Excellent transport maps are available free at Métro stations.

*** www.velib.paris.fr and www.4roues-sous-1parapluie.com

A selection of other locations within easy walking distance is given at the end of each chapter, and a list of opening times is at the back of the book.

1 These Shops are Different!

1st Arrondissement, a tour of idiosyncratic shops commencing with Julien Aurouze at 8 Rue des Halles
Métro 1, 4, 7, 14 Châtelet

When it comes to shopping few European cities rival Paris. All the major fashion brands and luxury labels are here. Unfortunately, this has rendered the appearance of some streets indistinct from those elsewhere. It is therefore reassuring to know that Paris retains many idiosyncratic specialist retailers staffed by knowledgeable people, passionate about their products.

Stuffed rats in the window of the pest control shop Julien Aurouze on Rue des Halles

Take for instance Julien Aurouze at 8 Rue des Halles (1st). Since 1872 it has been the city's specialist in pest control. This is the place to come for your mouse traps, insecticides, and disinfectants. Indeed, it is worth visiting just to marvel at the stuffed rats hanging in the window! The taxidermist theme is continued by Deyrolle at 46 Rue du Bac (7th), which was established in 1831 by Jean-Baptiste Deyrolle, a keen entomologist. Part shop, part museum it is an extraordinary place where household accessories rub shoulders with a menagerie of stuffed animals.

Unsurprisingly, many specialist shops in Paris are dedicated to the finer things in life. Goyard, for example, at 233 Rue Saint-Honoré (1st) has been making luggage since the 1850s. On display is a steamer trunk made for Sir Arthur Conan Doyle, incorporating a clock, barometer, and thermometer. M. G. W. Segas at 34 Passage Jouffroy (9th) specialises in antique walking sticks, whilst Heurtault at 85 Avenue Daumesnil (12th) is the place for hand-embroidered parasols. For French crystal there is the glittering La Maison de Baccarat at 11 Place des États-Unis (16th), with a museum containing the brandy decanters commissioned by Prince Rainier of Monaco, when he married Grace Kelly. Cooks, meanwhile, will adore old fashioned kitchenware specialist E. Dehillerin at 18–20 Rue Coquillière (1st) selling everything from copper pans to duck presses. Even candles come with a pedigree in Paris as witnessed by the shop Cire Trudon at 78 Rue du Seine (6th). Established in 1643 it famously supplied the court of Louis XIV (1643–1715) with candles and today offers burning busts of Napoleon!

Continuing in a leisurely manner there is Detaille 1905 at 10 Rue Saint-Lazaire (9th). This elegant cosmetics shop was established a century ago by a countess, who disliked her skin drying out whilst driving one of the first motorcars in Paris. Equally venerable is Cassegrain at 422 Rue Saint-Honoré (8th), which supplies engraved personal stationery, and for the fountain pens to go with it there is no better place than Elysées Stylos Marbeuf at 40 Rue Marbeuf (8th). Perhaps one was used to inscribe the historic autographs on sale at Librairie de l'Abbaye-Pinault at 27 Rue Bonaparte (6th)? They sometimes include examples by Winston Churchill, who would have approved of À la Civette at 157 Rue Saint-Honoré (1st), where cigars have been purveyed since 1716 (the shop features a walk-in humidor). Pipe smokers will enjoy the old fashioned surroundings of Au Caïd at 12 Rue de la Sorbonne (5th).

There is every type of clothing shop in Paris, from the city's *Dépôt Ventes*, which sell the previous season's designer fashions second-hand, to bespoke suppliers such as Charvet at 28 Place Vendôme (1st) – probably the only shirt maker in the world to offer 300 shades of white – and the corset-maker François Tamarin at 1 Rue Marcel Sembat (18th), who is a member of an elite group of professionals called the Meilleurs Ouvriers de France. For scarves and other fashion accoutrements visit Hermès at 17 Rue de Sèvres (6th), housed inside a former *Art Deco* swimming pool.

Paris also contains some wonderfully old-fashioned toyshops, including Pain d'Épices at 29–33 Passage Jouffroy (9th). For real antique toys make an appointment to visit La Tortue Electrique at 7 Rue Frédéric Sauton (5th), with its tin-plate cars and vintage board games. And for the widest range of stuffed toys Toute en Peluche at 39 Rue Raymond Losserand (14th) is a must, offering everything from teddy bears and dogs to owls and even cockroaches! As its owner says, when there are problems in society people need something soft to hold onto.

When the shopping gets too much retreat to the Grande Herboristerie Parisienne de la Place Clichy at 87 Rue d'Amsterdam (9th), where white-coated pharmacists have dispensed herbal remedies since 1880. Alternatively, try Produits des Monastères at 10 Rue des Barres (4th), where veiled nuns in blue habits proffer goods manufactured in the monasteries and convents of the French countryside.

Other places of interest nearby: 2, 3, 15, 16

2   Living Art and Artists

1st Arrondisement, a tour of artists' studios
including 59 Rivoli at 59 Rue de Rivoli
Métro 1, 4, 7, 11, 14 Châtelet

Paris is the birthplace of modern art, and many of the studios where it happened are still in use. Together with the city's more recently legalised art squats they are clear evidence that the artists of Paris are still alive and kicking.

The city's most revolutionary artists during the early 20th century were usually poor, and they found shelter in two unique Paris locations. Initially they gravitated towards the rural slopes of Montmartre, after the former village was absorbed into Paris in 1860. There they occupied Le Bateau-Lavoir at 13 Place Emile-Goudeau (18th), a warren of impoverished studios tumbling down the hillside. From the 1890s onwards the studios were inhabited by the likes of Modigliani, Utrillo, and Dufy. Then in 1904 Picasso arrived and together with Brancusi conjured up the style known as Cubism (see no. 58).

The First World War changed everything, and by the time the artists regrouped they did so in Montparnasse. At 2 Passage de Dantzig

This paint-daubed doorway leads to the former art squat 59 Rivoli

(15th) they occupied equally modest studios in a very different building. La Ruche was a former wine pavilion designed by Gustave Eiffel (1832–1923) for the *Exposition Universelle de Paris de 1900* (see no. 92). It was reconstructed here by the sculptor and philanthropist Alfred Boucher (1850–1934), who divided the structure into numerous studios and rented them out for a pittance. The polygonal form of the building gave rise to its name: the beehive. Between 1912, when Picasso arrived, and 1939, when war once again disrupted the city's creative process, artists including Chagall and Zadkine established the Paris School here. Still used by artists it can be visited by appointment.

There are many other historic artists' colonies that are less familiar. Like La Ruche, some occupy buildings salvaged from world fairs, including the contemporary Cité des Arts at 21 Avenue du Maine (14th). The Cité des Fusains at 22 Rue de Tourlaque (18th) and the studios at 9 Rue Campagne-Première (14th) are located in structures reused from an earlier exposition of 1889. The oldest artists' colony is the leafy Cité Fleurie at 65 Boulevard Arago (13th), built using materials from the exposition of 1878. Rodin and Mailol both sculpted here. In common with other colonies, the artists here were subversives, and as early as the mid-1930s they operated an anti-Fascist library.

Modern counterparts to these historic studios are the city's legalised art squats. The element of reuse is again apparent in that they are located in once abandoned buildings. 59 Rivoli at 59 Rue de Rivoli (1st) is a fine example. Before being squatted in 1999 this onetime bank building had been empty for a decade. With help from the City of Paris it was renovated and the artists' presence legalised in 2006. Visitors are free to peruse the studios, which couldn't differ more from the galleries of the nearby Louvre. As one artist told the author, "That was a different time!" Similar is Les Frigos at 19 Rue des Frigos (13th) in a former 1920s cold-storage warehouse. The interior walls are decorated top to bottom by the many artists who have operated here since the mid-1980s.

There are numerous other concentrations of active artists in Paris. In Belleville (20th), for example, the area's 200 or so artists open their doors to the public for one weekend in May (www.ateliers-artistes-belleville.org). Details of other artists' communities doing likewise are listed at www.ateliersdemenilmontant.org, www.apla.fr, and www.anversauxabbesses.fr. With 184 studios, Montmartre aux artistes at 187–189 Rue Ordener ranks as the largest artists' community in Europe (www.montmartreauxartistes.org).

Other places of interest nearby: 1, 3, 4, 16

3 The Duluc Detectives

1st Arrondissement, Duluc Détective at 18 Rue du Louvre
Métro 7 Louvre – Rivoli (Note: the agency is open for official
business only)

Popular culture has long associated Paris with detectives, from Jules Maigret, the pipe-smoking investigator created by Georges Simenon (1903–1989), to the bungling Inspector Jacques Clouseau portrayed by Peter Sellers. Both characters work for the Paris branch of the Police Judiciaire, the criminal investigation department of the Police Nationale (formerly the Sûreté). Less well re-

Discreet snooping is practiced at Duluc Détective

membered is British writer A. E. W. Mason's fictional Inspector Gabriel Hanaud, who was based on two real-life heads of the Sûreté. Hanaud is usually cited as the first important fictional police detective of the 20th century.

Another fictional French detective is Monsieur Lecoq, created by the 19th century writer Émile Gaboriau (1832–1873), a pioneer of the detective genre. Whilst Gaboriau's sleuth would have a major influence on Sherlock Holmes, his own inspiration was Eugène François Vidocq (1775–1857). This real life master burglar changed his ways to become a policeman, and in 1813 was made the first director of the Sûreté!

In 1833 Vidocq founded the Bureau des Renseignements Universels pour le Commerce et l'Industrie, which is regarded as the world's first detective agency. Assisted by a team of ex-convicts his clients included both business people and private citizens. Although inevitably he made enemies amongst the ranks of the existing Paris police force (Préfecture de Police) Vidocq is still considered the father of modern criminology. He is credited not only with the introduction of undercover investigation but also pioneering work with ballistics, as well as introducing the practice of taking plaster-cast shoe impressions at crime scenes. Vidocq, who lived upstairs at 13 Galerie Vivienne (2nd), claimed never to have informed on anyone who had stolen out of real need.

The home of Duluc Détective
on Rue du Louvre

A glance at the Paris *Pages Jaunes* reveals that today there are a hundred or more detective agencies operating in Paris. One of the oldest is Duluc Détective at 18 Rue du Louvre (1st), which features fleetingly in Woody Allen's film *Midnight in Paris* (2011). It is identified by a green neon sign at first floor level, and a more sombre brass plaque on the door inscribed *Enquetes privées et commerciales filatures*. The agency was founded by Jean Duluc in 1913 at Place Saint-Georges (9th), and was transferred to Boulevard Montmartre by his daughter in the 1930s. It was then purchased by the father of the present owner, Martine Baret, and relocated to its current address in 1945. At the time there were only five private detectives in the entire Île de France, whereas today there are over 300.

The Duluc Détective website (www.duluc.tm.fr) lists the services offered by a modern French private detective agency. With a past success rate of 85% and an affordable hourly rate they certainly offer a tried and tested service. Duluc's passionate staff are available around the clock for a wide variety of work: locating missing persons; spying for companies concerned about employees breaking contracts; assisting worried parents who suspect their children are using drugs; and, inevitably, gathering evidence on cheating husbands for women preparing divorce cases. Since French law prohibits private detectives from carrying arms, searching properties, or interviewing suspects, discreet snooping is the name of the game for the Duluc detectives.

A further insight into the world of the Parisian private detective can be gained by reading the novels of Cara Black (www.carablack.com). Her main protagonist is the female sleuth Aimée Leduc (the name is a homage to Duluc Détective) and each book takes place in a different Arrondissement.

Other places of interest nearby: 1, 2, 4, 5

4 Paris by Covered Passage

1st Arrondissement, a tour of *Passages Couverts* beginning
with Galerie Véro-Dodat at 19 Rue Jean-Jacques-Rousseau
Métro 1 Louvre – Rivoli, Palais Royal – Musée du Louvre,
7 Palais Royal – Musée du Louvre

Until the mid-19th century Paris lacked sewers, proper pavements, and sheltered walkways, which meant that when it rained the streets became impossibly muddy. During the relatively peaceful and prosperous Bourbon Restoration (1814–1830) the city planners of Paris found an answer to the problem by creating a series of covered passages *(Passages Couverts)*. These not only enabled people to shelter from the rain but gave them a place to shop, eat, drink, and even bathe; they also provided women with a public space where it was acceptable for them to promenade. Often made using the new materials of the industrial age (namely iron and glass) they were the precursor of the shopping mall, and by 1840 more than a hundred had been erected. However, with the arrival of the city's first department store, Au Bon Marché, in 1852, their popularity began to wane. Some were destroyed when Haussmann constructed his boulevards but fortunately others remain, either meticulously restored or else left in a state of faded grandeur.

This walk demonstrates how it is possible to get from the Louvre right out to the 9th Arrondissement using *Passages Couverts* for much of the way. It starts at the Galerie Véro-Dodat at 19 Rue Jean-Jacques-Rousseau (1st), an elegant example with skylights, painted ceilings, and shopfronts with neo-Classical façades. The name comes from the two affluent *Charcutiers* who commissioned the passage to capitalise on passing trade between the wholesale food market at Les Halles and the smart shops in the arcades of the Palais Royal. The entrance to the arcades, which were used to such effect in the Audrey Hepburn film *Charade* (1963), is at 5 Rue de Valois, which can be reached by crossing Rue Croix-des-Petits-Champs and walking to the end of Rue du Driant. Dating to 1786 the arcades provided the original inspiration for the *Passages Couverts*.

Leave the arcades of the Palais Royal by Rue de Beaujolais, where at number 9 the writer Colette (1873–1954) spent her last years. From here three very different *Passages Couverts* can easily be reached. Admirers of the *Belle Époque* will delight in the Galerie Vivienne at 4 Rue des Petits-Champs (2nd), with its mosaic floors, stucco bas-reliefs, and leisurely cafés (Jean-Paul Gaultier opened his first boutique here).

Galerie Vivienne is a classic Parisian Passage Couvert

Galerie Colbert at number 6 is over-restored by comparison, and even has a security check (it is difficult to imagine a car workshop existed here as recently as the 1980s). Different again is the Passage de Choiseul, farther along at number 40, which is home to a more modest and perhaps authentic selection of shops and eateries. The poet Paul Verlaine (1844–1896) came here to drink absinthe.

The walk concludes with a trio of semi-connected *Passages Couverts*, reached by exiting the Passage de Choiseul onto Rue Saint Augustin, and then walking eastwards to join Rue Vivienne. The Passage des Panoramas at 10 Rue Saint-Marc was the first covered passage in Paris opening in 1800, and some of its original shop fronts still exist. Across Boulevard Montmartre is the entrance to the Passage Jouffroy at number 10 (9th), the last major passage to open, in 1847. Artist Toulouse Lautrec bought his walking sticks at M. G. W. Segas at number 34 and the wonderful Librairie du Passage is one of the oldest bookstores in Paris. The vibrancy here is in part because of its proximity to the Musée Grévin, which has told the history of Paris in waxworks since 1882. The walk concludes with the Passage Verdeau at 6 Rue de la Grange Batelière, a popular hang-out for book and art collectors.

The elegant Galerie Véro-Dodat offers respite from the busy streets

Other places of interest nearby: 1, 2, 3, 5

5 Da Vinci's Other Masterpiece

1st Arrondissement, Leonardo da Vinci's *La Vierge aux Rochers (Virgin of the Rocks)* in the Musée du Louvre on Rue de Rivoli
Métro 1, 7 Palais Royal – Musée du Louvre

No-one is sure about the etymology of the word 'Louvre' although it might derive from *œuvre*, which finds its origin in the Latin *opera* and *opus* meaning a superlative work. Certainly the sprawling former royal palace, which today contains the Musée du Louvre, has impressive origins. It was completed in 1200 by Philippe-August (1180–1223) as an imposing fortress to protect Paris against invaders (see no. 21). In the 14th century it was converted into a residence by Charles V (1364–1380), and in 1546 reworked in French Renaissance style by François I (1515-1547) to exhibit his collection of Italian paintings. That collection, like the building containing it, has been added to ever since.

The Louvre first opened to the public in 1793 during the French Revolution. It today contains one of the most important and most visited art collections in the world, with extensive holdings of European paintings and sculpture, archaeological artefacts, and decorative *objets d'art*. But for all the Louvre's dazzling variety there is one object that attracts more attention than any other: the *Mona Lisa (La Joconde)* by Leonardo da Vinci (1452–1519). Quite why this small portrait of the wife of a Florentine cloth merchant – the name is a contraction of Madonna Lisa del Giocondo – has become so recognisable is unclear, although many would say it's her enigmatic smile. The painting is so popular that it has been given its own wall in the Denon Wing.

But there is another masterpiece by Leonardo in the Louvre that's every bit as intriguing as the *Mona Lisa*. This is his *La Vierge aux Rochers (Virgin of the Rocks)*, which hangs in the corridor nearby. The first thing to note is that the painting actually exists in two versions (the other hangs in London's National Gallery), which is unusual since the polymath Leonardo rarely found time to finish anything. A likely explanation is that he was first commissioned to create the work in 1483, as part of an altar for the Confraternity of the Immaculate Conception in Milan. Probably completed within three years it has been suggested that because Leonardo was unhappy with his fee he instead sold the painting privately to Ludovico Sforza, Duke of Milan (the painting was then acquired by Louis XII (1498–1515) around 1500). He then took much longer to paint a second version of the painting for the Confraternity, finishing it only in 1508. This painting was eventually purchased by a British art dealer in the 18th century, and in 1880 it was sold to the National Gallery.

The subject matter of the painting is also unusual. Rather than producing a painting alluding to Mary's Immaculate Conception, as was expected by the Confraternity, Leonardo proffered a non-Biblical scene of Mary introducing a young Saint John the Baptist (on whose shoulder her hand is placed) to her son Jesus. The unprecedented setting is a grotto with distant views to a wilderness of streams and craggy peaks. The figures, including an accompanying angel, display Leonardo's mastery of the so-called *sfumato* technique, which

Leonardo da Vinci's mysterious *La Vierge aux Rochers* hangs in the Louvre

Leonardo described as being "without lines or borders, in the manner of smoke or beyond the focus plane".

Equally dreamy is the backdrop, which could be an example of Leonardo's documented advice to budding artists to gain parameters for their work by staring at the marks and stains on a household wall. By screwing up one's eyes the curiously shaped rocks and pockets of sky do seem to give credence to this notion. All in all it's a magical work.

Other places of interest nearby: 2, 3, 4, 6

6 A Haven for Book Lovers

**1st Arrondissement, a tour of bookshops
beginning with Librairie Galignani at 224 Rue de Rivoli
Métro 1 Tuileries**

Paris is a city for book lovers. Despite the advance of new technology there are still a hundred bookshops in the 5th Arrondissement alone, without mentioning the charming *bouquinistes* lining the Seine. New, specialist, antiquarian, Paris has them all.

A superlative example is Librairie Galignani at 224 Rue de Rivoli (1st), which was the first shop on mainland Europe to offer English-language books. During the 16th century the Galignani family helped pioneer the use of the printing press to distribute books to a larger audience. Based in Venice their earliest successes included a bestselling edition of Ptolemy's *Geographia* (1597). In the late 17th century Giovanni Antonio Galignani relocated the business to Paris, where in 1801 he opened an English-language bookshop and reading room on Rue Vivienne. He also launched a daily newspaper aimed at the English-speaking community, with contributions from Byron and Wordsworth.

In 1856 Galignani moved the shop to Rue de Rivoli (1st). Although the publishing stopped long ago, the bookshop remains in his descendants' hands and half of the stock is still English. The premises are a joy to visit with their 1930s-era fittings illuminated by a skylight. There is also a strong arts department created during the Second World War, when English books were banned.

In a recent survey of Europe's most beautiful bookshops the Librairie Auguste Blaizot at 164 Rue du Faubourg Saint-Honoré (8th) was high on the list. The premises of this long-established antiquarian bookseller are everything they should be, with magnificent wooden bookcases filled with rare books, first editions, and volumes with exquisite bindings. Matching display cabinets contain fine illustrations and literary *objets d'art*. The shop was founded in 1840 as the Cabinet de Lecture de Mademoiselle Boisselle, and passed into the hands of the Blaizot family in 1877. Specialising in French literature the shop has been at its current address since 1928.

The most storied bookshop in Paris is Shakespeare and Company at 37 Rue de la Bûcherie (5th). This Anglo-American bookshop has long been a Left Bank institution. It was opened in 1919 by American expatriate Sylvia Beach (1887–1962), initially at 8 Rue Dupuytren and then 12 Rue de l'Odéon (6th). There in 1922 Beach published James Joyce's *Ulysses*, and the shop became a home-from-home for writers such as Ezra Pound, Ernest Hemingway, and F. Scott Fitzgerald. Although the shop closed in 1940 (it is said because a German officer tried to buy Beach's last copy of Joyce's *Finnegan's Wake*) it was reopened a decade later at its present address by another American, George Whitman, who retained the name in tribute to Beach. It is probably the only bookshop in the world to offer beds to budding writers in return for a few hours manning the till! The former inn next door at number 39 with its large dormer windows is one of the last examples of the timber-framed buildings once common in 16th century Paris.

A contented browser in the English Department of Librairie Galignani on Rue de Rivoli

This tour finishes with Librairie Ulysse at 26 Rue Saint-Louis-en-l'Île (4th), a travel bookshop established in 1971. Its owners Catherine and Dominique Domain host the fabled Cargoclub here each first Wednesday in the month (except January) at 6.30pm to which travellers are welcome. As the shop itself is rather small the event takes place outside come rain or shine and attendees are encouraged to bring drinks and nibbles to share.

Not far away at 6 Quai d'Orléans is the Bibliothèque Polonaise, long the centre of Polish culture in Paris. Alongside the letters of Frédéric Chopin is a 16th century edition of Ptolemy's map of what is now Eastern Europe.

To see traditional bookbinding visit Atelier Houdart at 77 Rue Broca (13th), where gold-leaf tooling and marbling are practiced.

Other places of interest nearby: 4, 5, 45, 49

7 Egypt on the Seine

2nd Arrondissement, the Passage du Caire at 2 Place du Caire
Métro 10 Vaneau

Contrary to popular opinion the vogue for things Egyptian that swept Paris around the turn of the 19th century finds its origin *before* Napoleon's expedition to the Nile in 1798. From the mid-18th century onwards budding French artists sent to study in Rome were returning with engravings by Giovanni Battista Piranesi (1720–1778), who believed Etruscan art had its origins in Egypt. During the Revolution the new Republic, as well as the city's Freemasons, incorporated these Egyptian motifs into their own iconography (see no. 47). Napoleon's expedition therefore served only to accelerate an existing fashion.

Under Napoleon (1804–1815) the neo-Egyptian style took many forms, from furniture and sculpture to architecture. The west façade of the Cour Carrée in the Louvre (1st), for example, which was completed by Napoleon, incorporates a representation of the goddess Isis. The Hôtel Beauharnais at 78 Rue de Lille (7th), once occupied by Napoleon's adopted son Eugène de Beauharnais (1781–1824), has a porch based on the Kiosk of Trajan at Philae. Most extravagant is the Passage du Caire at 2 Place du Caire (2nd), a covered passage inspired by the souks of Cairo (it is today filled with fabric merchants). Opened in 1798 it has an entrance decorated with pharaonic-style reliefs and busts of the goddess Hathor, inspired by capitals found in the temple at Dendera. Not far away are Rues du Nil, d'Aboukir, and d'Alexandre, all of which recall Napoleon's Egyptian forays, as does Rue des Pyramides (1st).

The Fontaine du Fellah at 52 Rue de Sèvres (7th) is particularly interesting. Erected in 1806 it is one of 15 fountains commissioned by Napoleon to provide Parisians with drinking water. This one, however, served also to remind passers-by of the emperor's Egyptian achievements. It takes the form of a temple doorway from which emerges an Egyptian clutching a pair of water jugs. Although the word *fellah* means peasant farmer, the figure by Pierre-Nicolas Beauvalet (who also worked on Napoleon's column in Place Vendôme) is based on a Roman statue discovered in Emperor Hadrian's villa at Tivoli. On the lintel is carved an eagle, signifying Napoleon's imperial rule, rather than the usual Egyptian winged sun disk.

Another of Napoleon's Egyptian-style fountains is the Fontaine du Palmier on Place du Châtelet (1st), modelled after a Roman triumphal column, with palm leaves on top. The four sphinxes around the base were added in 1858 by Napoleon III (1852–1870). More than a hundred sphinxes watch over Paris today.

The taste for things Egyptian long outlived Napoleon. In 1829 a 23 metre-high granite obelisk taken from a temple at Luxor was presented by Muhammad Ali Pasha, Viceroy of Egypt, to Charles X (1824–1830), together with a dozen mummies. The obelisk was erected in 1836 in Place de la Concorde (8th), where it now acts as a *gnomon* for the world's largest sundial. The mummies meanwhile were re-buried in the Louvre gardens, where they were joined

Egyptian-style busts adorn the outside of the Passage du Caire

by the bodies of victims of the July 1830 Revolution. Louis-Philippe I (1830–1848) then removed the bodies to a vault beneath the Colonne de Juillet at Place de la Bastille (4th), although it wasn't until later that the inclusion of the mummies was noticed!

A more modest obelisk marks the grave of Jean-François Champollion (1790–1832) in the Cimetière du Père-Lachaise (20th). He established the Egyptian collection in the Louvre, and in 1822 unlocked the mystery of Egyptian hieroglyphics using the Rosetta Stone. His is one of a dozen Egyptian-inspired tombs in the cemetery, Ancient Egypt having long been associated with eternity.

Other places of interest nearby: 8, 9, 10

8   The Original Statue of Liberty

3rd Arrondissement, the *Statue of Liberty*
outside the Musée des Arts et Métiers
at 60 Rue de Réaumur
Métro 3, 11 Arts et Métiers

The *Statue of Liberty* in New York expresses well the American notion of freedom. A gift from France to the United States to mark the centenary of the American Declaration of Independence, it depicts the Roman goddess *Libertas* bearing a torch and a tablet on which is inscribed the date 4th July 1776. Visitors to Paris have the unique opportunity of seeing four scale models of *La Liberté* in the city where she was constructed.

First stop is the Musée des Arts et Métiers inside the former medieval abbey church of Saint-Martin-des-Champs at 60 Rue de Réaumur (3rd). Here stands the original 1/16 plaster model used by the French sculptor Frédéric Auguste Bartholdi (1834–1904) to create the statue in 1875–1884. Models depicting Bartholdi's men working on the statue's five metre-high head, which like the rest of the statue was first moulded in plaster on a wooden frame and then clad with sheets of beaten copper, are displayed in the museum's Construction Gallery. The finished statue, which stands 46 metres high, was then shipped across the Atlantic in pieces, where it was reassembled over an iron frame designed by the engineer Alexandre Gustave Eiffel (1832–1923). The statue was dedicated in October 1886 by President Grover Cleveland.

By arrangement with the Musée des Arts et Métiers a handful of bronzes have recently been cast from the original plaster model, one of which now adorns the museum plaza. It bears witness to Bartholdi's original vision, and acts as a reminder of the skill with which he made the finished statue appear solid by using invisible riveting. The seven rays of the statue's diadem, incidentally, represent the seven continents and oceans.

A much older 1/16th reproduction once stood in the Jardin du Luxembourg but has now been moved to the sculpture court of the Musée d'Orsay at 1 Rue de la Légion d'Honneur (7th). One of five it was cast for Bartholdi on 15th November 1889 (which explains the date on the statue's tablet), who then donated it to the City of Paris for display at the *Exposition Universelle de Paris de 1900*.

The fourth scale model is the largest and most dramatic. Placed at one end of the Île aux Cygnes (15th/16th), a narrow artificial island in the Seine, this quarter-size reproduction was given by the French community of the United States to mark the centenary in 1889 of the French Revolution. The statue's tablet contains the start dates of both the American and French Revolutions. Although the statue originally faced Paris it was turned around in 1937 to face New York.

A final location connected with the statue is a replica of its burning torch in the Place de l'Alma (8th/16th). It was given by the International Herald Tribune in 1989 in gratitude for French workers having recently restored the statue. The torch subsequently became a shrine to Diana, Princess of Wales, who died in the tunnel beneath it in 1997. Prior to the accident she visited the former home of

A scale model of the *Statue of Liberty* outside the Musée des Arts et Métiers

the Duke and Duchess of Windsor at 4 Rue du Champ d'Entraînement (16th), and ate her last meal at the Paris Ritz.

The treaty ending the American War of Independence was signed on 3rd September 1783 at 56 Rue Jacob (6th). One of the signatories was Benjamin Franklin, the American envoy to France during the Peace of Versailles. He also installed the country's first lightning conductor at his home at 66 Rue Raynouard (16th), where there is a memorial.

Other places of interest nearby: 7, 9, 10, 12

9 Little Wenzhou and Chinatown

3rd Arrondissement, the Little Wenzhou Chinese community
on Rues au Maire and Volta
Métro 3, 11 Arts et Métiers

One of the most distinctive communities of *Paris Mondial* – as multi-cultural Paris is known – is Asian Paris. Many of the city's Southeast Asians hail from the former French colonies of Indochina. Some came in 1954 at the end of the First Indochina War, which ended with the division of Vietnam, while others arrived in the 1970s after fleeing the Pol Pot regime in Cambodia; during the late 1970s Vietnamese boat people came after the fall of Saigon.

The events in Tiananmen Square in 1989 prompted the arrival of many ethnic Chinese, too, but their story is much older. During the First World War the French government recruited several hundred thousand Chinese volunteers, many from Wenzhou, a port in the eastern coastal province of Zhejiang, over which France had a concession. After the war some stayed on, settling on the Îlot Chalon, near the Gare du Lyon, where their presence is recalled by a wall plaque on Rue Chrétien de Troyes (12th). Throughout the 1920s and 30s they were joined by artisans from Wenzhou, who came looking for work. After the Second World War the community relocated to the Marais, occupying workshops left empty by deported Jews.

They are still there today, along Rues au Maire and Volta (3rd), where they have cornered the trade in tailoring and leather working, and converse in the Wenzhounese dialect. During Chinese New Year in late January/early February the normally discrete merchants stage a street parade and hang red lanterns outside their premises to bring good fortune. And they may need it because the old buildings of the Marais are gradually being renovated driving up rents in the process, which forces workers to move out to factories beyond the *périphérique*. Should this continue then Little Wenzhou, the oldest and only pure Chinese community in Paris, might be relegated to the history books. Walking slowly through the neighbourhood today, peering into doorways and down alleyways, reveals what a loss that would be.

Since the 1980s, when China reopened its borders, more Wenzhounese have arrived. Many have joined an existing *Quartier Chinois* (in truth a mixed East and Southeast Asian community) at the junction of Rue de Belleville and Boulevard de Belleville (20th), where there is a familiar array of Asian shops and restaurants. The largest Asian

Galerie C. T. Loo on Rue de Courcelles was built for a Chinese antiques dealer

A fresh coat of paint in Little Wenzhou

community, however, occupies a series of tower blocks called Les Olympiades between Avenues de Choisy and d'Ivry (13th), erected during the late 1960s to revitalise what was considered a rundown part of Paris. Built originally to attract young French professionals, Vietnamese, Laotians, Thais, and Cambodians began moving here in the mid-1970s. They have opened many enterprises including Tang Frères at 48 Avenue d'Ivry, part of the biggest Asian supermarket chain west of China.

Well concealed inside Les Olympiades are two welcoming and atmospheric Buddhist temples: the Temple de l'Association des Résidents d'Origine Indochinoise at 37 Rue du Disque, and the Temple de l'Amicale des Teochews de France at 44 Avenue d'Ivry (on the concourse Dalle des Olympiades above). The Teochew are Han people from the Guangdong province of China, most of who now reside outside China.

The *Quartiers Chinois* of Paris may be vibrant but beyond their temples their architecture is rarely traditional. For that visit Galerie C. T. Loo at 48 Rue de Courcelles (8th). It is housed in a red-painted pagoda built in 1926 for the Chinese antique dealer Ching-Tsai Loo. Once one of the most important galleries of Asian art in the West this extraordinary building has been immaculately restored and now serves as a combined sales gallery and events venue (www.pagodaparis.com).

Other places of interest nearby: 7, 8, 10, 11, 12

10 The Oldest House in Paris

**3rd Arrondissement, a tour of old houses concluding
with that of Nicolas Flamel at 51 Rue de Montmorency
Métro 4 Étienne Marcel, 11 Rambuteau, Arts et Métiers**

Of the many superlatives applied to Paris one of the most hotly debated is that of the city's oldest extant house. Putting aside religious, military, and public buildings there are several worthy contenders. But which is the true one?

The oldest civil dwellings date back to Roman times and are preserved in the Crypte Archéologique beneath the Place du Parvis-Notre-Dame (4th) (see no. 30). But these buildings cannot be termed extant since their ruined walls barely rise above the level of their under-floor heating systems.

Above ground, and not far away, stands a building at 4 Rue de la Colombe. This house was built in the early 1200s by a mason working on the cathedral. However, in 1220 a flood caused its collapse, and in 1240 it was reconstructed as a tavern. Only a fragment of this original medieval masonry remains (to the left of the present entrance) so again the building cannot be considered extant. The street name, incidentally, which means Dove Street, recalls a pair of doves that – as legend has it – nested in the building prior to its collapse. The female was trapped but kept alive by the male, which brought water and grain until she could be freed. Medallions depicting the doves appear on the building's façade.

The first serious contender for oldest extant house is the half-timbered building at 3 Rue Volta (3rd), which is said to date from around 1300. Curiously it doesn't contain a cellar, which would be usual for buildings in Paris of such antiquity (see no. 17). Despite authorities such as Larousse and Michelin once supporting the claim, the building has now officially been re-dated to 1644, and is most likely a reworking of an older building.

A similar story applies to a pair of buildings at 11 and 13 Rue François Miron (4th), which carry wall plaques dating them to the 14th century. Historians have again suggested a more likely date in the 17th century, with cynics even suggesting 1967, when the buildings were over-renovated in an effort to liberate the Marais from its grimy and more recent past!

Another contender can be found at 20 Rue Etienne Marcel (2nd). The Tour de Jean Sans Peur is named after the pro-English Duke of Bur-

These ancient-looking buildings on Rue François Miron are not the oldest in Paris

gundy, who on 23rd November 1407 ordered the assassination of Louis d'Orléans, brother of Charles VI (1380–1482), sparking a civil war between the Burgundians and the Armagnacs. Fearful for his life the duke is said to have built this fortified tower house in 1409, with his bedroom on the top floor! In reality, however, it was probably little more than a status symbol.

This leaves the weather-beaten building at 51 Rue de Montmorency (3rd). Constructed in 1407 by one Nicolas Flamel (1330–1418) it is officially the oldest house in Paris. According to legend Flamel was an alchemist capable of transforming lead into gold, which helps explains both his wealth and his name-check in *Harry Potter*! More likely he accrued his fortune from his wife's dowry, real estate speculation, and possibly the expropriation of assets belonging to Jews expelled from France. As a result Flamel became a benefactor to several hospitals and churches, and constructed boarding houses like this one for the destitute. Rents gained from ground-floor shops enabled him to offer free rooms upstairs, on condition prayers were recited for the dead, as recalled in the inscription on the façade: "Pastrenotre et un Ave Maria". The property today houses the Auberge Nicolas Flamel, which offers *Gigot d'Agneau Mijoté Sept Heures* cooked to a suitably medieval recipe.

Around the corner from Rue de Montmorency is the charming Passage de l'Ancre. Accessible from either 223 Rue Saint-Martin or 30 Rue de Turbigo (3rd) it is one of the oldest thoroughfares in Paris, and is where in the 1640's one Monsieur Sauvage set up the first horse drawn cab service at his inn, the Hôtel Saint-Fiacre. Later, Saint Fiacre became known as the patron saint of taxi drivers.

Other places of interest nearby: 7, 8, 9, 12

11 A Market for Everyone

3rd Arrondissement, a tour of markets beginning
with the Marché des Enfants-Rouges at 9 Rue de Beauce
Métro 8 Filles du Calvaire, Saint-Sebastien – Froissart,
11 Arts et Métiers, Rambuteau

Each Paris neighbourhood has its own market, and many sell more than just food. An added attraction is that their customers represent a cross-section of the local community. With over a hundred to choose from here are some of the more distinctive ones.

The Marché des Enfants-Rouges at 9 Rue de Beauce (3rd) is the city's oldest covered market and dates from the early 17th century. Tucked away in a quiet corner of the Marais its unusual name recalls the red-dressed orphans (a symbol of Christian charity) taken in by the Hôtel-Dieu de Paris, the city's oldest hospital. Liveliest on Saturdays the market contains several excellent food stalls and has a tiny vegetable garden attached.

A couple of streets north is the Marché du Temple on Square du Temple (3rd). Together with the Marché Saint-Pierre at 1 Rue Ronsard (18th) it is an example of a late 19th century glass-roofed market hall. Although both today fulfill different functions there is another example, the Marché Saint-Quentin at 85bis Boulevard de Magenta (10th), that still goes about its original business. The Marché Beauvau on Rue d'Aligre (12th) is another covered market, and a very Parisian one at that. Older inhabitants of this long-established artisans' district come face-to-face here with young Parisians, across stalls piled high with fresh produce.

Very different is the bustling Marché Bastille that stretches northwards from Place de la Bastille along Boulevard Richard Lenoir (11th). On two mornings a week the market appears here as if by magic: an example of a *Marché Volant* (flying mar-

Gilles Sellier is a regular at the Marché aux Puces de la Porte de Vanves

ket). Don't forget that the Canal Saint-Martin runs directly beneath it (see no. 74)! Rather more genteel is the Marché Rue Mouffetard (5th), an example of a *Rue Commerçante* where shops set out stalls on the pavement. Although popular with tourists the narrow street retains its charm, including Le Verre à Pied at number 118bis, an old market bar replete with nicotine-stained walls and cheap wine.

The world of Parisian food markets is filled out with the Marché Raspail, the city's first *Marché Bio* at 4 Boulevard Raspail (6th), as well as the vibrant African Marché Rue Dejean (18th), with its exotic fruits and spices. The former fish market at 69 Rue Castagnary (15th) is still identified by a real Breton lighthouse!

Several Paris markets offer specialist products. The Marché aux Fleurs et aux Oiseaux on Place Louis-Lépine (4th) is the last market in the city dedicated to both flowers (Mon-Sat) and caged birds (Sun). Elsewhere, the Marché aux Timbres on Cour Marigny (8th) serves philatelists, the Marché St-Pierre on Place St-Pierre (18th) is for fabrics, the Marché de la Création on Boulevard Edgar-Quinet (14th) is where artists sell their work directly to the public, and the Marché aux Livres on Rue Brancion (15th) sells secondhand books.

Fleamarkets have a long tradition in Paris stretching back a hundred years, when unwanted household items, including flea-ridden bed linen, were sold on the streets. A relaxed example is the Marché aux Puces de la Porte de Vanves on Avenue Georges Lafenestre (14th). By comparison the Marché aux Puces St-Ouen de Clignancourt on Avenue de la Porte Clignancourt (18th) is enormous, indeed with over 2,000 stalls it is the largest flea market in the world. At its heart is the Marché Vernaison and the bistro Chez Louisette, where diners are serenaded with Édith Piaf songs.

For seven centuries the stomach of Paris was fed by the wholesale food market of Les Halles on Rue Montorgueil (1st). Although it moved away in 1969 it is recalled on the walls of the Restaurant Cochon à l'Oreille at 15 Rue Montmartre.

Other places of interest nearby: 8, 9, 12, 13

12 The Most Extraordinary Museum in Paris

3rd Arrondissement, a tour of specialist museums including the Musée de la Chasse et de la Nature at 62 Rue des Archives
Métro 11 Rambuteau

Paris is perfect for those interested in offbeat museums, indeed half the city's Arrondissements boast a specialist collection. There's something for everyone from fairgrounds and fakes to magic and medicine (see nos. 18, 32, 56, 71).

Some of the collections are industry-backed. The Musée du Parfum-Fragonard at 9 Rue Scribe (9th), for example, which illustrates 5,000 years of perfume manufacture, is part of the Fragonard perfume factory in Grasse. And there's no getting away from the names behind the made-to-measure car showrooms of Renault and Citroën at 42 and 53 Avenue des Champs-Elysées (8th). Others are far less commercial and more the result of individual passions. They in-

A stag in the house at the Musée de la Chasse et de la Nature on Rue des Archives

clude: the Musée de l'Éventail at 2 Boulevard de Strasbourg (10th), where old fans are displayed and new ones made; the Musée du Fumeur at 7 Rue Pache (11th), with its opium pipes and antique snuff boxes; the Musée de la Fédération Française de Tennis at 2 Avenue Gordon Bennett (16th), housed in the former groundsman's cottage of the Roland Garros tennis stadium; the tiny Musée du Barreau de Paris at 25 Rue du Jour (1st), detailing the activities of the Paris Bar Council; and the Musée de la Musique at 221 Avenue Jean-Jaurès (19th), where visitors wear headsets to hear music played on the antique instruments displayed.

Located in the 3rd and 4th Arrondissements there are four more specialist museums. The Musée des Traditions de la Garde Republicaine at 18 Boulevard Henri IV (4th) illustrates the colourful history of the guards of honour established by Napoleon in 1802. The tiny Mariage Frères Musée du Thé at 30 Rue du Bourg-Tibourg (4th), which was created by a family firm that has been purveying fine teas since 1854, features antique teapots and tea caddies (400 types of tea are sold in the shop in which the museum is housed). Different again is the Musée de la Poupée in Impasse Berthaud at 22 Rue Beaubourg (3rd), which contains a private collection of dolls and dolls' houses (tucked away alongside it is the Jardin Anne Frank, a hidden garden at the entrance to which is a Chestnut tree planted in memory of the celebrated Jewish diarist and victim of the Holocaust).

Most unusual of all is the Musée de la Chasse et de la Nature at 62 Rue des Archives (3rd). By rights this museum of hunting should be an old fashioned place, with a dwindling number of visitors. Instead, its various stuffed creatures, antique weapons, and artworks reflecting the natural world have been artfully arranged in some unexpected ways. Thus, a wood-panelled living room containing a tapestry of a stag hunt has a real stag standing alongside it. To one side is a room containing traditional paintings by Breughel and Rubens but with a ceiling covered with feathery owls' heads. And a mysterious dimly-lit chamber in the corner illustrates the quest to prove the existence of mythical beasts such as the unicorn.

Other rooms are dedicated to specific creatures, including wild boar and hawks, with associated objects explaining their relationship to humans. The display about hunting dogs includes not only a collection of ornate metal collars but also a kitschy little dog kennel. This most extraordinary of museums concludes with a picnic scene attended by a pair of gorillas, a trophy room reinvented with a brightly-painted ceiling, and a curious but cosy hunter's log cabin.

The Musée de la Chasse et de la Nature is located inside the only extant town house (Hôtel Particulier) designed by the architect François Mansart (1598–1666), which accounts for its distinctive Mansard roof.

Other places of interest nearby: 9, 10, 11, 15

13 From the Parisii to Proust

The Marais is renowned for its many grand town houses called *Hôtel Particuliers* built during the 17th and 18th centuries by French nobles as temporary lodgings when in Paris (see no. 20). Two such *Hôtels* on Rue de Sévigné (3rd) are now home to the eclectic Musée Carnavalet, which illustrates 5,000 years of Paris history.

The museum is entered through the Hôtel Carnavalet at number 23, which was built in 1548 and named after the widow of one François de Kernevenoy, who purchased the building in 1578. In 1677 it became home to Madame de Sévigné, the *Grand Dame*

This sign from the cabaret *Le Chat Noir* hangs today in the Musée Carnavalet

of the Marais. She is remembered not only for her prodigious letter-writing, evoking aristocratic life in the neighbourhood, but also her extravagant lifestyle. Perhaps it is not surprising that her body was exhumed during the Revolution and decapitated!

On the advice of Georges-Eugène Haussmann (1809–1891), whose redevelopment of Paris during the second half of the 19th century destroyed so many old buildings, the Hôtel Carnavalet was purchased by the City of Paris for use as a museum. Opulent interiors salvaged from demolished *Hôtels* were brought here, including a ceiling from the Hôtel de la Rivière painted by court artist Charles Le Brun (1619–1690). The city's redundant street signs also found a home here and today make for a very colourful collection on the ground floor (see no. 25).

From the first floor a corridor leads to the neighbouring Hôtel Lepeletier at number 29, which is equally storied. Also built in the mid-16th

century it was acquired by Louis-Michel Lepeletier, Marquis de Saint-Fargeau. He was a representative of the nobility in the Estates-General, an assembly convened in 1789 by Louis XVI (1774–1791) to resolve the French government's financial problems. It collapsed when members left to form the National Assembly, signalling the outbreak of the French Revolution. In 1793, Lepeletier voted for the execution of the king, and was murdered for doing so, on the day of the king's execution.

The Hôtel Lepeletier was annexed and opened to the public in 1989. Its orangery contains three canoes made from hollowed-out tree trunks *(Pirogues)* found during construction work for the city's Méteor line in 1990. Carbon-dated to 2800–2500 BC they provide the earliest evidence for human habitation in the Paris area. The tribes that used the boats for fishing eventually gave way to the Celtic Parisii, who settled on the Île de la Cité around 250 BC. They were in turn ousted by the Romans in 52 BC, who established their own settlement of Lutetia Parisorum (see no. 30).

On the first floor of the Hôtel Lepeletier there are further reconstructed rooms, including an *Art Nouveau* jeweller's shop by the Czech artist Alfons Mucha (1860–1939), and a magnificent 1920s ballroom from the Hôtel de Wendel. Also here is the bedchamber occupied by the novelist Marcel Proust (1871–1922) at 102 Boulevard Haussmann (8th), where he laboured on his massive *À la Recherché du Temps Perdu*. So he could sleep by day and work at night he sound-proofed the room with cork tiles. On the second floor are objects relating to the French Revolution, including Robespierre's last letter and a model of the Bastille made out of a stone from the original fortress (see no. 19).

Square Georges-Cain around the corner on Rue Payenne contains the museum's large-scale architectural fragments, including pieces from the Palais des Tuileries and Hôtel de Ville, both of which were destroyed by the Communards in 1871. Similar fragments lie in the Jardins du Trocadéro (16th).

Another *Hôtel Particulier* in the Marais is the Hôtel Salé in the Rue de Thorigny. Built in the 1650s for Pierre Aubert, a tax farmer who became rich collecting the *gabelle* or salt tax, it is considered one of the finest old houses in the area. The building has had a colourful life serving as the Embassy of the Republic of Venice, a school in which Balzac studied, and eventually the Musée de Picasso. The museum arose out of a law that permitted heirs to pay inheritance taxes with works of art instead of money and features works by the artist from all his various 'periods' and in all media. It also includes Picasso's personal collection of works by other artists.

Other places of interest nearby: 11, 12, 14, 17, 18

14   In Paris Pletzl

4th Arrondissement, Jewish life around Rue des Rosiers
in the Marais
Métro 1 Saint-Paul

The story of the Jews of Paris, as elsewhere in Europe, has often been
a painful one. Of the numerous locations bearing witness to it several
are located in the Marais, where the community has long been con-
centrated.

The first Jewish community in Paris was established by Sephar-
dim from the Iberian Peninsula during the 6th century AD. In the 10th
century they built a synagogue on the Left Bank, and by the 12th century France had become a centre of Jewish learning. Persecution was
rife, however, especially in the wake of
the First Crusade, and in 1182 Philippe
Auguste (1180–1223) expelled the
Jews from Paris, only to recall them
after realising their worth as money-
lenders. He permitted them to re-settle
in the Marais, a marshy area outside
his city wall, straddling what is today
the 3rd and 4th Arrondissements (see
no. 21). In 1306, with his treasury
empty, Philip IV (1285–1314) again
banished the Jews, seizing possession
of their assets. Perhaps with a mind
to repeating Philip's actions, Louis X
(1314–1316) recalled the Jews in 1315,
although they were not exiled again
until 1394 by Charles VI (1380–1422).

This time the Jews did not return
until the 17th century but prejudice
persisted. Together with Protestants,
actors, and suicides, for example, they
could not be buried in public cemeteries. Only in 1780 was permission
granted for the Sephardic community
to open their own cemetery at 44 Avenue de Flandre (19th), albeit with the
proviso that burials took place noctur-

Rabbis watch over fresh bread at the Kosher
bakery Murciano on Rue des Rosiers

nally. Although the little cemetery was abandoned in 1810, when Napoleon (1804–1815) opened all city cemeteries to the Jews, it can still be found behind modern apartment buildings.

During the Revolution France became the first European country to emancipate its Jewish population. Judaism was placed on an equal footing with other faiths, and Jews soon occupied high positions in French society. During the late 19th century their numbers were bolstered by Ashkenazi Jews fleeing persecution in Eastern Europe, and the Marais became known unofficially as Pletzl (Yiddish for 'little place'). They worshipped together in the Synagogue des Tournelles at 21bis Rue des Tournelles until 1913, when the Ashkenazis built their own synagogue at 10 Rue Pavée (designed by the *Art Nouveau* architect Hector Guimard). The story of both communities is told in the Musée d'Art et d'Histoire du Judaisme at 71 Rue du Temple.

Between 1942 and 1944 history was reversed, when the Nazis and their Vichy French collaborators sent 76,000 Parisian Jews to death camps in Poland. The victims are remembered in the Mémorial de la Shoah at 17 Rue Geoffroy-l'Asnier, and another memorial on Place des Martyrs Juifs du Vélodrome d'Hiver (15th), where French police rounded up 12,000 Jews in a cycling stadium prior to deportation.

After the war a wave of Sephardic Jews arrived from France's North African colonies and settled in Belleville (20th). Anti-Semitism continued due to the country's close ties with Israel, resulting in 1982 in a terrorist attack by pro-Palestinians on Goldenberg's, a popular Ashkenazi restaurant at 7 Rue des Rosiers. The restaurant is gone now – turned into one of the fashion boutiques now filling the Marais – but several other Jewish concerns remain on the same street. They include the Librairie du Temple, which sells Hebraic sacred texts, several falafel shops, a school, and the kosher bakers Finkelsztajn, Korcarz, and Murciano, where *Challah*, the braided bread eaten on the Sabbath, is baked. All of which is a reminder of the tenacity of Jewish life in Paris Pletzl.

Other places of interest nearby: 13, 15, 17, 18

15 Through Quiet Cloisters

4th Arrondissement, a tour of former religious cloisters
beginning with the Cloître des Billettes at 24 Rue des Archives
Métro 1 Hôtel de Ville, Saint-Paul, 11 Hôtel de Ville, Rambuteau

The Cloître des Billettes is an unexpected sight on Rue des Archives

This thematic journey brings together the city's former religious cloisters, and is for those seeking tranquillity. A cloister (from the Latin
claustrum meaning 'enclosure') is a courtyard surrounded by an ar-
caded walkway. As part of a medieval monastery or convent its purpose was to provide a study area for the religious community separate
from the outside world. Although long since secularised the cloisters
of Paris continue to offer a world apart.

The only medieval cloister in Paris is the Cloître des Billettes at
24 Rue des Archives (4th). It was built in 1427 as part of the monastery
of the Frères Hospitaliers de la Charité de Notre-Dame, known as the
Billettes on account of the little heraldic figures adorning their habits.
Legend has it that the monastery originated as a chapel erected in 1294
to expiate the sins of a Jewish moneylender. In the late 19th century
the monastic buildings were converted into a school, and the cloister
now serves as an occasional art gallery. The difference in atmosphere
between the pensive arcades and the busy road outside is tangible.

Another Right Bank cloister at 150 Rue du Faubourg-Saint-Martin

Magnificent vaulting at the Ancien Collège des Bernardins on Rue de Poissy

(10th) once formed part of the Couvent des Récollets, established for the Franciscans by Marie de Médicis in the early 17th century. Like other religious establishments the convent was closed during the Revolution, and used thereafter for secular purposes. The old fabric was gradually reduced until in 1968 the remains became the Maison de l'Architecture, offering studios and exhibition space to architects.

On the Left Bank, and in a similar spirit, a former Augustinian cloister built by the first wife of Henry IV (1589–1610) was incorporated in 1816 into what is now the École des Beaux-Arts at 14 Rue Bonaparte (6th). As the Cour du Mûrier it was transformed into a Florentine-style atrium (recalling the Graeco-Roman origins of medieval cloisters) and used to display the academy's plaster casts of the Parthenon friezes. It is worth noting that between 1368 and 1540 Rue Bonaparte was a canal, cut by the monks of the nearby Abbaye de Saint-Germain-des-Prés, to keep its fields *(Prés)* separate from those used by the Sorbonne. Although much of the abbey has gone its church remains as the oldest in Paris, together with two cloisters at 12 and 13 Rue de l'Abbaye.

A little further south are more cloisters, including that of the former Séminaire de Saint-Sulpice at 9 Place Saint-Sulpice (6th), now a tax office. The magnificent Cloître du Val-de-Grâce at 1 Place Alphonse-Laveran (5th) once belonged to a royal abbey established by Anne of Austria in thanks for giving birth to a son after many years of marriage to Louis XIII (1610–1643). It is today a military hospital containing the Musée du Service de Santé des Armées. Equally impressive is the Cloître de Port-Royal at 123 Boulevard de Port-Royal (14th), formerly part of a Cistercian convent of 1625, and today the maternity wing of the Hôpital Cochin. Tantalising glimpses of the cloister garden are available from outside.

The tour finishes with the Couvent des Bénédictines Anglaises at 28 Rue des Tanneries (13th), which served as a prison during the Revolution but now contains apartments and studios.

A magnificent example of secular Gothic vaulting is the recently-restored Ancien Collège des Bernardins at 18–24 Rue de Poissy (5th). Established in 1248 by Cistercians as a seat of learning it is impossible to believe that after the Revolution this glorious 70 metre-long columned hall served as a fire station!

Other places of interest nearby: 12, 13, 14, 17

16 On the Way of Saint James

4th Arrondissement, the Tour Saint-Jacques
on Square de la Tour Saint-Jacques
Métro 1, 4, 7, 11, 14 Châtelet

A great slab of stone lies to one side of the entrance to the Église Saint-Julien-le-Pauvre at 79 Rue Galande (5th). Unearthed in 1926 it once formed part of a Roman road constructed during the 4th century AD. The road later became the Rue Saint-Jacques, which as its name suggests is part of the Chemin de Saint-Jacques (Way of Saint James), a Catholic pilgrimage route leading all the way to northwestern Spain.

Legend holds that the remains of Saint James, the first bishop of Jerusalem, who was stoned to death for his Christian convictions, were taken by boat to northwestern Spain for burial. Before landing a storm hit the boat and the body was swept into the ocean. Sometime later, and seemingly miraculously, it was washed ashore undamaged, protected by a layer of scallop shells. It was then buried in what is now the city of Santiago de Compostella in Galicia.

For at least a thousand years pilgrims have been making the journey to Santiago de Compostella to venerate the saint, encouraged in the knowledge that they might receive a plenary indulgence for doing so. By the Middle Ages the place ranked alongside Rome and Jerusalem as one of the most important Christian pilgrimage destinations. The Black Death, however, as well as the Protestant Reformation and political unrest during the 16th century, saw pilgrim numbers dwindle. Today, however, more than a hundred thousand people make the journey annually, with twice that number during Holy Compostelan Years (when Saint James's day (July 25th) falls on a Sunday).

The earliest record of French pilgrims to Compostella dates from to the mid-10th century. One of the great 12th century proponents of the pilgrimage was Pope Calixtus II, and his *Codex Calixtus* lists four starting points in France: Paris, Vézelay, Arles, and Le Puy. All converge at Puente la Reina from where a single route crosses northern Spain to Compostella.

The Paris route commences at the Église Saint-Jacques-de-la-Boucherie on Square de la Tour Saint-Jacques (4th). Unfortunately, all that remains of this magnificent 16th century church is its 52 metre-high Gothic tower, the rest having been damaged during the Revolution and then demolished. The unusual name of the church recalls its patrons, the wholesale butchers of the nearby Les Halles market, and the tower's glorious sculptural decoration is evidence of their wealth. The tower continues to act as a landmark for pilgrims *(Pèlerins)*, and since the 19th century a statue of Saint James has stood at its summit.

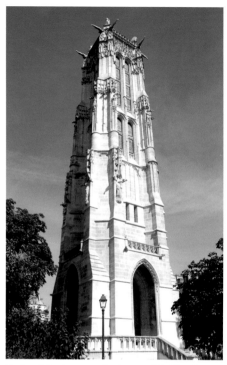

The Tour Saint-Jacques marks the start of the Way of St. James pilgrimage route

Budding pilgrims set off southwards from the tower along Rue Saint-Jacques, passing on the way the Hôtel de Cluny, a former Gothic abbots' residence at 6 Place Paul Painlevé (5th). It is today the Musée de Cluny – Musée National du Moyen Âge and includes examples of pilgrims' travel chests and other paraphernalia (see no. 26). The scallop shells *(Coquilles)* on the building's façade recall the story of Saint James, and indeed pilgrims still return from the shores of Galicia with a seashell as proof of their journey. A little further on the Église Saint-Jacques-du-Haut-Pas also owes its existence to the pilgrimage route, which from here leads out along Rues du Faubourg-Saint-Jacques and de la Tombe-Issoire, and eventually all the way to Tours and beyond.

Modern pilgrims should pause at 27 Rue Saint-Jacques to admire a sundial engraved by Salvador Dalí in 1966. It depicts a human head in the shape of a scallop shell!

Other places of interest nearby: 1, 2, 15, 21

17 Descent into a Gothic Underworld

4th Arrondissement, the Maison d'Ourscamp
at 44–46 Rue François-Miron
Métro 1 Saint-Paul, 7 Pont Marie

This atmospheric Gothic cellar lies beneath Maison d'Ourscamp on Rue François-Miron

Underground Paris for many city explorers consists of the late 18th century catacombs and the 19th century sewer system (see nos. 44, 84). There is, however, another far older aspect to the subterranean city. It is represented by a superbly vaulted Gothic cellar beneath the Maison d'Ourscamp at 44 Rue François-Miron (4th).

The origins of the Maison d'Ourscamp go back to the 12th century, when abbeys across France were both rich and powerful. It was usual at the time for abbots to establish a *Pied-à-Terre* for themselves in the capital, where they could reside when visiting. This would also be where goods and produce from their abbeys could be stored, prior to being sold in the city's markets. The Cistercian Abbaye Notre-Dame d'Ourscamp in northern France was no exception, and in 1248 its abbot commissioned the construction of the Maison d'Ourscamp.

Given its great age it is not surprising that the building seen today on Rue François-Miron is very different from the original, since it has been reworked many times over the years. By contrast, its vaulted cellar remains much as it was. Even after the Revolution, when both the house and abbey were expropriated, the cellar continued to be used for storage by local tradesmen.

By the mid-20th century, however, the southern part of the Marais in which the Maison d'Ourscamp stands had been designated an *Îlot Insalubre Parisien*, and scheduled for demolition. Fortunately the building was saved after the architectural importance of its cellar was highlighted in the early 1960s by the Association Paris Historique, a voluntary organization dedicated to protecting the city's historic fabric. The group has been based in the building ever since, and has spent many years restoring the cellar to its former glory.

Visiting the cellar today is an unexpected joy. A steep stone staircase leads down from street level and immediately a world of Gothic architecture opens up. The cellar consists of a single room stretching beneath what is now 44–48 Rue François-Miron. The cellar and the three houses above it were once a single structure, which was subdivided for rental purposes when the building was reworked in the late 16th century (today only the houses at 44 and 46 are conjoined). It was at the same time that the building received its present façade. The cellar's vaulted ceiling is supported on six columns, and it's worth remembering that until the room was cleared by the association the accumulated debris reached up to the column capitals!

An even older vaulted ecclesiastical building lies hidden inside a courtyard at 19 Rue des Ursins (4th). The Chapelle Saint-Aignan was built in the 1120s within the bounds of Notre-Dame, and was one of several places of worship at the eastern end of the Île de la Cité. Built just prior to the arrival of the Gothic style in Paris the chapel is defiantly Romanesque. Mass was celebrated secretly here during the Revolution after which it served as a storeroom and stable. Now a chapel once more it contains a statue of the Virgin and Child, the 13th century original of which is in Notre-Dame, where it serves to recall the many similar statues removed from there when Gothic became passé during the Renaissance. (Note: the chapel is only open during the Journées du Patrimoine on the third weekend in September.)

Other places of interest nearby: 14, 15, 18, 21

18 A Truly Magical Museum

4th Arrondissement, the Musée de la Magie
at 11 Rue Saint-Paul
Métro 1 Saint-Paul, 7 Sully – Morland

When strolling in the Marais look out for the red-painted doorway at 11 Rue Saint-Paul (4th). Above it a pair of curtains is drawn permanently back to reveal an intriguing name: *Académie de la Magie*. Cross the threshold and behold the two ancient Egyptians illuminating the gloom. Beneath them a narrow staircase leads down into a truly magical world.

The Musée de la Magie is a fascinating private collection illustrating the long and secretive history of magic and illusion. The address itself is a suitably ancient one: the 16th century building was originally used as a caravanserai by travellers (when the area still lay outside the city walls), and was later home to the notorious aristocratic libertine, the Marquis de Sade (1740–1814).

The history of magic stretches back as far as the priests of ancient Egypt, who used magical formulae in preparing the dead for the afterlife. When Christianity became the dominant religion of the Roman Empire during the 4th century magicians were considered no better than witches, and many were persecuted. Amongst the tenets of the *Lex Salica* commissioned by the first king of the Franks, Clovis I (509–511), were tough penalties for those practicing magic.

It was not until the Renaissance that travelling magicians were eventually permitted to entertain the aristocracy with tricks and illusions. Around the same time the first books of magic were published, one of the earliest being *Premiere Partie d'Inventions Subtiles et Delicieuses* (1584) by Frenchman Jean Prevost. By the 18th century magic as entertainment was well established in Europe, and practitioners from Harry Houdini to David Copperfield have ensured it has stayed that way ever since.

The Musée de la Magie occupies a series of stone-vaulted chambers, the atmosphere of which is enhanced by the use of blood red carpets. The objects on display are grouped thematically, for example a collection of intricately-carved wooden containers with secret compartments used for table top trickery. A painting on a wall nearby shows such an illusion in progress, with a suitably dumbfounded observer! In another room a collection of optical illusions are presented, including antique magic lanterns, a zootrope, and an ingenious device

The Musée de la Magie on Rue Saint-Paul boasts blood-red carpets and a mummy's sarcophagus!

that generates the image of a gold ring that can't be picked up. Very frustrating! Another room contains a wooden box with hinged doors used during the 1920s by the American magician Howard Thurston to saw a woman in half. It was the first time this now-popular illusion had been performed, and this is Thurston's original apparatus.

Adorning the walls are colourful posters advertising performances by 19th century French magicians, the most famous of whom was Jean Eugène Robert-Houdin (1805–1871). A watchmaker by trade he fell into magic after purchasing by accident a book on scientific amusements. The book is displayed together with some of his original equipment, including the *Inexhaustible Bottle*. It was Houdin, incidentally, who inspired the name of the escapologist Houdini (real name Erik Weisz) (1874–1926).

A separate collection within the museum, the Musée des Automates, contains many examples of automata. After being wound up these mechanised human figures entertain the operator with everything from a bar room brawl to a series of risqué peepshows. An especially effective one is in the form of a sphinx, in which questions posed by the onlooker are answered by a pair of real human hands that emerge from the sphinx's sleeves!

Visits to this most magical of museums are rounded off with a performance by a real-life magician.

Other places of interest nearby: 14, 17, 19, 20

19   What Remains of the Bastille?

**4th Arrondissement, the remains of the Bastille
in Square Henri-Galli
Métro 7 Sully – Morland**

The Bastille is a legendary name in history, and not only for the French. The storming of this medieval fortress, a symbol of royal authority in Paris, was a key moment in the French Revolution. The subsequent fall of the Bourbons sparked a series of copycat revolutions across Europe, and ultimately inspired the major socialist revolutions of the 20th century. That so little remains of the Bastille today only adds to its legend.

The Bastille was built in 1370 by Charles V (1364–1380) to protect the Porte Saint-Antoine on the eastern edge of Paris (see no. 21). In the 17th century it was converted into a prison by Cardinal Richelieu, Louis XIII's chief minister. Then in 1784 Louis XVI (1774–1791) closed it for financial reasons and planned to replace it with a square in his own honour (much as Place Vendôme honoured Louis XIV). Work had not started when the storming of the Bastille took place on 14th July 1789, the revolutionaries drawn by rumours of much-needed gunpowder.

Within days of the attack the decision was taken to demolish the Bastille, and a team of 800 men set to work. Some of the stones were carted away to help build the Pont de la Concorde (7th/8th), with others used to build houses locally. There was also a brisk trade in souvenirs, one Pierre François Palloy (1754–1835) selling models of the fortress carved from original stones. An example of his work is displayed in the Musée Carnavalet at 23 Rue de Sévigné (3rd) (see no. 13).

Within three years the Bastille had disappeared from view. The site today is occupied by the busy Place de la Bastille, with seemingly little evidence left of the once formidable fortress – but look a little closer. Outside 1 Rue Saint-Antoine there is a line of bricks in the ground indicating where it once stood, its position relative to today's streets inscribed conveniently on the wall at nearby 3 Place de la Bastille. Furthermore, during excavation work for the Métro in 1899 some undemolished footings from one of the Bastille's eight towers were uncovered. These were relocated to nearby Square Henri-Galli (4th) at the end of Boulevard Henri-IV, where they can still be seen. Also found was a stretch of masonry once used to strengthen the outer slope of the defensive ditch *(Counterscarp)* surrounding the fortress, which has

These few old stones on Square Henri-Galli are all that remains above ground of the Bastille

A model of the Bastille in the Musée Carnavalet is made from one of the prison's original stones

been left *in situ* on the platform of Line 5 of the Bastille Métro station (direction Bobigny).

It is little wonder that the words *Quatorze Juillet* still fire the French imagination and that the annual Fête Nationale is celebrated with such gusto. Outside France it is known as Bastille Day but this is a misnomer. What the French are celebrating is not the destruction of the Bastille but rather the first anniversary of the event, when Louis XVI accepted a constitutional monarchy – and the French nation was born.

The victims of two further revolutions are commemorated at Place de la Bastille. In July 1830 three days of street fighting occurred at the barricades in Faubourg Saint-Antoine, at the end of which Charles X (1824–1830), the reactionary Bourbon king, was dethroned and replaced by Louis-Philippe I (1830–1848), the last King of the French. The event is commemorated by the Colonne de Juillet in the centre of the square. Eighteen years later and the barricades were up again. This time Louis-Philippe was replaced by the Second Republic, which soon gave way to the Second Empire. The victims of both revolutions are memorialised in a crypt directly beneath the column.

Other places of interest nearby: 17, 18, 20

20 Where the Hashish Club Met

**4ᵗʰ Arrondissement, the Hôtel de Lauzun
at 17 Quai d'Anjou
Métro 7 Pont Marie, Sully – Morland**

Peaceful Île Saint-Louis (4ᵗʰ) dates from the 17ᵗʰ century, when two flood-prone islands, used only for fairs and duels, were sold by the canons of Notre-Dame for development. The islands were joined together and given quays along which elegant town houses were constructed. Called *Hôtels Particuliers* many were designed by Louis Le Vau (1612–1670), a favoured architect of Louis XIV (1643–1715). The island was not a place for the aristocracy, however, but for ambitious bourgeoisie, who made their fortunes administering the king's court.

One was Charles Gruyn des Bordes, a wealthy financier grown wealthier by being general commissioner of cavalry during the civil disorders of the Fronde. He had a *Hôtel* built at 17 Quai d'Anjou on the island's fashionable north side and although closed to the public it is worth pausing outside to reflect on its long and colourful history.

Designed by Le Vau the building was completed in 1657, with rich fittings by Charles Le Brun (1619–1690) (it is one of the few Paris *Hôtels* to retain its original interior). The decor incorporates Gruyn's initial 'G' interlaced with the letter 'M' for his wife, Geneviève de Mony. After Gruyn was imprisoned for selling non-existent fuel to the army she retained the house, bequeathing it later to her son.

An ornate drain pipe adorns the Hôtel de Lauzun on Quai d'Anjou

Meanwhile, over at the Palais du Luxembourg, Anne Marie Louise d'Orléans, Duchess of Montpensier (1627–1693), was looking for a husband. The wealthiest woman in the world she was called Le Grande Mademoiselle because of her size, and eventually fell for the penniless adventurer and philanderer Antoine Nompar de Caumont (1632–1723). Although Caumont was known to Louis XIV as a captain of the Musketeers the match was deemed unsuitable. Indeed the very idea was enough to see Caumont imprisoned in the Bastille, and he was only released when the duchess relinquished two valuable estates to the king. Banned from court thereafter Caumont purchased the *Hôtel* from the de Mony's, which he then used as a venue for his numerous affairs and gambling parties. Legend has it that the duchess would visit by boat and chase him around the house! After the couple's separation Caumont resumed his career and became Duc de Lauzun, which explains the name over the door.

Following the Revolution the building was divided and rented to writers and artisans, including the poet Charles Baudelaire (1821–1867), who wrote much of his *Les Fleurs du Mal* in the attic. A few years later the Romantic poet Théophile Gautier (1811–1872) joined him, and together they founded the Club des Haschischines. Foreign visitors included Rilke, Sickert, and Wagner, and a hashish smoke-blackened patch of wallpaper from the time is preserved in the East Room.

Since 1928 the Hôtel de Lauzun has been owned by the City of Paris and used for official receptions. Queen Elizabeth II was entertained here in 1957 during which guests were attended by footmen wearing eighteenth-century clothing.

After Henry IV (1589–1610) commissioned the Place des Vosges (4ᵗʰ) the Marais became the fashionable place for Parisian nobility to build their *Hôtels*. But when Louis XIV relocated his court to Versailles many were abandoned and became warehouses, factories, and shops. Those remaining today include the Hôtel de Beauvais at 68 Rue François Miron, where Mozart gave his first Paris recital, and the Hôtel Donon at 8 Rue Elzévir, which today contains the Musée Cognacq-Jay, a collection of 18ᵗʰ century art. Similar collections exist in the Musée Nissim de Camondo at 63 Rue de Monceau and the Musée Jacquemart-André at 158 Boulevard Haussmann (8ᵗʰ).

Other places of interest nearby: 18, 19, 27

21 The Seven Walls of Paris

4ᵗʰ Arrondissement, a tour of the city walls beginning
at 6 Rue de la Colombe
Métro 4 Cité

The casual observer could be fooled into thinking that Paris was never fortified, so few and far between are the remains of its walls. In reality the city has been protected seven times over the past 2,000 years, both for military and mercantile reasons, and on each occasion with a wall greater than the one before. This extended journey takes in evidence for all of them.

The first wall dates from the time of the Romans after they settled in 52BC on the Île de la Cité. As Lutetia Parisorum the town initially prospered and spread onto the Left Bank. By 400AD, however, it was little more than a garrison town occupying the island alone, with the first wall erected around it to afford protection against Germanic invaders. The line of the wall is marked in the street outside 6 Rue de la Colombe (4ᵗʰ) and fragments of it can be seen in the Crypte Archéologique beneath the Place du Parvis-Notre-Dame (see no. 30). When complete it stood around eight metres high, with a crenelated walkway on top.

Leave the Île de la Cité now by means of Île Saint-Louis and the

The Roman city wall in the Crypte Archéologique beneath the Place du Parvis-Notre-Dame

Pont Louis-Philippe to reach Place Saint-Gervais. Here stands the Église Saint-Gervais-Saint-Protais, one of the oldest churches in Paris. A church had already stood here for six centuries when the second wall of Paris was built during the 11th century. The front steps of the church still give an impression of the hillock which protected the church from river floods. The Rue de Barres behind it follows exactly the line taken by the wall, which was 1,700 metres in length.

Now walk upstream as far as Rue des Jardins-Saint-Paul, where an impressive stretch of the third wall of Paris still stands to its original height. It was commissioned by Philippe Auguste (1180–1223) to protect Paris against pirates and other invaders, and encompassed what are today the 1st, 4th, 5th, and 6th Arrondissements. North of the Rue des Jardins-Saint-Paul the wall ran along the south side of the Rue des Francs-Bourgeois before reaching its northernmost point at a gateway, which stood at the junction of Rue aux Ours and Boulevard de Sébastopol. From there it turned south-west to meet the Seine near the Louvre, which finds its origins in a moated defensive outpost completed in 1200 (its impressive foundations still exist beneath the Cour Carrée and when extant it would have resembled the Conciergerie on Île de la Cité). Before the wall's demolition in the 16th century it ran for 5,400 metres and was punctuated by four main gates and more than 60 towers.

In 1356 and with King John le Bon (1350–1364) in prison the provost of the merchants of Paris commenced work on a fourth city wall, to safeguard the commercial heart of the city from attack by the English. He had only completed a gate, the Porte Saint-Antoine, on the eastern edge of the city when he was killed for conspiring with the English. The wall was continued by Charles V (1364–1380) from the gate (which was now protected by the Bastille fortress) in a moated semicircle all the way to the Louvre. Although the wall was lower than the previous one (six instead of ten metres high) it stood on a massive earthen embankment wide enough to confound modern cannonballs.

At the same time the marshy area between the Porte Saint-Antoine and the earlier wall of Philippe Auguste was drained to create the Marais, and it was to here that the king moved his royal residence from the Île de la Cité. A reminder of the former royal compound is the ruined tower of the Église Saint-Paul at the corner of Rues Saint-Paul and Neuve Saint-Pierre.

Of the massive wall itself surprisingly little remains beyond a length of counterscarp to protect the Bastille on the platform of Line 5 at the Bastille Métro station (direction Bobigny), which can be reached

The wall of Philippe Auguste on Rue des Jardins-Saint-Paul

by walking to the top of Rue des Jardins-Saint-Paul and turning east along Rue Saint-Antoine (see no. 19). Suffice to say that the *Grands Boulevards* of Louis XIV (1643–1715), which stretch north from Bastille, follow the line of the wall, rising and falling as they cross its former bastions (the steps in the narrow Passage Sainte-Foy at 263 Rue Saint-Denis (2nd) do likewise).

Commencing in 1543 during the reign of Francis I (1515–1547) and continuing until 1640 under Louis XIII (1610–1643) the wall of Charles V was extended westwards by the Enceinte Fossés Jaunes, so-called because of the yellow earth used in its construction. This, the city's fifth wall, extended from the Porte Saint-Denis (today a marooned archway at the junction of the Boulevards Saint-Denis and de Sébastopol) to the Place de la Concorde. To see the only remaining piece of this wall take Métro Line 1 from Bastille to Concorde, where the remains of a bastion stand in the basement of the Musée de l'Orangerie in the Jardin des Tuileries (1st).

The sixth wall of Paris was very different to those preceding it. Called the Enceinte des Fermiers Généraux (Tax Farmers' Wall) it was constructed between 1785 and 1790 by order of Louis XVI (1774–1792), to ensure that taxes *(Octroi)* could be levied on all goods entering the city. An idea of its great size can be gauged from the fact that Métro Lines 2 and 6 follow exactly its former 24 kilometre-long course. Since the wall was not defensive it was only ever three metres high. Although it was demolished in 1860 four of architect Claude-

Remains of the medieval louvre lie beneath the Cour Carrée

Nicolas Ledoux's neo-Classical tollhouses built to collect the taxes are still standing, including one at the northern entrance to Parc Monceau (8th). It can be reached by taking Métro 1 from Concorde to Charles de Gaulle Étoile, and then Métro 2 to Monceau.

The seventh and final wall around Paris dates to the 1840s, and was a response to the occupation of Paris by Prussian forces in 1814–15. Designed by Adolphe Thiers, Prime Minister to Louis Philippe I (1830–48), it is the greatest wall of all, stretching 34 kilometres and defining the city's Arrondissements as they exist today. However, despite having earthworks 140 metres wide the Thiers Wall did little to halt the Germans during the Franco-Prussian War (1870), and it was demolished in 1919. The military road that once serviced it is now occupied by the Boulevards des Maréchaux and the Boulevard Périphérique. A solitary remnant of the once-mighty wall has been revealed in a modern courtyard garden at 23 Rue Albert-Roussel (17th), which can be reached by taking Métro 2 to Place de Clichy and then Métro 13 to Porte de Clichy, from where it is a short walk along Boulevard Berthier.

Other places of interest nearby: 16, 22, 23, 24, 25

22 The Real Hunchback of Notre-Dame

4th Arrondissement, Notre-Dame de Paris
on Place du Parvis-Notre-Dame
Métro 4 Cité

The publication in 1831 of *Notre-Dame de Paris* by Victor Hugo (1802–1885) created much more than a bestseller – it altered the fabric of the city. Using the 12th century cathedral as a backdrop to his story, Hugo made a plea for the preservation of Gothic Paris and its decaying architecture (it should be remembered that during the Revolution Notre-Dame had been vandalised and used as a food store). The great popularity of the book helped promote the nascent historical preservation movement in France, leading ultimately to a major restoration of the cathedral by the Gothic Revivalist Eugène Viollet-le-Duc (1814–1879) at the behest of Napoleon III (1852–1870).

Notre-Dame today appears much as Viollet-le-Duc left it, with its grimacing gargoyles, distinctive steeple, and Galerie des Chimères, which can be seen at close quarters during a 387-step ascent of the South Tower. The romantic story still retains its power, too, in which the deaf hunchback bell ringer, Quasimodo, gives refuge to the beautiful gypsy girl Esmeralda after she is branded a witch. Although Hugo set his tale in the 15th century he used it to comment on his own times, notably a condemnation of the absolutist rule of Charles X (1824–1830), the last Bourbon king of France.

It has long been assumed that Quasimodo was a figment of Hugo's imagination. That view was altered, however, in 2010, when Adrian Glew, head of archives at London's Tate Collection, revealed that the character might have been based on a real person. The revelation came about after the memoirs of a little-known 19th century British sculptor, one Henry Sibson (1796–1877), were discovered in an attic in Cornwall, England. Sibson recounted how he had been employed on repairs at Notre-Dame in 1820 but after falling out with his employers sought new work at a government-sponsored studio, where a team of artisans were crafting large stone figures for the cathedral. There he encountered a sculptor called Trajin, who told Sibson that his foreman was a reclusive character nicknamed Le Bossu – meaning the hunchback!

Considering Hugo's strong interest in the restoration of Notre-Dame, and the fact that he regularly visited the cathedral, it is quite

Notre-Dame de Paris bristles with gargoyles and other carved ornaments

possible that Hugo and Messrs Trajin and Le Bossu were acquaintances. The theory is bolstered by the studio being linked to the École des Beaux-Arts in the 6th Arrondissement, an area where Hugo lived during the early 1820s. It has also been revealed that an early draft of *Notre-Dame de Paris* included a character by the name of Jean Trejean, which Hugo later changed to Jean Valjean. With all this in mind it seems entirely plausible that Hugo was inspired by both men, although it should be noted that Trajin and Le Bossu were actually employed on an earlier neo-Classical restoration of the cathedral led by the architect Etienne-Hippolyte Godde (1781–1869), which Hugo vociferously opposed.

But the story doesn't end there. In 1821 Sibson was hired by Trajin and Le Bossu to work with them on a project in Dreux, west of Paris, the very town where Hugo proposed to his wife in July of the same year. Can this really be just another coincidence or was Hugo paying the masons a visit? The truth may never be known, and the real name of the enigmatic Monsieur Le Bossu remains a mystery. However, if indeed he did provide the inspiration for Quasimodo then it is a further example of Hugo's marvellous ability to take elements of real life and weave them into magical literature.

Other places of interest nearby: 21, 23, 24, 25

23 Saint Vincent and the Crown of Thorns

4th Arrondissement, the monthly presentation
of the True Crown of Thorns in Notre-Dame de Paris
on Place du Parvis-Notre-Dame
Métro 4 Cité

Despite containing a great number of churches Paris is not a city renowned for its religious relics. Many were removed or destroyed
during the Revolution, when the city's Catholic places of worship
were secularised. Of those remaining, however, two are very special
indeed.

The first is the body of Saint Vincent de Paul (1581–1660) in the
Chapelle des Prêtres de la Mission Lazariste at 95 Rue des Sèvres (6th).
Born into a family of Gascon peasant farmers de Paul dedicated his
life to serving the poor. He spent his last years in Paris at the Maison
Saint-Lazare on Place Franz Liszt (10th), where after his death his work
was continued by a society of missionary priests known as Vincentians
or Lazarists.

When the Maison Lazariste was requisitioned as a prison during
the Revolution the priests were ousted. They eventually relocated to
Rue des Sèvres, when the chapel there was constructed in 1827. Of
course they brought the body of de Paul with them and it can still

Saint Vincent de Paul in his casket on Rue des Sèvres

A depiction of the Crown of Thorns in the treasury of Notre-Dame

be seen today inside an ornate silver and glass casket high above the altar. The skeleton is clothed in vestments, the hands and face restored in wax, giving the very real impression that the saint is merely sleeping.

In 1633 de Paul helped found the Daughters of Charity, a society for women within the Catholic Church. They are based today at 140 Rue du Bac (7th), where de Paul's incorruptible heart is stored in the Chapelle de la Médaille-Miraculeuse. The chapel's name honours Saint

Catherine Labouré to whom the Virgin Mary appeared in 1830, instructing her to strike medallions that would bring grace to those wearing them. Her equally incorrupt body is also preserved in the chapel. (The Daughters' former *Potager*, the lovely Jardin Catherine-Labouré, is around the corner at 29 Rue de Babylone.)

The greatest religious relic in Paris is in the city's greatest place of worship, namely Notre-Dame de Paris on Place du Parvis-Notre-Dame (4th). As one of the most famous churches in the world much has been written about the building yet few visitors are aware that it is home to the True Crown of Thorns. The peregrinations of medieval Christendom's second most important relic after the Shroud of Turin would make a book in itself. Suffice to say the Crown is first documented in the year 409, when Saint Paulinus of Nola lists it amongst relics on Mount Zion in Jerusalem.

To protect them from invading Persians the relics were shipped to Byzantium, where in 1238 they were pledged as security on a loan to Venetian bankers by the financially pressed Latin Emperor Baldwin II. They were never returned and instead purchased by the French King Louis IX (1226–1270), who commissioned a glorious Gothic reliquary in Paris to house them. The Sainte-Chapelle at 4 Boulevard du Palais (1st) was completed in 1244 and used to store the Crown and other relics until the French Revolution, when they were entrusted to the Archbishop of Paris.

The Crown is today stored in the treasury of Notre-Dame, and displayed to worshippers each first Friday of the month at 3pm (also each Friday in Lent, and Good Friday 10am–5pm). It is said that when the reliquary containing the crown was opened in 1940 the vegetation inside was still green. Despite its name, however, it contained no thorns, suggesting this was perhaps a second crown made from rushes into which thorns were inserted, then placed on Jesus' head by Roman soldiers to mock him as King of the Jews.

There is another relic in Paris that even the city's Catholics have almost forgotten about. In the crypt of the Église Saint-Leu-Saint-Gilles at 92 Rue Saint-Denis (2nd) are the bones of Empress St. Helena (250–330AD). She helped spread Christianity throughout the Roman Empire and was the first to bring Christian relics back to Rome. The bones were brought to France by a travelling monk and later entrusted to the Knights of the Holy Sepulchre in Paris, where today they are stored in a reliquary and venerated by the Russian Orthodox community.

Other places of interest nearby: 21, 22, 24, 25

24 An Historic Jazz Cellar

5th Arrondissement, Le Caveau de la Huchette
at 5 Rue de la Huchette
Métro 4 Saint-Michel

Paris has been crazy about jazz ever since the First World War, when black American ragtime and jazz bandleader James Reese Europe led an army-band tour across France, kick-starting a dance-hall craze. American GIs reignited the craze after the Second World War, and these days it is performed in a variety of venues from smoky piano bars to smart concert halls. Undoubtedly the most historic is Le Caveau de la Huchette in an atmospheric cellar at 5 Rue de la Huchette (5th).

Situated in the Quartier Latin the Rue de la Huchette is one of the oldest streets on the Left Bank. Fortunately the area was spared Baron Haussmann's wrecking ball after he lost his job during the upheavals of 1870; he only got as far as demolishing the buildings around Rue de la Harpe as part of an unfulfilled plan for road-widening. This left amongst others number 10, where a young and unknown Napoleon Bonaparte lived in 1795.

The narrow street is first documented in 1200 as Rue de Laas because it ran alongside a vineyard known as the Clos de Laas. During the 1280s it then took the name of a house on the street belonging to the Notre-Dame chapter *À la Huchette d'Or*. The origin of the word *Huchette* is obscure although it may be derived from *Hutchet*, being an old term for a bugle.

The building in which the Caveau de la Huchette is located dates from the 16th century but its cellar is much older. It is alleged to have been used as a secret meeting place by the Knights Templar during the late 13th century and the Freemasons in the 1770s. It also served as a prison, court, and place of execution during the Revolution, and was a hiding place for resistance fighters during the Second World War.

During the 1920s and 30s the building became a hotel and was frequented by the American author Elliot Paul (1891–1958); his novel *The Last Time I Saw Paris* recalls many of the street's characters from that time. Paul was a great admirer of the work of fellow American and Francophile Gertrude Stein (1874–1946), equating her "feeling for a continuous present" with the jazz genre. It seems therefore entirely fitting that in 1948 the hotel was transformed into the city's first jazz club.

Since then the ancient cellar walls of the Caveau de la Huchette

Jazz music has been played at the Caveau de la Huchette since just after the Second World War

have vibrated to the music of American jazz legends such as Sidney Bechet, Count Basie, Lionel Hampton, and Art Blakey. Other jazz stalwarts have included swing drummer Panama Francis and his Savoy Sultans, trombonist Gene "The Mighty Flea" Conners, pianist Wild Bill Davis, and trumpeter Harry "Sweets" Edison. Of course leading French jazz musicians have performed here, too, including Claude Luter, Sacha Distel, and Claude Bolling. The venue appears in Marcel Carné's film *Les Tricheurs* (1958), and American blues pianist Memphis Slim memorialised it in his composition *Stomping at the Caveau de la Huchette*.

French vibraphonist Dany Doriz currently owns the club, opening his doors each night to both regulars and visitors. He is certainly the man for the job having toured with both Lionel Hampton and Stephan Grapelli. The timeless atmosphere recalls the Cotton Club and the Savoy in their glory days: vibrant and urgent but with the intimacy of belonging to something very exclusive.

The subterranean jazz experience continues at the Caveau des Oubliettes at 52 Rue Galande (5th), where a surprising sight is a guillotine said to have been used on members of the so-called Chouannerie, who staged a revolution *against* the Revolution!

Other places of interest nearby: 22, 23, 25, 26, 33

25 House Signs and Street Names

5th Arrondissement, some unusual street details
around Rue Saint-Séverin
Métro 4 Saint-Michel

Away from the galleries and museums of Paris a more intimate history of the city is provided by easy-to-miss street details such as ancient house signs and curious street names. For *Flâneurs* and city explorers alike these are a joy to discover.

To make navigation easier when illiteracy was commonplace and house numbers non-existent, houses were identified by figurative signs, some of which involved a play on words *(Calembours)*. Several examples, which appear cryptic to modern onlookers, remain in the ancient streets around Rue Saint-Séverin (5th). At 13 Rue Saint-Séverin, for example, there is a 14th century inn sign depicting a swan wrapped around a crucifix. The word swan in French is *Cygne*, a homophon for *Signe*, which together with the crucifix signifies "The Inn at the Sign of the Cross". On the corner opposite at number 24 note how the letters "ST" (for Saint) have been chiselled away from the street name. This was done during the Revolution, when it was every citizen's duty to remove all symbols of religion and royalty.

Turn up onto Rue Xavier Privas now, which was known formerly as Sac à Lie after the wine dregs (lees) once used to clean leather hides and parchments here. A reputation for insanitary conditions saw the street later re-named Squalie, rendered as Zacharie in a faded inscription at number 19.

At the end of the street turn right onto Rue de la Huchette, where at number 14 there is another house sign. The present building occupies the site of a 15th century sewing shop *(Mercier)*, and the letter "Y" in an oval frame that still adorns its façade represents either a needle on a thread or else the tie for a gentleman's breeches. Additionally, the number inscribed at the building's corner with Rue du Chat-qui-Pêche refers to the divisions of Paris before the creation of *Arrondissements*, whilst the street name itself recalls an old sign that once identified a fish shop.

Cross onto Rue de la Bûcherie and turn right past the Église Saint-Julien-le-Pauvre to reach Rue Galande, where the oldest house sign in Paris can be found at number 42. Dating to 1380 it depicts a husband and wife rowing a boat, with another figure in between them. The scene recalls the legend of Saint Julien l'Hospitalier, the son of a nobleman and a keen hunter, who one day encountered a talking stag. It informed him that he would kill his own parents if he did not renounce hunting. This he did and instead married and settled down but inevitably he returned to hunting. Sometime later whilst he was away an elderly couple visited his home and his wife offered them the marital bed. When Julien returned he misread the situation and slew the

The oldest street sign in Paris is on Rue Galande

pair. They were, of course, his parents. Heartbroken and repentant he took to ferrying people across the Seine with his wife, offering them lodgings in a guesthouse *(Hôpital)* on the shore (documentary evidence exists for such an establishment on the site of the church during the 6th century). One dishevelled customer to benefit from Julien's new-found kindness was an angel (the third figure on the house sign), who forgave Julien his sins.

Elsewhere in Paris royal symbols adorn the façades of certain buildings, including a delightfully prickly porcupine, the emblem of Louis XII (1498–1515), at 82 Boulevard de La-Tour-Marburg (7th). A series of altogether more mundane royal monograms can be seen in the Cour Carrée du Louvre (1st), signifying the various monarchs responsible for the building's various wings. "LMT", for example, appears on a wing erected by Louis XIV (1643–1715) and his queen, Maria Theresa of Spain. Indicative of the eighteenth century street scene are the decorative devils' heads known as *Mascarons* seen grinning above many windows. Finally, from the nineteenth century come novelties such as the great gilded snail identifying L'Escargot, a long-established restaurant at 38 Rue Montorgeuil (1st).

By the 16th century the narrow streets of Paris were cluttered with signs advertising all manner of establishments and services. Fashioned from wrought iron or painted on metal panels they were frequently noisy and a danger to traffic. Some wonderful examples are preserved in the Musée Carnavalet at 23 Rue de Sévigné (3rd) (see no. 13).

Other places of interest nearby: 22, 23, 24, 26, 33

26 The Lady and the Unicorn

5th Arrondissement, the Musée de Cluny – Musée National
du Moyen Âge at 6 Place Paul Painlevé
Métro 10 Cluny – La Sorbonne

The Musée de Cluny – Musée National du Moyen Âge at 6 Place Paul
Painlevé (5th) contains some remarkable medieval objects, including
Limoges enamels, children's toys, and pilgrims' travel chests. It occupies two separate structures, one of which is a partially-ruined Roman
bathhouse erected around 200AD. The other is the Hôtel de Cluny,
a residence built in 1500 by the abbots of Cluny for their use during
visits to Paris, which is a rare example of a Gothic secular building in
Paris – another is the Hôtel de Sens at 1 Rue du Figuier (4th) containing the Bibliothèque Forney – and is adorned with carved seashells,
emblems of the Chemin de St-Jacques that commences nearby (see
no. 16).

A highlight on the ground floor of the museum is a collection of
battered stone heads of the Kings of Judah, unearthed in 1977 behind
the Opéra Garnier. They once adorned the façade of Notre-Dame but
were hacked off by the Communards, who mistook them for the Kings
of France! The room next door is the former Roman *Frigidarium* (cold
bath), which contains the so-called Boatmen's Pillar, the oldest piece
of sculpture in Paris. It originally graced a Roman temple on the site
of Notre-Dame, where it was dedicated to Jupiter by the League of
Paris Boatmen during the reign of the Emperor Tiberius (14–37AD)
(the league held a monopoly on river traffic between Montereau and
Mantes).

For many visitors, however, the highlight of the museum is undoubtedly the magical tapestry cycle called *La Dame à la Licorne* (The
Lady and the Unicorn). Consisting of six separate scenes it hangs on
the walls of a rotunda on the first floor, where the light is kept deliber-
ately low to protect it. It is thought that the tapestry was designed in
France during the late 15th century and probably woven in the southern
Netherlands. In each scene an elegantly-dressed lady wearing a jewelled collar is depicted with an attendant. The figures are flanked by a
lion and a unicorn, and beside them stand the banners of the de Viste
family from Lyons, for whom it is supposed the tapestries were made
as a gift. The rich red floral backdrop is of the *Mille-Fleurs* (thousand
flowers) type popular during the Middle Ages.

The first five tapestries are allegories of the senses. For 'Sight' the

Part of the tapestry cycle *La Dame à la Licorne* in the Musée de Cluny

unicorn lies with its hooves in the lady's lap and gazes into a mirror; for 'Hearing' the lady plays a portable organ, pumped by her attendant; for 'Taste' the lady takes a sweet from a bowl, and will perhaps give it to the parakeet perched on her left hand; for 'Smell' she sniffs a bloom taken from a bouquet, while a monkey does likewise behind her; and for 'Touch' she holds one of the banners as well as the unicorn's horn. All this is understood – but what about the sixth tapestry? It depicts the lady at the open door of a tent on which is written *À mon Seul Désir*. She is shown removing her jewelled necklace to place in a box, as the unicorn raises its horn in salute. If this is a scene of renunciation what is the lady foregoing? Or is it the Virgin Mary taming the noble savages? Or maybe just a simple allegory for love? No-one knows for sure. Perhaps the answer lies in the medieval-style garden to one side of the museum, which is inspired in part by these intriguing scenes.

The heraldic emblem of Paris is a boat and its motto, *Fluctuat nec Mergitur*, means 'it tosses but it does not sink'. Its origins date back to Roman times and by the medieval period the guild of boatmen and dockers was one of the city's most powerful. They built the first Paris quay in the sixteenth century for the trans-shipping of goods. Later during the nineteenth century the quays also provided a location for dance halls and drinking dens known as *Guinguettes*. In the 1950s and 60s the old quays were replaced by the controversial *Voies sur berge* enabling motor traffic to access the heart of the city as quickly as possible. In 2013 the stretch between Pont de l'Alma and Pont Royal was reclaimed for use as "Les nouvelles Berges", where not only freight barges but also walkers, cyclists, and other pleasure-seekers can once again use the quays for their original intended purpose.

Other places of interest nearby: 24, 25, 32, 33

27 Journey to the Centre of the Earth

5th Arrondissement, the Collection de Minéraux
de l'Université Pierre et Marie Curie at 4 Place Jussieu
Métro 7 Jussieu

The science fiction novel *Voyage au Centre de la Terre* by Jules Verne (1828–1905) was published to much acclaim in 1864. It was one of the first in a long series of books by the author called *Les Voyages Extraordinaires*, commissioned by Verne's publisher to "outline all the geographical, geological, physical, and astronomical knowledge amassed by modern science and to recount, in an entertaining and picturesque format...the history of the universe".

The story concerns a German professor and his attempt to demonstrate the existence of volcanic passages penetrating the Earth's core. Whilst most of Verne's ideas about the interior of the planet have subsequently been refuted he did manage to give his readers an idea of modern geology, which by this time was replacing the Biblical explanation for the creation.

Prior to becoming successful Verne spent ten years in Paris, studying law whilst also writing poems and libretti for operettas. He only turned to full time writing in 1863 after the success of his *Cinq Semaines en Ballon*, thereafter relocating to Auteuil and eventually Amiens. Surprisingly there are no memorials recalling Verne's time in Paris although several locations are associated with him. They include the submarine-like Arts et Métiers Métro station, the Restaurant Le Jules Verne at the Eiffel Tower, and the Librairie Jules Verne at 7 Rue Lagrange (5th).

Of great interest to readers of *Voyage au Centre de la Terre* will be the city's three geological museums. The one most redolent of Verne's age is the Musée de Minéralogie at 60 Boulevard Saint-Michel (6th). Established in 1794 this old-fashioned collection is housed in a hundred metre-long gallery in the Hôtel de Vendôme, a former private home and convent, which has been occupied by the École des Mines de Paris (Mines ParisTech) since 1814. The 19th century display cabinets contain 80,000 minerals, 700 gemstones, and 400 meteorites, making it one of the ten largest geological collections in the world. Access is by means of a magnificent staircase decorated with murals of the French Alps.

Perhaps more suited to Verne's vision of the future is the ultramodern Collection de Minéraux de l'Université Pierre et Marie Curie at 4 Place Jussieu (5th), which was established just after the creation of the Chair of Mineralogy at the Sorbonne in 1809. Since 1970 it has been housed in the basement of the Campus Universitaire de Jussieu, where 1,500 rare and precious specimens are displayed in specially-lit glass cases designed not only to show them off but also to protect them from deterioration. One of the collection's rarest minerals is

A glittering specimen of calcite in the Collection de Minéraux de l'Université Pierre et Marie Curie

Cuprosklodowskite, named in honour of Marie Curie (1867–1934), whose maiden name was Skłodowska.

A third geological collection is the Galerie de Minéralogie et de Géologie in the Muséum National d'Histoire Naturelle at 36 Rue Geoffroy-Sainte-Hilaire (5th). It was established in 1625, when minerals with medicinal properties were deposited in the Jardin des Plantes, which at the time was a royal medicinal herb garden (see no. 45). Of related interest is the staggering collection of fossils to be found in the museum's Galerie d'Anatomie Comparée et de Paléontologie at 2 Rue Buffon.

In 1863 Verne wrote a novel called *Paris au XXe Siècle* describing the city as it might appear in 1960. He successfully predicted glass skyscrapers, high-speed trains, gas-powered cars, and calculators but the book's overall pessimism prompted his publisher to suggest the book be shelved for twenty years. Verne put the manuscript in a safe, where it was only discovered by his great-grandson in 1989.

Other places of interest nearby: 20, 28, 29, 30

28 An Englishman and his Fountains

5th Arrondissement, the Wallace Fountain at the corner
of Rue Geoffroy-Sainte-Hilaire and Rue Cuvier
Métro 7 Place Monge, Jussieu, 10 Jussieu

Scattered across Paris in all but three arrondissements are green-painted public drinking fountains known to Parisians as *Les Fontaines Wallace*. Installed during the late 19th century and often adorned with graceful *caryatids* they are a distinctive aspect of the Paris scene.

The story of the Wallace fountains dates back to the time of the Franco-Prussian War and the Siege of Paris (1870–71). Living in the city at the time was an Englishman, Sir Richard Wallace (1818–1890), whose father the 4th Marquess of Hertford had until his recent death occupied the Chateau Bagatelle in the Bois de Boulogne. Wallace inherited his father's fortune and achieved the admiration of Parisians by financing field hospitals during the siege, to treat both French wounded and sick Britons. As Prussian artillery rained down Wallace elected to remain in the city and help distribute supplies to the needy.

One of the results of the siege, and the violence resulting from the Commune that followed, was the destruction of the city's aqueducts, which resulted in an increase in the price of water. The lower classes had to pay for their water and there was a risk that some would turn instead to cheap liquor. Wallace therefore decided to continue his philanthropic work by financing the installation of a city-wide network of public drinking fountains, which even today provide a reliable source of fresh water for the homeless.

Wallace designed the fountains himself and intended them to be functional as well as beautiful. With this in mind he made them high enough to see from afar (but not so high as to be unsightly), affordable so that at least 50 of them could be installed quickly, cast in iron to guarantee durability and ease of manufacture, and painted green so that they fitted harmoniously in squares, parks, and tree-lined streets.

Wallace drafted two designs himself and had them reworked by the sculptor Charles-Auguste Lebourg (1829–1906). The first and most recognisable was based loosely on the Fontaine des Innocents on Place Joachim-du-Bellay (1st), the oldest monumental fountain in Paris. Weighing 600kg it consists of an octagonal pedestal on which stand four *caryatids*, their arms supporting a reservoir decorated with dolphins (the *caryatids* represent kindness, simplicity, charity, and sobriety). The water flows down from the reservoir and was originally collected using a tin cup attached by a chain. These were removed for health reasons in 1952 although the hooks to which the chains were attached can still be seen.

The second, slightly smaller model was designed to be attached to a wall, and comprises a semi-circular pediment from which the head of a *naiad* issues water into a basin placed between two pillars. Very few of these were ever made and only a single example survives today at the corner of Rues Geoffroy-Sainte-Hilaire and Cuvier (5th) (an example of the more common larger model stands not far away at the corner of Rue Poliveau and Rue de l'Essai).

A thirsty traveller is refreshed at a Wallace Fountain on Rue Geoffroy-Sainte-Hilaire

The Wallace Fountains were later supplemented by columnar and pushbutton versions, which whilst less elaborate are in their way no less elegant. All of them operate from mid-March to mid-November and are re-painted every few years. For his efforts Wallace was given a Legion d'Honneur and is buried in the Cimetière du Père-Lachaise (20th).

Other places of interest nearby: 27, 29, 30

29 Mint Tea Beneath a Minaret

**5th Arrondissement, the Grande Mosquée de Paris
at 2bis Place du Puits-de-l'Ermite
Métro 7 Place Monge, Censier – Daubenton**

In 2005 a Saudi prince pledged 17 million Euros to the Musée du Louvre to help build a new gallery in which to exhibit Islamic art. It was the largest gift ever made to the world's largest museum. The result is a state-of-the-art exhibition space in the Cour Visconti, which has been given a sail-like roof that reminded the prince of a flying carpet.

The prince's gift highlights French relations with the Islamic world, and the belief that an increased awareness of Islamic art might help bridge the cultural gap made apparent by the events of 11th September 2001. The objects on display are certainly impressive: a delicate 10th century ivory box from Córdoba, a 14th century inlaid bronze platter from Syria, a 17th century Persian *kilim* with poems embroidered in silver. But the Louvre is only a museum, and to relate more intimately to Islam as a living faith a visit should be made to the Grande Mosquée de Paris at 2bis Place du Puits-de-l'Ermite (5th).

The green-roofed mosque with its 33-metre high minaret is currently the largest in Paris and was constructed by the French government in the 1920s, to honour the many Muslims who died for France in the First World War. Realised in the Hispano-Moorish style it echoes the grand mosques of the Maghreb, whence the Muslims of Paris first hailed in the late 19th century. Although the prayer hall is only open to worshippers, non-Muslims are welcome to enjoy the glorious garden (from where the prayer hall can be glimpsed), and to sip *Thé à la Menthe* in the leafy courtyard of the neighbouring La Mosquée restaurant.

Once used only by scholars the mosque's prominence in Parisian life has grown over the years, especially after the Algerian *Mufti* Dalil Boubakeur became rector. No shrinking violet, Boubakeur has roundly condemned French multiculturalism, saying it has failed Europe's largest Muslim community, as well as the rest of the population. In his opinion, neither *laissez-faire* permissiveness nor draconian governmental measures help the two communities live peaceably together. Only by promoting integration and keeping religion out of politics will mutual suspicion and discrimination lessen.

Boubakeur has his detractors, of course. Cynics view him as a

The minaret of the Grande Mosquée de Paris

Muslim for the French and a Frenchman for the Muslims, highlighting the conflicting interests faced by religious and political leaders in deciding how best to accommodate Islam in France. And it shouldn't be forgotten that most Muslims in Paris worship in far more modest premises than the Grande Mosquée. For these Muslims a most press-

A tranquil corner of the mosque's water garden

ing concern is overcrowding in mosques, which saw them take to the streets with their prayer mats in 2011. Critics regarded it as a threat to French secularism, which was made law in 1905, as a result of which street prayers (as well as the wearing of *Burqas* and *Niqabs* in public) have been outlawed.

Perhaps an improvement can be affected by the Institut du Monde Arabe at 1 Rue des Fossés-Saint-Bernard (5th). Unveiled in 1987 to increase cultural contact between the Arab world and the West it contains a museum and library, and hosts a busy programme of activities. One can't help thinking, however, that real progress will only occur by forging real, grass roots relationships out in the suburbs, where conflicts and prejudices are felt most keenly.

The unusual lens-like apertures that make up the façade of the Institut du Monde Arabe open and close automatically to regulate the building's light levels, and are a modern take on traditional Arabian latticed windows *(Mashrabiyah)*.

Other places of interest nearby: 27, 28, 30

30 The Ruins of Roman Lutetia

5th Arrondissement, a tour of Roman remains including
the Arènes de Lutèce at 49 Rue Monge
Métro 7 Jussieu, Place Monge, 10 Cardinal Lemoine, Jussieu

In 52BC the armies of Julius Caesar conquered the Paris basin and established a permanent settlement called Lutetia Parisiorum. It was not the Romans, however, that inspired the city's modern name but rather a Celtic Iron Age tribe. The Parisii had occupied this part of Gaul since around 250 BC, and they made a spirited but unsuccessful attempt to defend their stronghold on the Île de la Cité. Thereafter and for the next five centuries the fortunes of the Roman town ebbed and flowed, and since the 19th century archaeologists have been revealing what remains of it.

Like the Parisii the Romans established their military headquarters on the Île de la Cité, with official buildings at the west end and temples to the east (one of these on the site of Notre-Dame was dedicated to Jupiter). For his personal residence the Roman governor favoured the Montagne Sainte-Geneviève on the Left Bank, where all the public buildings expected of a Roman town were constructed. Laid out in a grid pattern these included a forum (between what is now the Jardin du Luxembourg and the Panthéon) and several thermal baths, the remains of one of which are today incorporated into the Musée de Cluny at 6 Place Paul Painlevé (5th) (see no. 26).

Lutetia Parisiorum also boasted paved roads of which the stone slab in front of the Église Saint-Julien-le-Pauvre at 79 Rue Galande (5th) is a reminder (the city's central axes were the present-day Rue Saint-Jacques and Rue Soufflot). It laid claim to the first sewer system in Paris, too, receiving fresh water along a covered acqueduct from springs rising in Rungis, 16 kilometres to the south (fragments are displayed in the Musée Carnavalet at 23 Rue de Sévigné (3rd)). Although Lutetia lacked its own mint, plenty of Roman coins have been discovered during excavations, and some are displayed in the Musée de la Monnaie de Paris at 11 Quai de Conti (6th).

Later during the 3rd and 4th centuries Left Bank Lutetia was sacked repeatedly by Germanic invaders, prompting the Roman authorities to abandon that part of the city. Instead they erected a wall around the Île de la Cité, and converted it into a military outpost. Fragments of the wall have been revealed in the Crypte Archéologique beneath the Place du Parvis-Notre-Dame (4th) (see no. 21). Despite this in 476 the

A ruined roman bath house today comprises part of the Musée de Cluny

The roman amphitheatre on Rue Monge

Franks ousted the Romans from Paris – Lutetia had changed its name in 360 – and built their own fortress. Twenty years later their king, Clovis I (481–511), converted to Catholicism and in 508 he established his capital here. He also laid the foundations of the first Notre-Dame. For the first time Paris became the capital of France, albeit a France that stretched little further than the Île de France.

By the late 12th century the ruins of Roman Lutetia had disappeared beneath a new Left Bank city wall erected by Philippe Auguste (1180–1223). There they remained until 1869, when the remains of a Roman amphitheatre were revealed during construction of the Rue Monge (5th). With support from the writer Victor Hugo the site was secured and later excavated and partially restored. Constructed in the late 2nd century it once held 16,000 spectators making it the largest amphitheatre in Roman Gaul. Today it is a place where people come to laze in the sun and gently play *Pétanque* but close your eyes for a moment: it's not too difficult to imagine the gladiatorial and theatrical displays that once occurred here.

Other places of interest nearby: 27, 28, 29, 31

31 Extraordinary Events in the Panthéon

5th Arrondissement, the Panthéon on the Place du Panthéon
Métro 10 Cardinal Lemoine

In 1744 the Bourbon King Louis XV (1715–1774) recovered from a grave illness while commanding his armies in the War of the Austrian Succession. Grateful to be alive he commissioned a church in honour of Genevieve, the patron saint of Paris, whose intercession had saved him. The resulting neo-Classical structure on the Montagne Sainte-Geneviève – now Place du Panthéon (5th) – features a cupola inspired by Louis XIV's Dôme at Les Invalides and Saint Paul's Cathedral in London.

When the church was completed in 1789 the French Revolution was underway. As a result it was converted into a secular mausoleum where the tombs of suitable French notables could be placed. Renamed the Panthéon it was returned to the Church in 1806 by Napoleon (1804–1815), only to be secularised and then desecularised again before becoming a civic building in 1885. Today its atmospheric crypt still contains the remains of Voltaire, Rousseau, Dumas, Hugo, Zola, Braille, and both Curies.

During its checkered history the Panthéon has played host to two extraordinary events. The first occurred in 1851 when the French physicist Léon Foucault (1819–1868) demonstrated to the French public that the Earth spins on its own axis. Following a successful experiment at the Observatoire de Paris Foucault suspended a heavy metal ball from the dome of the Panthéon by means of a long wire. Once set in motion the ball continued to swing in the same plane, while the ground rotated several degrees each hour beneath it, the motion being recorded on a circular track on the floor. Known as Foucault's Pendulum the demonstration provided the first dynamic proof of the Earth's rotation.

By comparison the second extraordinary event was a secretive one. In September 2005 an underground cultural guerrilla group calling itself Untergunther UX took up residence in the Panthéon without anyone knowing it. As part of their brief to restore France's unloved cultural heritage they set about repairing a 19th century wall clock that had not worked since the 1960s. Not only did they establish a clandestine workshop behind the clock face but they also tapped into the local electricity grid, and even installed easy chairs to relax in! With several new parts made from scratch the group eventually spent a total of 4,000 Euros and untold hours on the project.

In October 2006, with restoration of the clock complete, the group revealed itself to the Panthéon's curator. They did this less for the publicity value and more because they relied on the staff of the Panthéon to keep the newly-restored clock wound in the future. Not surprisingly the Centre des Monuments Nationaux, the French heritage agency whose perceived inadequacies motivated the group's actions in the first place, were embarassed by the ease with which the group were able to remain in the Panthéon after hours. Legal action was sought against the group but when the case came to court in 2007 all charges were dismissed. The clock has remained unwound ever since.

The controversial clock inside the Panthéon

Untergunther UX was formed in the 1980s, when as students in the Quartier Latin they held secret parties in tunnels under the city; since then they claim to have conducted more than a dozen covert restorations. Whatever one thinks of them it should be remembered that their activities continue a freethinking tradition stretching all the way back to the 12th century, when the theologian and philosopher Peter Abelard led a student exodus from Notre-Dame to the Église Saint-Julien-le-Pauvre on the Left Bank (see no. 92).

Other places of interest nearby: 26, 30, 32

32 Illustrated Histories of Medicine

**6th Arrondissement, some medical museums
including the Musée de l'Histoire de la Médecine
on the second floor of the Université Paris Descartes
at 12 Rue de l'École-de-Médecine
Métro 4 Odéon, 10 Odéon, Cluny – La Sorbonne**

In early medieval France the people with any knowledge of medicine were mostly monks. In 1131, however, an ordinance banned them from studying, which meant France had no trained doctors until the establishment of several small schools in Paris around 1220. In 1331 these were merged by Philippe VI (1328–1350) into the Faculté de Medécine, one of four faculties making up the old Université de Paris (known popularly as the Sorbonne). Although the university was suppressed for a century following the Revolution, and later replaced by the Université de France, the faculty's original anatomical theatre built in 1744 is still standing at 13 Rue de la Bûcherie (5th).

With such a long history it is not surprising that Paris contains several specialist medical museums. One of the most memorable – but certainly not one to everyone's taste – is the Musée Dupuytren at 15 Rue de l'École-de-Médecine (6th). This collection of anatomical specimens illustrating diseases and malformations was established in 1835 with a bequest from Guillaume Dupuytren (1777–1835), a surgeon renowned for having treated Napoleon's haemorroids! Housed originally in the Gothic refectory of the Couvent des Cordeliers the collection was mothballed in the 1930s and only reopened in a different part of the medical faculty in 1967. On display is the skeleton of Marco Cazotte (1757–1801) – known as Petit-Pepin – whose hands and feet grew directly from his hips and shoulders. There is also the pickled brain used by anatomist Paul Pierre Broca (1824–1880) to locate the speech areas in humans.

The full history of medical practice stretching back to the ancient Greeks is illustrated in another museum on the opposite side of the street. The Musée de l'Histoire de la Médecine is housed in a dramatic 19th century glass-roofed hall on the second floor of the Université Paris Descartes at 12 Rue de l'École-de-Médecine. Amongst the dangerous-looking surgical implements are oddities such as the scalpel of Louis XIV's personal surgeon Charles François Felix, the medical bag belonging to one Dr. Antommarchi, who was entrusted with Napoleon's autopsy, and a table made from human body parts, including four ears and a foot!

The Musée de l'Histoire de la Médecine contains a table made from human body parts!

Belonging to the same university – one of thirteen autonomous universities established in Paris during the 1960s – is another important collection of anatomical samples. The Musée de l'Anatomie Delmas-Orfila-Rouvières on the eighth floor at 45 Rue des Saints-Pères contains two century's worth of viscera all modelled in wax. The museum was opened in 1794 by the anatomist Honoré Fragonard (1732–1799), whose own extraordinary collection of flayed figures *(Écorchés)* is displayed in the Musée Fragonard just outside Paris.

Yet another university collection is the Musée de Matière Médicale at 4 Avenue de l'Observatoire, which is crammed with samples of medicines culled from the analysis laboratories of the Faculté de Pharmacie. Alongside the museum is a hidden botanical garden containing plants used in the production of medicines and cosmetics.

Away from the university, the Musée des Moulages at 1 Avenue Claude-Vellefaux (10th) is part of the Hôpital Saint-Louis. Built originally to quarantine plague victims the hospital initiated the study of dermatology, and its museum provides an opportunity to examine its collection of life-like dermatological casts. Equally specialist is the Musée d'Art Dentaire at 22 Rue Emile Ménier (16th), with its collection of vintage tooth extractors. It is today administered by the Musée de l'Assistance Publique at 47 Quai de la Tournelle (5th), which itself illustrates the huge advances made in the treatment of sick Parisians since the Middle Ages.

Other places of interest nearby: 24, 25, 26, 31, 33, 37

33 The Beat Hotel and Other Accommodations

6th Arrondissement, a tour of distinctive places to stay finishing with the Relais-Hôtel du Vieux Paris at 9 Rue Gît-le-Cœur
Métro 4 Saint-Michel

Paris offers its visitors over 2,000 places to stay from modest cosy hideaways to glittering converted palaces. Here are a few of the more memorable ones.

Best known of the city's luxury hotels is the Paris Ritz at 15 Place Vendôme (1st). Opened in 1898 it was the first European hotel to offer *en suite* facilities and a telephone in every room. Subsequently its bar became legendary and its Suite Impériale declared a French National Monument. Equally glamorous is the Paris Le Grand at 2 Rue Scribe (9th), which opened in 1862 to the sound of composer Jacques Offenbach's orchestra. Designed by the architect of the Opéra Garnier it exudes Second Empire elegance, and was once the biggest hotel in the world. Another example is the Hôtel de Crillon at 10 Place de la Concorde (8th), which was commissioned in 1758 by Louis XV (1643–1715) as one of a pair of state palaces. With its *Ancient Régime* flair still intact it was transformed into a hotel in 1909. And don't forget Le Bristol at 112 Rue du Faubourg Saint-Honoré, which was once home to the Count of Castellane (since 1925 his private theatre has served as the restaurant). During the Second World War the hotel became a safe haven for Americans in Paris because of its air raid shelter.

For those seeking a more discreet hideaway there is plenty of choice. The Pavillon de la Reine, for example, at 28 Place des Vosges (3rd) is a romantic, ivy-clad hotel in the heart of the Marais. It is named after Anne of Austria, the mother of Louis XIV (1643–1715), who stayed nearby. The Hôtel Caron de Beaumarchais at 12 Rue Vieille du Temple (4th) is decorated in Louis Quatorze style, and named after Pierre-Augustin Caron de Beaumarchais (1732–1799), who penned the stage comedy *Le Mariage de Figaro* at number 47. The delightful Hôtel des Grandes Écoles stands in its own walled garden at 75 Rue du Cardinal-Lemoine (5th), a far cry from Ernest Hemingway's first address along the road at number 74. And equally well-hidden is the Hôtel de l'Abbaye at 10 Rue Cassette (6th), a former convent which tempts customers with its open fire, and the Relais Christine at 3 Rue

The author reads Burroughs in the so-called Beat Hotel on Rue Git-le-Cœur

Christine (6th), built on the site of a 13th century abbey (the breakfast room retains some impressive vaulting).

Some hotels offer novel accommodation, including the racy Hôtel Amour at 8 Rue Navarin (9th) with its erotic literature, the futuristic Hotel Kube at 1–5 Passage Ruelle (18th) with its black toilet paper (!), and the Hotel Seven at 20 Rue Berthollet (5th) featuring James Bond and Alice in Wonderland suites. Quite the opposite are the 20 bedrooms of the Hôtel de Nesle (6th) at 7 Rue de Nesle, each painted with murals based on historical themes from ancient Egypt to Molière.

This tour concludes with two hotels that have come up in the world. The smart L'Hôtel at 13 Rue des Beaux-Arts (6th) was once the modest Hôtel d'Alsace, where Oscar Wilde died in poverty in November 1900. The shabby florid wallpaper which he famously decried was only taken down a century later. It is equally difficult to imagine that during the late 1950s the comfortable Relais-Hôtel du Vieux Paris at 9 Rue Git-le-Cœur (6th) was an unnamed hostel used by the writers of the Beat Generation. There was only a single bathtub for the 40 rooms, and the bedsheets were changed but once a month. A wall plaque records that William Burroughs and Allen Ginsberg both spent time here in what is known unofficially as the Beat Hotel. Their photos and books are displayed in the hotel foyer.

Other places of interest nearby: 24, 25, 26, 32, 34

34 Zinc Bars and Philocafés

**6th Arrondissement, some distinctive bars and cafés
including La Palette at 43 Rue de Seine
Métro 4 Odéon, Mabillon, 10 Odéon, Mabillon**

During the late 19th and early 20th centuries so-called Zinc bars were common in Paris. These unpretentious establishments frequented by artists and the working class were named because of the cheap galvanized metal used to waterproof their countertops (grander venues opted for marble). Customers used the dull grey surface not only to rest their drinks on but also to lay down their payment. Émile Zola mentions *Le Zinc* in his novel *Le Ventre de Paris*, and the name soon became synonymous with the typical neighbourhood bar.

Although many bars had their zinc removed during the Second World War a few originals still remain, and they retain something of their original atmosphere. Nestled amongst art galleries near the heart of the Left Bank, La Palette at 43 Rue de Seine (6th) is a fine example. This quintessential café-bar and bistro opened in 1903 and comprises two rooms, a smaller front one containing the bar and a larger back one for dining. Gallery owners and art students are regulars here, explaining both the name of the place as well as the artists' palettes hanging on the wall. Pull up a chair in a corner and enjoy a glass of wine or a *Café au Lait*. You'll be in good company since not only Picasso, Braque and Cézanne were here but later also Hemingway, Jim Morrison, and Catherine Deneuve.

Another Zinc with a story to tell is Aux Tonneau des Halles at 28 Rue Montorgueil (1st). Its name recalls the barrels that became a common sight after Philippe Auguste (1180–1223) created a covered market here in 1183. Dubbed "the belly of Paris" by Émile Zola the Les Halles wholesale food market remained in business until its closure in 1969. Market workers would frequent the bar for an early breakfast of *Steak Frites* and bone marrow, washed down with a glass of red wine. Although the workers may have gone the warm welcome remains the same.

A third Zinc is La Belle Hortense at 31 Rue Vieille-du-Temple (4th), which doubles as a bookshop and art gallery (the name comes from a novel by Jacques Roubaud). This part of the Marais contains numerous other idiosyncratic bars, too, including Au Petit Fer à Cheval directly across the street at number 30. Established over a century ago it is named after its distinctive horseshoe-shaped bar, and features recycled Métro seats in the back room.

A couple of streets away at 41 Rue du Temple (4th) is Café de la Gare, in reality the city's most famous fringe theatre established in 1968. Housed in a former 17th century mansion it was for a time a hostel favoured by the poet Guillaume Apollinaire (1880–1918), who coined the term Surrealism. His fellow Surrealists congregated at Les Deux Magots at 6 Place Saint-Germain-des-Prés (6th), while he and Picasso had tables at Café de Flore at 172 Boulevard Saint-Germain. The Existentialists Jean-Paul Sartre and Simone de Beauvoir also frequented the café and it is no coincidence that today it is a *Café Philosophique*, where public debates are held on the first Wednesday evening of the month. The first *Philocafé* was Café des Phares at 7 Place de

La Palette on Rue de Seine is an original Zinc bar

la Bastille (4th), where a lively Sunday morning debate has been held since 1992. All are welcome!

The oldest café in Paris is Café Procope established in 1686 at 13 Rue de l'Ancienne Comédie (6th). A wall plaque records notable customers including Voltaire, Napoleon, and Benjamin Franklin.

Other places of interest nearby: 2, 5, 33, 35

35   At Home with Natalie Barney

6th Arrondissement, the former home of Natalie Barney at 20 Rue Jacob
Métro 4 Saint-Germain-des-Prés, 10 Mabillon
(Note: the property is not open to the public)

Paris has long offered freedom of expression to expatriate writers, including Gertrude Stein, Henry Miller, James Joyce, and Samuel Becket. One of the most colourful and certainly the most beautiful was Natalie Barney (1876–1972), who provided a rallying point for Paris literati at her home at 20 Rue Jacob (6th). It was also from here that she spearheaded a literary movement that championed women's rights.

Barney was born into a wealthy American family and visited Europe from an early age. As a teenager she was dubbed The Amazon owing to her expertise as a horsewoman, as well as her knack of seducing beautiful women. An early conquest was the renowned courtesan and *Demimondaine* Liane de Pougy, whom Barney first encountered in 1898 whilst out riding in the Bois de Boulogne. A year later Barney presented herself at de Pougy's residence, claiming to be a "page of love" sent by Sappho. De Pougy fell for Barney's charms, despite being wooed by many wealthy and titled men, and chronicled their ensuing relationship in her novel *Idyll Sapphique*. The liaison also prompted Barney's first published literary effort entitled *Quelques Portraits-Sonnets de Femmes*.

Barney's father disapproved strongly of his daughter's activities and demanded her return to America. Along the way she became engaged for just three weeks to Lord Alfred Douglas, the man behind Oscar Wilde's downfall. By the time she reached America her father had died and Barney inherited his sizeable fortune. Returning quickly to Paris she commenced a turbulent relationship with the poet and novelist Renée Vivien, whose real name was Pauline Tarn (1877–1909).

In 1909 Barney set up home in a 17th century pavilion at 20 Rue Jacob (6th), where for the next six decades she hosted a Friday literary salon. The pavilion is still there, albeit not open to the public, set in a courtyard concealed behind the anonymous street frontage. Here in privacy Barney brought together *avant garde* writers and artists and lived out her libertarian lifestyle. In the garden there stands a tiny Doric Greek temple, where she hosted discussions. It is a so-called *Temple d'Amitié* erected as a meeting house during the Revolution to replace the church (the entrance to a similar venue can be found

A portrait of Natalie Barney, *L'Amazone*, by her mother, Alice Pike Barney

The Temple d'Amitié at 20 Rue Jacob

around the corner at 34 Rue de Seine). The letters "DLV" inscribed on the temple pediment remain an enigma. They could be an acronym for "Dieu-Le-Veut" meaning "God wants it" or else they could signify the number 555 in Roman numerals, a number significant to Freemasons (see no. 47).

Barney received some of the greatest writers of the age on Rue Jacob: Apollinaire, Truman Capote, Jean Cocteau, T. S. Eliot, F. Scott Fitzgerald, Hemingway, Joyce, Ezra Pound, and Proust. Of the women who came, including Josephine Baker, Djuna Barnes, Sylvia Beach, Colette, Isadora Duncan, and Marguerite Yourcenar, several were at one time or another her lovers. Alice B. Toklas, who co-hosted another renowned salon with Gertrude Stein at 27 Rue des Fleurus (6ᵗʰ), was here, too. And on one famous occasion Mata Hari rode a bejewelled white horse through the garden!

Through it all Barney's great love was the American portrait painter Romaine Brooks (1874–1970), whose striking portrait of Barney entitled *L'Amazone* hangs in the Musée Carnavalet at 23 Rue de Sévigné (see no. 13). The pair remained together for 50 years.

A rare photo of Liane de Pougy at the time of her affair with Barney is displayed in the Musée de l'Erotisme at 72 Boulevard de Clichy (18ᵗʰ). The Bois de Boulogne, where the pair first met, is home to the Auteuil steeplechase course, with year-round meetings and family Sundays known as Les Dimanches au Galop (www.france-galop.com).

Other places of interest nearby: 5, 33, 24, 36

36 The Best Bistro in Paris?

6th Arrondissement, Le Bistrot d'Henri at 16 Rue Princesse
Métro 4 Saint-Sulpice, Odéon, 10 Mabillon, Odéon

There are 40,000 places to eat in Paris! With so much choice it is not surprising that the city considers itself the gastronomic heart of Europe. But for all the choice on offer it is the humble bistro that still encapsulates for many the romantic notion of eating out in Paris.

A bistro is a small restaurant serving simple, moderately-priced meals in a modest setting. While the chalkboard menu, aproned waiter, and chairs on the street are an important part of its appearance, it is the traditional home-cooked food that really matters. Robust dishes such as *Bœuf Bourguignon* and *Coq au Vin*, and slow-cooked ones such as bean *Cassoulet* are the staples of most bistro menus.

No-one knows the origin of the word. In Montmartre they'll tell you it came about after the Russians occupied the heights in 1814, indeed a wall plaque at 6 Place du Tertre (18th) says as much. Cossacks eager to celebrate their success were heard ordering food and drink using the word *bystro* (быстро) meaning 'quickly'. This colourful explanation seems unlikely, however, since the word is not documented

Typical bistro fare at le Bistrot d'Henri in Saint Germain-des-Prés

LE 30 MARS 1814
LES COSAQUES LANCERENT ICI
EN PREMIER, LEUR TRES FAMEUX "BISTRO"
ET, SUR LA BUTTE, NAQUIT AINSI
LE DIGNE ANCÊTRE DE NOS BISTROTS.
180ᵉᵐᵉ ANNIVERSAIRE
SYNDICAT D'INITIATIVE DU VIEUX MONTMARTRE

A wall plaque in Montmartre giving a spurious origin for the word 'bistro'

until 1884. It is more likely to be Parisian slang, derived perhaps from the aperitif *Bistrouille*. What is certain is that the bistro developed out of the basement kitchens of Parisian apartment houses, where tenants paid for both their room and board. Astute landlords supplemented their income by opening up their kitchens to the public. Simple foods that could be prepared in quantity and reheated were the obvious choice, and as demand increased so limited space was supplemented with chairs on the pavement.

So where is the best bistro in Paris? For this author there are three worthy candidates. The first is Le Bistrot d'Henri on a narrow side-street at 16 Rue Princesse (6th). One of the few real neighbourhood bistros left in Saint Germain-des-Prés it offers a dozen tables, a defiantly conservative menu, and unfussy service. Fresh haricot bean salad as a starter, succulent slow-cooked lamb shank for main, and the perfect crème brûlée to finish, washed down with a glass of Bordeaux.

Second choice is La Ravigote at 41 Rue Montreuil (11th) run by a husband-and-wife team. They are passionate about the country cooking of southern France *(Cuisine de Terroir)* and their house speciality is *Tête-de-Veau*. Not a dish for the faint hearted!

For a bistro with a modern twist, the third choice is L'Entredgeu at 83 Rue Laugier (17th). One of the new breed of chef-owned *Bistronomiques*, this place combines the comfort and reliability of a neighbourhood restaurant with robust yet refined dishes. Typical main courses include stuffed leg of quail and seared fillet of cod with slow-cooked vegetables.

A singular restaurant appreciated as much for its appearance as its food is Le Train Bleu at the Gare de Lyon (12th). This hundred year-old railway buffet retains its glorious *Belle Époque* interior, with wall paintings depicting the cities served by trains departing from here. Such old fashioned splendour is normally reserved for the city's brasseries, such as the magnificent La Fermette Marbeuf 1900 at 5 Rue Marbeuf (8th), Le Grand Colbert at 2 Rue Vivienne (2nd) and Brasserie Bofinger at 5–7 Rue de la Bastille (4th), with its unforgettable *Art Nouveau* dolphin's head men's urinals!

Returning to the subject of the classic Parisian bistro, several other reliable ones can be mentioned here. Like Le Bistrot d'Henri, Le Mesturet at 77 Rue de Richelieu (2nd) is a traditional corner bistro offering a legitimate 'Old Paris' dining experience. Equally cosy is Auberge de la Reine Blanche at 30 Rue Saint-Louis-en-l'Île, and Benoît at 20 Rue Saint-Martin (both 4th). And don't forget Bistrot du Peintre out at 116 Avenue Ledru-Rollin (11th), with its dizzying *Art Nouveau* decoration, in the heart of what was once the furniture-makers' district east of Bastille.

Paris has several renowned single-dish restaurants: Le Relais de l'Entrecote at 20 Rue Saint-Benoit (6th) has long specialised in tender *Steak Frites* with a secret recipe herb sauce (another good choice is the tiny Poulette bistro at 3 Rue Etienne Marcel (3rd) with its zinc bar and *Belle Époque* tiled wall scenes celebrating beer and coffee); Huîtrerie Régis at 3 Rue de Montfaucon (6th) sells the best freshly-shucked Brittany oysters; Au Pied de Cochon at 6 Rue Coquillière (1st) has been serving onion soup and pig's trotters day and night since 1946; and since 1890 La Tour d'Argent at 15–17 Quai de la Tournelle (5th) has served up more than a million Challandais ducks!

Other places of interest nearby: 32, 35, 37, 39

37 A Revolutionary Form of Measurement

6th Arrondissement, the Metre stone at 36 Rue de Vaugirard
Métro 4 Saint-Sulpice, Odéon, 10 Mabillon, Odéon

Most historians agree that the French Revolution (1789–1799) was one of the most important events in world history. Its rallying cry was "Liberté, Égalité, Fraternité" although in this context fraternity should perhaps be defined as kinship rather than brotherhood, since women also used the Revolution to improve their lot.

The main aims of the Revolution were to rid France of the hereditary class system of the *Ancien Régime*, and to replace the absolutist monarchy with a republic in which every citizen would have a say. The Revolution's exact legacy has long been debated but it is fair to say that it helped spread democratic ideals throughout Europe and the world. Although the French subsequently lost some of their hard won rights after the collapse of Napoleon's First Empire they never forgot the feeling of being part of the political process. Or as the American historian Lynn Hunt so cleverly put it: "Revolution became a tradition and republicanism an enduring option".

It is easy to forget that one of the by-products of the Revolution was the introduction in 1793 of the Metre as the official French unit of length. The revolutionaries were scrupulous in replacing all units of measure that made reference to the human body – the inch, the foot, the ell – since the body in question had traditionally been that of the ruling monarch! One year earlier the National Convention of the First French Republic (1792–1795) had stripped Louis XVI of all his political power. Now another vestige of the king's former might was shorn away.

The Metre was first defined in 1791 by the French Académie des Sciences as one ten millionth of the distance covered by a meridian passing through Paris between the North Pole and the Equator. Favoured over an English notion based on the movement of a pendulum this particular length was picked for historical reasons because it was discovered to be similar to a traditional unit of length, the Parisian *Aune*, used by textile merchants.

Between February 1796 and December 1797 the French Directory (1795–1799), which succeeded the Convention but preceded the French Consulate (1799–1804), installed 16 slabs of marble each a

The Metre stone on Rue de Vaugirard

Metre long at various points across the city, to help the public acquaint themselves with the revolutionary new measure. The only one still in its original position can be found at 36 Rue de Vaugirard (6th).

Seventeen other nations signed up for the Metre in 1875, since when its exact length has been further refined as scientific knowledge has advanced. Initially the Academy dispatched an expedition to measure exactly the meridian arc between a belfry in Dunkerque and a castle in Barcelona. This was later discovered to be inaccurate by one fifth of a millimetre because the flattening of the Earth had not been taken into account. The latest refinement occurred in 1983 when a Metre was defined as the distance travelled by light in a vacuum in $1/299,792,458$th of a second!

A second Metre stone is attached beneath a window of the Ministère de la Justice at 13 Place Vendôme (1st), to where it was moved in 1848 from the Agence des Poids et Mesures.

At the corner of Place Vendôme and Rue de Castiglione is a very different inscription marking the former site of the Embassy of Texas. After gaining independence from Mexico in 1836 Texas was an independent state until its annexation by the United States in 1845.

Other places of interest nearby: 32, 36, 39

38 Some Not So Famous Addresses

**6th Arrondissement, the Musée Zadkine
at 100bis Rue d'Assas
Métro 4 Vavin**

More than any other city Paris has made a habit of preserving the former homes and workplaces of its luminaries. They include those of literary giants such as Victor Hugo at 6 Place des Vosges (4th), illustrating his unusual taste in furniture, and Honoré de Balzac at 47 Rue Raynouard (16th), with a side door used to evade debt collectors; the dreamy studios of sculptor Rodin in the Hôtel Biron at 79 Rue de Varenne (7th), and the artist Delacroix at 6 Rue de Furstenberg (6th); and the more prosaic dwellings of President Georges Clemenceau at 8 Rue Benjamin-Franklin (16th), Russian revolutionary Lenin at 4 Rue Marie-Rose (14th) (not open to the public), and scientist Louis Pasteur (see no. 94). Musicians' homes have become museums, too, including the singer Édith Piaf at 5 Rue Crespin-du-Gast (11th) and the *avant garde* composer Erik Satie at 6 Rue Cortot (18th) (again unfortunately not open to the public) (see no. 66).

Other addresses are less well-known, including that of Valentin Haüy at 5 Rue Duroc (7th), who founded the city's first school for the blind, genre-defying artist Gustave Moreau at 14 Rue de la Rochefoucauld (9th), electronics inventor Édouard Branly at 21 Rue d'Assas (6th), and Positivist philosopher Auguste Comte at 10 Rue Monsieur-le-Prince (6th). (Europe's only Positivist temple stands at 5 Rue Payenne (3rd).)

One address, however, warrants special attention. The Musée Zadkine at 100bis Rue d'Assas (6th) is where the Russian-born sculptor Ossip Zadkine (1890–1967) lived and worked for the last 40 years of his life. Open to the public since 1982, after his widow the painter Valentine Prax bequeathed 300 of her husband's works to the City of Paris, it is an oasis of calm.

Zadkine emigrated to Paris in 1910 and lived initially in the artists' colony of La Ruche in Montparnasse (see no. 2). He didn't like it there though and found nothing romantic in its squalid living conditions. After serving as a stretcher-bearer during the First World War Zadkine returned to Paris, and in 1928 moved into the house-cum-studio on Rue d'Assas. Well concealed from the street and surrounded by its own garden this is where he found a much-needed sense of peace. "Come see my pleasure house," he wrote to a friend, "and you will understand how much a man's life can be changed by a dovecote, by a tree."

Paradoxically, the idyllic surroundings did not prompt Zadkine to celebrate the joys of nature in his art. Rather they offered him the freedom to express in dramatic form his anguish over the human condition. The house, studio, and garden provide a backdrop for Zadkine's striking sculptures, paintings, and lithographs. They reveal his progress as an artist from Cubism to his own idiosyncratic style influenced partly by African art. One memorable piece is the model for his *Torse de la Ville Détruite*, created as a memorial to the Second World War victims of Rotterdam. It

Rebecca ou La grande Porteuse d'Eau in the Musée Zadkine

consists of a bronze figure with its arms outstretched, the torso pierced by a jagged hole.

Other personal addresses include Sarah Bernhardt's dressing room in the Théatre de la Ville at 16 Quai des Gesvres (4ᵗʰ), the desk in the Cercle Suédois at 242 Rue de Rivoli (1ˢᵗ) on which Alfred Nobel conjured up his eponymous prize, and the former home and studio of glassmaker René Lalique at 40 Cours Albert I (8ᵗʰ), with its unique front door made of glass panels moulded like ferns.

Other places of interest nearby: 39, 40, 87

39 A School for Beekeepers

6th Arrondissement, the Beekeepers' School (Rucher-École)
in the Jardin du Luxembourg on Boulevard Saint-Michel
Métro 12 Notre-Dame-des-Champs

There are over 400 public green spaces in Paris, including formal gardens, planted squares, sprawling parks, and deep forests. Many contain something unusual, such as the specialist plants of the Jardin Alpin, the Masonic symbolism of Parc Monceau, the manmade romanticism of the Parc des Buttes-Chaumont, and the wilderness of the Jardin Naturel (see nos. 45, 47, 75, 79). Another example is the Jardin du Luxembourg on Boulevard Saint-Michel (6th). As well as featuring in Victor Hugo's novel *Les Misérables*, and being where a penniless Ernest Hemingway caught pigeons to eat, one of its more unusual claims to fame is that it contains a school for beekeepers.

The Jardin du Luxembourg is the second largest public park in Paris after the Jardin des Tuileries, and it shares that garden's penchant for symmetry. It was first laid out by Marie de Médicis (1575–1642), widow of Henry IV, to adorn the Palais du Luxembourg, which she had built in imitation of the Palazzo Pitti in her native Florence. The palace is still standing – it is today the seat of the French Senate – as is Marie's grotto-style Medici Fountain, fed originally by a Roman aqueduct revived by her engineers in 1623 (see no. 77). Until 1904 the aqueduct's flow was monitored through a vaulted manhole *(Regard)* in the Maison du Fontanier at 42 Avenue de l'Observatoire (14th).

The original garden consisted of 2,000 elm trees and a system of formal Florentine terraces and *Parterres* ranged around an octagonal basin navigated today by model yachts. Later monarchs largely neglected the garden, and in 1780 the Comte de Provence, the future Louis XVIII (1795–1824), sold off the eastern part for real estate development. Following the Revolution, however, the garden was restored and expanded, and during the second half of the 19th century statues of queens, saints, writers, and artists were installed, as well as a scale model of the *Statue of Liberty* (see no. 8). The period feel was completed by the addition of new ornamental gates, polychrome brick garden houses, a marionette theatre, greenhouses, and a series of beehives *(Ruches)*.

Located in the southwestern corner of the garden the beekeeping school (Rucher-École) was founded in 1856 and offers diplomas in beekeeping. It is worth noting that the temperature in the city is on average about three degrees warmer than in the surrounding countryside, and the bees thrive on it. The official Keeper of the Hives, who is available on Wednesdays and often Saturdays, is happy to provide further details. Observing the hives from a safe distance can be a zen-like experience as the bees to and fro with nectar collected from nearby chestnut, acacia, and orange trees, as well as lavender plants. Like all good things, however, the clear, golden honey they produce takes time and it is only sold once a year at the autumn honey festival in the garden's *Orangerie*. But it's certainly worth the wait!

The Beekeepers' School in the Jardin du Luxembourg

The Jardin du Luxembourg is not the only place in Paris where bees are hard at work. There are hives in several of the city's parks and cemeteries, including Parc Kellermann, Parc Georges Brassens, Parc de la Villette, and the Cimetière de Picpus. And surprisingly around 2,000 kilos of honey are produced annually on the rooftops of the Opéra Garnier and the Opéra Bastille (jars are sold in the opera boutiques). For honey products and beekeeping accessories visit Les Abeilles at 21 Rue de la Butte-aux-Cailles (13th).

Other places of interest nearby: 36, 37, 38, 40

40 A Rich, Restless, Magnificent Life

6th Arrondissement, the former home of Henry de Monfreid
at 31 Rue Saint-Placide
Métro 4 Saint-Placide (Note: the interior of the building
is not open to the public)

It is commonplace in Paris to honour the city's luminaries with museums in their former homes and workplaces (see no. 38). At the very least a wall plaque is installed, as is the case at 31 Rue Saint-Placide (6th), where no less than three former inhabitants are memorialised. Undoubtedly the most colourful of them was author and adventurer Henry de Monfreid (1879–1974).

De Monfreid was only young when his family moved here from the village of La Franqui on the Mediterranean coast. His father, an art dealer and friend of Gauguin, enrolled him at the city's Alsatian School but it was soon apparent that the boy craved a more exciting life. In 1889, inspired by a performance given by Buffalo Bill at the *Exposition Universelle de Paris*, he performed a balancing act on the balcony railings outside the family's fifth floor apartment!

Following his parents' divorce in 1892 de Monfreid took on a variety of professions including chauffeur, chemist, and dairy farmer, and relocated to the Rue du Parc Montsouris (14th). There he made contact with an African merchant who was planning to import coffee from the Horn of Africa. It was the opportunity de Monfreid was looking for and by 1911 he was living in Djibouti, which at the time was a French possession. Soon tiring of colonial life, however, he exchanged the coffee trade for a more lucrative line in gun running. He also converted to Islam and adopted the name Abd-al-Hai ("Slave of Life").

With the start of the First World War de Monfreid swapped guns for hashish and for the next three decades led a raffish, exciting life racing up and down the Red Sea in his dhow *Altair*. He would be first to admit that his business exploits were merely a means to an end. In his heart he longed only to be with "the sea, the wind, the virgin sand of the desert". When not at sea he converted the scribbled contents of his log books into a series of travel books, which proved popular outside his native France. They included exciting titles such as *The Secrets of the Red Sea* and *Hashish: Smuggling under Sail in the Red Sea*.

A cross between Arthur Rimbaud and Lawrence of Arabia, de Mon-

Henry de Monfreid in later life at home in the village of Ingrandes

freid was no stranger to controversy. He was banned from Aden by the British authorities during the First World War, and in the early 1930s he was expelled from Ethiopia by Emperor Haile Selassie. His support for Italy during the Second World War resulted in the British placing him under house arrest in Kenya.

De Monfreid eventually returned to France in 1947, moving into a comfortable house in the village of Ingrandes in Indre-en-Berry (in true Parisian style it today contains a museum); he also maintained a *Pied-à-Terre* in Paris at 33 Rue Erlanger (16th). But even late in life he remained a restless spirit. Until discovered by the authorities he grew opium poppies in his garden and he continued writing non-fiction accounts of his peripatetic life, as well as novels inspired by the exotic locations he once frequented. And when his book royalties fell short he sold off his father's collection of Gauguin paintings, which were eventually revealed to be fakes! Shortly before his death aged 95 he summed it all up by saying "I have lived a rich, restless, magnificent life".

Other places of interest nearby: 36, 37, 38, 39, 92

41 The Angel of Nagasaki

7th Arrondissement, the grounds of UNESCO
at 7 Place de Fontenoy
Métro 6 Cambronne, 10 Ségur
(Note: visits by appointment only)

The Paris headquarters of UNESCO – United Nations Educational, Scientific and Cultural Organisation – are located at 7 Place de Fontenoy (7th). As its name implies, the purpose of the organisation is to contribute to international peace and security through education, science and culture. Additionally the UNESCO building and gardens are home to some surprising works of art.

Inaugurated in 1958 the UNESCO building was designed in the International Style by three architects of different nationalities: Frenchman Bernard Zehrfuss, Italian Pier Luigi Nervi, and Hungarian Marcel Breuer. They in turn were overseen by an international committee of world class architects, including American Walter Gropius and Swiss-born Charles-Édouard Jeanneret-Gris (better known as Le Corbusier). The result is an unusual Y-shaped building, seven storeys high and set on concrete stilts. This is the Secretariat where representatives from almost 200 UNESCO member states do their business.

The two largest artworks at UNESCO sit in the garden directly in front of the Secretariat, and were installed as part of the original design. They are Henry Moore's *Silhouette au Repos* and the mobile *Spirale* by Alexander Calder. Two collaborations between Catalan painter Joan Miró and ceramicist Josep Llorens Artigas *(Les Murs de la Lune et du Soleil)* have since been brought under cover to protect them from the elements. Other works displayed inside include a huge mural by Picasso called *La Chute d'Icare* and Alberto Giacometti's sculpture *L'Homme qui Marche*.

To the rear of the Secretariat lies another green space, where the kinetic work *Signaux Éoliens* by Greek artist Vassilakis Takis can be found. Beyond, and in front of one of the ancilliary buildings, is the *Square de la Tolérance*. It features an olive tree and a stone wall engraved in ten languages with an extract from UNESCO's constitution. The square was a gift from Israel in 1996 in memory of the country's murdered Prime Minister, Yitzhak Rabin. On the wall of another building is Jean Bazaine's mosaic *Les Rhythmes d'Eau*.

Next to the square is the *Jardin Japonais*, which is unusual in that it was designed by a sculptor, Isamu Noguchi. It was given by the

Japanese government to signify harmony between nature and the work of Man, a message reinforced by the garden's *Fontaine de la Paix*.

Attached to a wall at the far end of the Japanese garden is something extraordinary. It is the stone head of an angel found miraculously intact amongst the ruins of Nagasaki in August 1945. The use of the atomic bomb on the city helped bring an end to the Pacific War but it also claimed 80,000 lives in the process. The angel once adorned a Roman Catholic church in the town of Urakami on the outskirts of the city, which before its destruction was one of the largest Christian churches in the Far East. The City of Nagasaki donated the angel to UNESCO to help mark its 30th anniversary in 1976.

Another anniversary is marked at the far end of the Japanese Garden. The so-called

The Angel of Nagasaki in the grounds of UNESCO

Espace de Méditation by Japanese architect Tadao Ando is a cylindrical single-storey structure commissioned by UNESCO to commemorate the 50th anniversary of the adoption of UNESCO's constitution. Inside are a couple of chairs where one should pause and think about the price of peace, whilst looking out over a pavement of granite slabs brought from the city of Hiroshima.

Other places of interest nearby: 95, 96

42 Some Towering Statistics

7th Arrondissement, La Tour Eiffel on Champ-de-Mars
Métro 6 Bir-Hakeim

La Tour Eiffel on Champ-de-Mars (7th) is one of the most recognisable manmade structures on the planet. Named after the engineer Gustave Alexandre Eiffel (1832–1923) it formed the entrance to the *Exposition Universelle de Paris de 1889*, a world's fair marking the centenary of the French Revolution. The original plan to demolish the tower after 20 years was abandoned when it found a new use as a telegraphic relay station. Since then over 250 million visitors have climbed the tower making it the world's most visited paid monument.

There are many well-known facts concerning the Eiffel Tower but for each there is another more arcane. When completed, for example, it was the world's tallest tower, a title it retained until the construction in 1930 of the Chrysler Building in New York. But few know that if the 324 metre-high tower was melted down it would only rise a mere 6cm above its own footprint!

Long before the tower was complete it was fiercely decried by 19th century aesthetes such as Gounod and Maupassant. Conversely Paul Gauguin and Le Corbusier loved it, and Jean Cocteau called it the "Notre-Dame de la Rive Gauche". The tower is painted every seven years by 25 people using 60 tonnes of paint. But who knew that three separate shades are used, with the darkest at the top so as to appear uniform from the ground?

The tower weighs 10,100 tonnes but is actually much lighter than the heaviest metal framework in Paris, which supports the roof of the Grand Palais on Avenue Général Eisenhower, which was created for the *Exposition Universelle de Paris de 1900*. Some of the names inscribed around the tower are the scientists who made such magnificent structures possible.

Eiffel is remembered as the architect of the tower but he was assisted by many less well known engineers. The original idea dates to 1884, when two of Eiffel's assistants, Maurice Koechlin and Emile Nouguier, proposed a 300 metre-high structure. Eiffel's experience with railway bridges made him an ideal candidate to realise the plan but he also knew the tower needed an aesthetic touch. For this he turned to fellow architect Stephen Sauvestre (1847–1919), who suggested the graceful arches around the base, a glass pavilion at first floor level, and the cupola at the top. The little-known Sauvestre was

The Eiffel Tower from the backstreets

A memorial to Gustave Eiffel at the foot of his tower

thus instrumental in transforming what was in essence a lattice of pig-iron held together by 2.5 million rivets into a structure of considerable elegance.

There have been many unusual ascents and descents of the tower. People have raced up it, cycled down it, flown under it, and bungee-jumped off it. Inevitably, there have been many suicides, too. In 1912 a man died testing a homemade parachute and in 1989 a tight-rope walker crossed successfully to the tower from the Palais de Chaillot. Of the celebrities who have visited, Charlie Chaplin and Buffalo Bill were made very welcome. Adolf Hitler less so, with locals cutting the lift cables to prevent him going to the top. In 1925 con man Victor Lustig even managed to sell the tower to a gullible scrap merchant!

On a clear day Chartres Cathedral is visible from the top but don't forget the base of the tower, where there is a 19th century grotto, a secret military bunker, and the engine room that powers the original hydraulic lifts (visits by appointment only). It's also worth remembering that if Eiffel hadn't changed his German surname in 1879 the tower would now be called La Tour Bönickhausen!

A recent addition to what is already one of the most visited attractions in Paris is a glass floor inserted at the tower's first floor level, which affords a breathtaking view of the ground 57 metres below.

Immediately prior to working on his famous tower, Gustave Eiffel was commissioned to design the Bibliothèque Sainte Geneviève at 10 Place du Panthéon (5th). At its heart is the magnificent Labrouste reading room with curved iron roof braces very much in the style of the Eiffel Tower.

Other places of interest nearby: 43, 44, 45, 52

43 A Curious Crystal Skull

7th Arrondissement, the Musée du Quai Branly
at 37 Quai Branly
Métro 6 Bir-Hakeim, 8 École Militaire,
9 Alma – Marceau, Iéna

With vigorous support from President Jacques Chirac the Musée du Quai Branly opened in 2006 at 37 Quai Branly (7th). Constructed on stilts to a design by Jean Nouvel its purpose is to give the indigenous arts of Africa, the Americas, Asia, and Oceania a platform in Paris as impressive as those devoted to Western art. Visually stunning the museum has inevitably fuelled controversy over how such objects are displayed in a post-colonial era.

Amongst the 3,500 objects on display, including Ethiopian prayer scrolls, Fijian bamboo headrests, and Vietnamese ceremonial machetes, there are inevitably curiosities. One is a beguiling trophy skull from New Guinea, with white feathers for hair and a red-beaded nose. It was used either to venerate an ancestor or memorialise an enemy. Equally captivating is a skull hewn from a single piece of quartz – but this is very rarely displayed. Known as the Paris Skull it is one of a handful of similar objects around the world purported to be pre-Columbian in date. Only recently have most of them been revealed as fakes.

The Paris Skull first appeared in 1875, when the French explorer Alphonse Pinart (1852–1911) purchased it from the antiquarian Eugène Boban (1834–1908). Three years later Pinart donated the skull to the newly opened Musée d'Ethnographie du Trocadéro in the the Palais du Trocadéro (16th). When this was demolished in the 1930s and replaced by the Palais de Chaillot, the museum was replaced by the Musée de l'Homme, where the skull remained until it was transferred to the Musée du Quai Branly.

But where did Boban acquire the skull? Perhaps it was when he led an expedition to Mexico to acquire ancient artefacts for Napoleon III (1852–1870). Napoleon had supported the Habsburg Emperor Maximilian I of Mexico, who was executed by Republican forces the same year. With a Mexican provenance seemingly likely, the skull was for a long time displayed as being a masterpiece of Aztec carving.

In recent years such thinking has been abandoned. Boban was as much a dealer in antiquities as an archaeologist, and more than one crystal skull passed through his hands. An example known today as

A New Guinea trophy skull in the Musée du Quai Branly

the British Museum Skull first appeared without any provenance in his shop window in Paris in 1881. After relocating his business to New York this skull was bought at auction by Tiffany, who in turn sold it in 1897 to the museum in London.

Recent microscopic analysis of both skulls has revealed traces of abrasion using modern rotary tools. It now seems almost certain that they were made in the German town of Idar-Oberstein, where during the late 19th century many decorative objects were carved from imported Brazilian quartz.

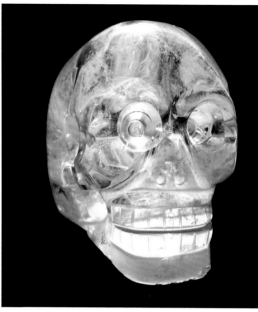

The crystal skull in the Musée du Quai Branly

The only real mystery therefore is why such skulls were carved in the first place, and why the Musée du Quai Branly chooses not to exhibit its own example, albeit as a fascinating fake. Its absence only serves to fuel the legends surrounding the skulls, as well as a thriving business in New Age books, and even an Indiana Jones film!

The Palais de Chaillot on Place du Trocadéro (16th) is today home not only to the Cité de l'Architecture et du Patrimoine, which contains scale models of historic French buildings, but also the Musée National de la Marine, where the transportation by sea of the Luxor obelisk from Egypt to Paris is illustrated. Maritime enthusiasts will also enjoy the *Argonaute*, a 1950s submarine in the Cité des Sciences et de l'Industrie at 30 Avenue Corentin-Cariou (19th). The largest science museum in Europe, the Cité des Sciences is one of many attractions in the Parc de la Villette. In amongst the various museums, galleries and theatres here can be found the recently-opened Philharmonie de Paris, a 2,400-seat concert hall designed by the architect Jean Nouvel.

Other places of interest nearby: 42, 44, 45, 52

44 Tout à l'Égout!

7ᵗʰ Arrondissement, the Musée des Égouts
opposite 93 Quai d'Orsay
Métro 9 Alma – Marceau

When the composer Frédéric Chopin arrived in Paris in 1831 he wrote of "the greatest splendour, the greatest filthiness" – and it's easy to understand why. The city contained palaces and grand buildings but lacked proper pavements and a sewer system. Parisians at the time relied on the time-honoured waste disposal method known as *Tout à la Rue* – everything to the street! When eventually a comprehensive waste water system was inaugurated 30 years later it was such a revelation that Victor Hugo devoted 50 pages to it in his *Les Misérables*.

The Romans were the first to give Paris a sewer system and fragments remain beneath their ruined bath buildings in the Quartier Latin (see nos. 26, 30). It wasn't to last long though and with the abandonment of that part of Roman Lutetia around 300AD the city reverted to using the Seine for both its drinking water *and* for depositing its waste. Initially the river was able to process the waste biologically, the major problem being the use of open ditches to transport it, which contributed to the spread of plague in 1348. In 1370 the first stone-lined sewer was laid along Rue Montmartre although it wasn't until the early 1800s that Napoleon commissioned the first sewer network. The burgeoning population, however, meant that it was too little, too late. The Seine was now dangerously polluted and following a deadly outbreak of cholera in 1832 it became necessary to find a permanent solution.

The answer came in 1852 when Napoleon III (1852–1879) instructed his Prèfet de la Seine, Georges-Eugène Haussmann (1809–1891), to create a modern, revolution-proof city. Haussmann believed that the provision of a proper sanitary system was just as important as the construction of wide boulevards to provide the emperor's police with sight lines. Whilst his herculean efforts above ground are there for all to see, those of his waterworks engineer Eugène Belgrand (1810–1878) remain hidden.

Belgrand's brief was to extend the city's sewer system and increase the number of homes with running water. He achieved this by building tunnels large enough to discharge waste water safely downstream, to contain separate pipes for the delivery of fresh water, and to facilitate easy maintenance. The new sewers mirrored exactly the streets above and were kept clean (as they still are today) by deliberate and regular

Inside the Musée des Égouts on Quai d'Orsay

flooding. Both streets and sewers were given the same names to assist the *Égoutiers* with their work.

The Paris sewers have drawn the curious since 1867, when public tours were first made available. Initially visitors were hauled through the tunnels on specially-constructed waggons; later, between 1920 and 1975, they made the same journey by boat. Today's visitors to the Musée des Égouts opposite 93 Quai d'Orsay (7th) make their way by foot but it's still an adventure since the path crosses an active sewer canal.

In 1894 a new law required that all waste be sent to the sewers, and Parisians were delighted that everything was now officially *Tout à l'Égout!* The Paris sewers were hailed as a technological marvel heralding the modern age, and by 1878 had reached a length of 600km (if laid end-to-end today they would reach as far as Istanbul). It is little wonder that the main gallery of the Musée des Égouts is named in Belgrand's honour. Anyone still in doubt about what he achieved should use the museum's own toilets, and then try to imagine what they would be like without a sewer beneath them!

Other places of interest nearby: 42, 43, 45, 52

45   Passionate about Plants

8th Arrondissement, the Jardin de la Vallée Suisse
at the junction of Avenue Franklin D. Roosevelt and Cours
de la Reine
Métro 1, 9 Franklin D. Roosevelt, 1, 13 Champs-Élysées –
Clemenceau

At least a hundred public gardens in Paris are *insolite*: quirky, unfamiliar spaces that transport the visitor to another world (see nos. 41, 47, 79). The result of singular gardening passions they are united only by their diversity. Consider the Jardin de la Mission Etrangère de Paris at 28 Rue de Babylone (7th), containing plants brought back by French missionaries, or the presbytery garden of the Église Saint-François-Xavier at 39 Boulevard des Invalides (7th), made up of plants with religious significance. By contrast the rose-filled Jardin Saint-Gilles-Grand-Veneur on Rue des Arquebusiers (3rd) is a celebration of traditional gardening practices, as is the walled Clos des Blancs-Manteaux at 21 Rue des Blancs-Manteaux (4th). Others are thematic: the Jardin d'Acclimation (16th) contains the Asian-style Jardin du Seoul symbolising friendship between the Korean capital and Paris; the Parc Georges Brassens (15th) includes a scented garden for the visually impaired; and the Jardin Atlantique at the Gare Montparnasse (14th) follows a maritime theme, reflecting the fact that trains depart here for the coast.

For sheer escapism there is little to beat the Jardin de la Vallée Suisse at the corner of Avenue Franklin D. Roosevelt and Cours de la Reine. That such a magical garden exists in such a busy spot is a revelation. The entrance is marked by a dreamy statue of the 19th century poet Alfred de Musset (1810–1857), who is remembered for his love affair with George Sand (see no. 51). To one side a rickety stone path leads down into a miniature alpine valley. This surprising illusion was created in the late 19th century by Jean-Charles Adolphe Alphand (1817–1891), a city engineer who did much to beautify Paris under Napoleon III (1852–1870). The natural-looking rocks and wooden footbridge are all formed from concrete. The plants are real enough, though, including lilacs, ivy, and a hundred year-old weeping beech. The pond is fed by the Seine, which seems to please the slow-moving carp.

Continuing the alpine theme is the Jardin Alpin. It can be found in the Jardin des Plantes at 36 Rue Geoffroy-Sainte-Hilaire (5th), which was itself established as a royal medicinal herb garden by the phy-

The sylvan setting of the magical Jardin de la Vallée Suisse

sician of Louis XIII (1610–1643). Today it comprises numerous individual gardens of which the craggy Jardin Alpin is perhaps the finest. Created in 1931 to illustrate the diversity of plant life in mountainous regions it contains more than 2,000 species from North America to the Himalayas. The garden is set three metres below the surrounding land to protect it from extremes of temperature. When visiting look out for the 18th century pistachio tree used by the botanist Sébastien Vaillant (1669–1722) in his work on plant reproduction.

For the record, the oldest tree in the Jardin des Plantes is an acacia planted in 1636. The oldest tree in Paris stands on Square René Viviani (5th) and dates back to 1601.

In 1739 the naturalist Georges Louis Leclerc, Comte de Buffon (1707–1788) became curator of the Jardin des Plantes and transformed it into a preeminent scientific institution. After the Revolution it was reorganised as the Muséum National d'Histoire Naturelle, which today includes galleries devoted to mineralogy, palaeontology, and entomology (see no. 27). A patriarchal statue of Buffon faces the museum's Grande Galerie de l'Évolution, with its astounding taxidermic stampede. Buffon was also responsible for acquiring the 18th century Cabinet de Curiosités in the museum library at 38 Rue Geoffroy-Sainte-Hilaire. The full history of the garden is given in the Cabinet d'Histoire du Jardin des Plantes at 57 Rue Cuvier.

Other places of interest nearby: 6, 42, 43, 44, 52

46 An Arch and its Secrets

8th Arrondissement, the Arc de Triomphe
on Place Charles de Gaulle
Métro 1, 2, 6 Charles de Gaulle – Étoile

As Emperor of the French Napoleon Bonaparte (1804–1815) transformed France, and for a while Europe, too. Although many of the grand monuments he planned for Paris were never realised he did commission a pair of triumphal arches on the Champs-Élysées, which had been laid out as a triumphal way during the 17th century. The largest of them, the Arc de Triomphe, is today well-known, and yet it still manages to retain a few secrets.

The Arc de Triomphe is sited perfectly on a subtle rise at the top of the Champs-Élysées, where a dozen Haussmann-era avenues converge, enabling troops to be easily deployed in the event of civil disorder. What few visitors realise, however, is how different it might have looked. The first idea for a monument on this spot actually came from an engineer called Ribart, who suggested in 1758 that Louis XV (1715–1774) might like a giant elephant built here. Ribart envisaged a staircase leading up to a banqueting hall inside the elephant's body, with space in the ears for musicians, and a royal throne inside the head. A fountain would pour from the trunk, and on the elephant's back would be a pedestal supporting a statue of the king. What a shame it never materialised!

Instead it was left to Napoleon to conjure up a less colourful concept. The first and smaller arch – the Arc de Triomphe du Carrousel – was erected as an entrance to the Palais des Tuileries in 1807. Inspired by the Arch of Septimus Severus in Rome it celebrated Napoleon's victory at Austerlitz (1805). The gold *Quadriga* stolen by the French from Saint Mark's Basilica in Venice was for a while displayed on top.

Constructing the Arc de Triomphe, which honoured those who died for France during the Revolution and the Napoleonic Wars, proved more problematic. The ground was chalky and unstable, and costs soared as extra foundations were required. This meant that the arch would not be ready in time for Napoleon's wedding to Marie Louise of Austria in 1810. Instead, the architect Jean Chalgrin (1739–1811) built a full-scale model of the arch using scaffolding and painted canvas, and it was beneath this that the newly-weds passed on their big day. The makeshift arch dominated the Paris skyline for the next 22 years, and only in 1832 did work recommence on the real thing. It was finally completed in 1836 by which time Napoleon was long dead. Four years later his body was wheeled through the arch on its way for burial at Les Invalides (7th).

Standing 50 metres high and 45 metres wide the Arc de Triomphe dwarves the Roman Arch of Titus on which it is modelled. At the end of the First World War a pilot flew his biplane through it, indeed it remained the largest triumphal arch in the world until 1982, when one even bigger was erected in Korea. On its completion several sculptors were commissioned to add four monumental bas-reliefs, with that of François Rude facing the Champs-Élysées considered the finest. Some

The Arc de Triomphe is instantly recognisable

say the shifty-looking fellow on the right is the Mayor of Paris, with whom Rude had fallen out at the time.

Details aside perhaps the best place to view the Arc de Triomphe is through the arch of its little brother in the Jardin du Carrousel, from where Napoleon's triumphal way can really be appreciated, all the way out to the Grande Arche of La Défense five kilometres away.

47 Mysterious World of the Freemasons

8th Arrondissement, Parc de Monceau
on Boulevard de Courcelles
Métro 2 Monceau

The 17th century origins of Freemasonry still baffle historians. Some have suggested a re-emergence of the Knights Templar after their suppression three centuries earlier. It seems more likely, however, that it stemmed from groups of specialist medieval masons working in freestone, who established guilds to protect their skills. This would explain the many Masonic sites in Paris, a city famous for its medieval stonework. Indeed, the word 'Freemason' may be derived from *Frère Maçon* or *Franc Maçon* meaning a skilled mason permitted to work unregulated.

Modern Freemasons, who are today builders only in a philosophical sense, claim their interests lie in charity work and the preservation of good human values, their insistence on the use of arcane handshakes and ritualised meetings designed only to protect their membership. Such secretive behaviour, however, means that Masonic locations retain an air of mystery. One such is Parc de Monceau on Boulevard de Courcelles (8th), which was created by Philippe, Duke of Orléans (1747–1793). During the Revolution he shrewdly reinvented himself as Philippe-Egalité but it didn't save him and he quickly followed his cousin, Louis XVI (1774–1791), to the guillotine.

Fifteen years earlier the duke had employed the artist Louis Carrogis Carmontelle to design Parc de Monceau as a fantasy garden. It contained follies created by the duke's architect, Bernard Poyet, representing scaled-down examples of world architecture. They included a Roman colonnade, a Venetian bridge, a Chinese fort, and a Turkish tent, all peopled by servants dressed in exotic costumes. Especially interesting is a miniature Egyptian pyramid still standing today. It is known that the duke and his architect were Freemasons, and so the pyramid is taken to be a Masonic symbol for immortality. Incidentally, it was here in the park in 1797 that the first ever parachute jump – from a balloon – was made.

Elsewhere in Paris there are further cryptic references to Freemasonry including a flaming star carved on a façade at 12 Rue de Buci (6th), where the city's first Masonic lodge was established in 1732 (the star represents the second level in Freemasonry hierarchy). The Temple du Droit Humain established in 1893 at 5 Rue Jules-Breton (13th) is unusual not only for its Egyptian-style façade – Freemasons have long included ancient Egyptian motifs in their iconography – but also for being a Freemasons' Lodge accepting female members.

To uncover the history of Freemasonry in France visit the fascinating Musée de la Franc-Maçonnerie at 16 Rue Cadet (9th), part of the Grand Orient de France, the oldest and largest Masonic Order in mainland Europe. A masonic dinner service is diplayed and tours of the temple are available by appointment. One of the Order's former Grand Masters was behind the extraordinary Rights of Man monument

This mysterious pyramid stands in the Parc de Monceau

in front of the Eiffel Tower on Champ-de-Mars (7th). After leaving the lodge visit the Masonic book specialist Detrad at number 18.

Before his execution Louis XVI was imprisoned in the Temple Tower (3rd), once the European headquarters of the Knights Templar, where the Temple Métro station now stands. Its demolition in 1808 took with it the truth surrounding the mysterious death of the king's son and heir, who died there in 1795. It is no longer thought he is buried in a common grave in the former cemetery of the Église Sainte-Marguerite at 36 Rue Saint-Bernard (11th), where there is a mysterious headstone inscribed "L XVII". His very real heart, however, is preserved in the Cathédrale Royale de Saint-Denis (formerly the Abbaye de Saint-Denis), north of Paris.

48 The Bones of Louis XVI

8ᵗʰ Arrondissement, the Chapelle Expiatoire
on Square Louis-XVI
Métro 9 Saint-Augustin

Half way along bustling Boulevard Haussmann is Square Louis XVI (8ᵗʰ). A public park since 1862 it provides sanctuary in a busy area, and a history lesson from the French Revolution. It was here in 1793 that the body of its namesake king was hastily buried after losing his head to the guillotine.

The area occupied by the square was first carved out in 1720 as a cemetery for the parish of Sainte-Madeleine de la Ville-l'Évêque. In 1770 more than a hundred bodies were brought here, victims of a stampede at a fireworks display marking the wedding of the future king Louis XVI (1774–1791) and his wife Marie Antoinette, Archduchess of Austria. No-one at the time could imagine that the king would himself end up here one day.

On 10ᵗʰ August 1792, with the French Revolution in full swing, more than 300 Swiss Guards were massacred whilst attempting to defend the Palais des Tuileries. They too were buried in the Cimetière de la Madeleine, their sacrifice enabling Louis and his queen to escape briefly to Versailles. Louis was arrested three days later and by the end of September the monarchy had been abolished, and France declared a republic.

Louis met his own end on 21ˢᵗ January 1793, when he was guillotined before a large crowd on Place de la Révolution (later Place Louis XVI, now Place de la Concorde). Afterwards his body was placed in an open coffin and transported to the cemetery. There it was covered with quicklime to accelerate decomposition and buried in an unmarked pit. Later that year Marie Antoinette met the same fate and joined him, her frivolous lifestyle symbolising much of what the revolutionaries despised about the *Ancien Régime*. Until the closure of the cemetery in March 1794 many more victims of the guillotine would also be buried here.

Twenty years later during the Bourbon Restoration Louis XVIII (1814–1824) identified the bones of his elder brother and sister-in-law, and had them removed to the Abbaye de Saint-Denis, the traditional burial place of French kings (see no. 61). He then ordered that a chapel be erected on the site of the former cemetery. Known as the Chapelle Expiatore it was designed in sombre neo-Classical style, with a crypt containing an altar on the spot where the king's remains had been found. In front of the chapel are two rows of cenotaphs memorialising the many other victims buried here.

The Cimetière de la Madeleine was eventually cleared during the 1840s and the remains taken to the Paris Catacombs (see no. 84). The site of the parish church that originally served the cemetery is now ocupied by the Église de la Madeleine.

Inside the Chapelle Expiatoire on Square Louis-XVI

The guillotine was first used on 25th April 1792 on Place de Grève (now Place de l'Hôtel-de-Ville) (4th) after which it was trundled around the city pursuing its bloody business. Over 1,100 people were guillotined on Place de la Révolution, and a further 1,300 on Place du Trône-Renversé (now Place de la Nation) (12th), their bodies taken to the Cimetière de Picpus for burial (see no. 69). The guillotine returned to Place de Grève in 1794, and remained there until 1832, when it was moved to Place Saint-Jacques (14th). In 1851 it was relocated to the prison of La Grand Roquette, where five foundation stones at the junction of Rues de la Roquette and de la Croix-Faubin (11th) still mark the spot (see no. 67). In 1900 the guillotine was moved finally to La Santé prison (14th) (see no. 85).

Other places of interest nearby: 49

49 The Lair of the Phantom

9th Arrondissement, the Opéra Garnier on Place de l'Opéra
Métro 3, 7, 8 Opéra (Note: the cellars beneath the Opéra
Garnier are not open to the public)

The most grandiose building commissioned by Napoleon III (1852–1870) during the Bourbon Restoration must surely be the Opéra Garnier. Unveiled on Place de l'Opéra (9th) in 1875 it was designed and named after a relatively unknown architect, Charles Garnier (1825–1898).

A visit to the opera should not only be for a performance, since the building itself is a marvel. The façade is merely an *entrée*, a typically *Beaux-Arts* mishmash of neoclassical styles and gilded rooftop sculptures (little wonder it is also called the Palais Garnier). The real glories are inside, namely the marble and onyx Grand Staircase, the opulently mirrored Grand Foyer, and the auditorium itself, a sea of red velvet, gold leaf, and cherubs. It is illuminated by a bronze and crystal chandelier weighing seven tons.

The chandelier is famous for more than just shedding light though. On 20th May 1896 a counterweight used to raise it into the cupola for cleaning broke free, killing a worker below. The incident inspired a famous scene in Gaston Leroux's gothic love story *Le Fantôme de l'Opéra* (1910). Despite selling poorly the book would eventually inspire Andrew Lloyd Webber's hugely successful musical *The Phantom of the Opera*.

The novel opens with a prologue in which Leroux states that the Phantom was a real person, a deformed genius who helped construct the opera house, thereafter finding refuge beneath it on the shore of a mysterious lake. Cue the entrance of the lovely Christine, a member of the opera chorus. The Phantom woos and encourages her with his beautiful singing, and eventually absconds with her down into his lair, only to be rejected when she removes his mask.

The Phantom, of course, is fictional – but what about the lake? When the foundations for the opera were dug in 1861 the groundwater was so bad that the engineers were forced to construct a coffer dam to keep it out. To alleviate the pressure on the walls of the dam they filled it with water and then roofed it over to create a cistern. On top of this a conventional cellar was constructed in which to stable the horses used to raise the scenery, and the opera house proper was built on top of that.

The work inevitably sparked rumours that a subterannean lake had

The auditorium of the Opéra Garnier

been discovered and Leroux couldn't resist perpetuating the myth by incorporating it into his story. Even the very real burial in 1907 of a time capsule containing gramophone records in the cellar of the opera finds its way into his book. And there are other ghosts in the gloom, too, since during the 1871 Siege of Paris the cellar doubled as a prison, hospital, and food store.

Tours beneath the opera are only exceptionally available because the cellar is occupied today by theatre workshops, and the cistern is used occasionally by the police to practice nightime diving. But just knowing that such a world exists below one's feet surely adds to the experience of a night at the opera.

Almost as grand as the Opéra Garnier is the near-contemporary Hilton Paris Opera at 108 Rue Saint Lazaire (8th). Rooms are expensive but it's worth a visit just to admire the sumptuously-appointed Le Grand Salon, with its lofty frescoed ceilings, granite columns and arched balconies.

Also located in the Opéra Garnier is the Bibliothèque-Musée de l'Opéra National de Paris, which contains models of opera and ballet sets, an old-fashioned library of music scores, and numerous extravagant costumes.

For an impression of life when Parisian high society was centred on the Opéra Garnier and *Les Grands Boulevards* visit the glittering neo-Rococo ballroom in the Musée d'Orsay at 1 Rue de la Légion d'Honneur (7th), preserved exactly as it appeared in 1900.

Other places of interest nearby: 48, 50

50 A Discreet Armenian Community

9th Arrondissement, the Armenian Quarter around Rue La Fayette
Métro 7 Cadet

One of the least obvious immigrant communities in Paris is that of the city's Armenians. Represented by barely a dozen shops, restaurants, and institutions it is an aspect of the city too few people are aware of.

The story of the Armenian diaspora is a long and tragic one. During the 16th century the country was divided between the Ottoman Empire and Persia, at which time many Armenians were forcibly resettled. Although the Ottomans granted their Armenian subjects a measure of autonomy they discriminated against them as Christians, and when Armenians pushed for rights in the 1890s many more died. Later during the First World War Armenia was centre-stage in the conflict between the Ottoman and Russian Empires. When Armenia provided a contingent of volunteer troops to Russia the Ottomans massacred at least half a million of the country's inhabitants, an act for which the word 'Genocide' was first coined.

With the eventual collapse of the Ottoman Empire Armenia reformed but it didn't last long. In 1920 the fledgling republic collapsed at the hands of the Turks, and the spoils shared with Russia. Executions and deportations continued under Stalin, and it wasn't until 1990 that Armenia successfully declared independence from the Soviet Union.

The first major influx of Armenian refugees into France arrived in Marseilles between 1915 and 1930. Many of today's 400,000-strong community are still there, while a minority continued northwards to Paris, settling alongside Greeks and Ashkenazi Jews in the Marais, Belleville, and the Quartier Latin. Here they set up as jewellers, lapidarists, shoemakers, and tailors, although few remain today. Instead there are memories. A wall plaque at 36 Rue Monsieur-le-Prince (6th), for example, opposite the Oriental bookshop Librairie Samuelian, marks where Shahnour Vaghenag Aznavourian was born in 1924, known to the world as singer Charles Aznavour. Another at 19 Rue au Maire (3rd) is where the Armenian poet and Communist partisan Missak Manouchian hid from German soldiers during the Second World War.

Only around the Cadet Métro station in the 9th Arrondissement does the Armenian community retain a visible presence, although it

The Armenian liturgy is practiced in the beautiful Cathédrale Saint-Jean-Baptiste on Rue Jean Goujon

is difficult to believe that until the 1970s it was as prominent as today's Turkish community on Rue du Faubourg Saint Denis (10th). Rue La Fayette was once home to many Armenian jewellers recalled by the name of the plush Armenian restaurant Les Diamantaires, which was established at number 60 in 1929. A surviving Armenian jeweller is Ishkan at nearby 40 Rue de Trévise. On the same street at number 26 is the grocers Massis & Chirag, offering provisions from Armenia as well as Greece and Lebanon. A similar range has been offered since 1930 by Heratchian Frères at 6 Rue Lamartine, which for the uninitiated is like entering another world. Spread around the floor are large sacks bursting with grains, pulses and dried fruits, and the walls are lined with shelves heavily laden with exotic tinned and other goods.

Inside Heratchian Frères on Rue Lamartine

Other discreet addresses in the neighbourhood include the Association Arménienne d'Aide Sociale at 77 Rue La Fayette, founded in 1890 to support refugees, and the Centre de Recherches sur la Diaspora Arménienne (C.R.D.A.) at 9 Rue Cadet (9th). Tiny Place Chavarche Missakian honours the founder of *Haratch*, the first European newspaper to be printed in a foreign language in 1925.

Elsewhere in Paris the ancient rite of the Armenian Apostolic Church is practised in the beautiful Cathédrale Saint-Jean-Baptiste at 15 Rue Jean Goujon (8th). The Bibliothèque Nubar at 11 Square Alboni (16th) contains many documents pertaining to Armenian life, and was founded in 1928 by the Union Générale Arménienne de Bienfaisance, with which it shares premises. The fascinating Musée Arménien de France can be visited online at www.le-maf.com.

Other places of interest nearby: 7, 49, 51

51 George Smoked her Cigars Here!

9th Arrondissement, the Musée de la Vie Romantique
at 16 Rue Chaptal
Métro 2 Blanche, Pigalle, 12 Pigalle

Amantine Aurore Lucile Dupin (1804–1876), better known by her pseudonym George Sand, was a most unconventional Frenchwoman. A cigar-smoking proto-feminist, as well as a prolific writer, she split her time between her country estate in Nohant, and Paris, where she was a major presence on the Salon scene. "What a brave man she was, and what a good woman," observed the Russian novelist Ivan Turgenev (1818–1883).

Sand's early life gave little indication of what was to come. Raised in a wealthy family she married Baron Casimir Dudevant when she was just eighteen, and bore him two children. Less than a decade later, however, and tired of married life in the country she relocated to Paris, where she became a journalist, a profession then dominated by men. A liaison with the novelist Jules Sandeau not only heralded her literary debut (the pair collaborated on her first novel) but also resulted in the *Nom de Plume* that was to make her famous: George Sand.

Around the same time Sand began wearing a top hat, trousers, and boots, which she claimed were more comfortable (and cheaper) than women's clothing. The outfit allowed her to socialise more freely at a time when women were barred from many venues. Equally unconventional was Sand's use of tobacco in public, and she was rarely seen without a cigar, a cigarette, or a hookah.

Sand also raised eyebrows with her numerous relationships, including one with the Polish composer Frédéric Chopin (1810–1849), who arrived in Paris around the same time as she did. Their nine-year relationship from 1838 to 1847 was the happiest and most productive period of Chopin's short life. For several winters the pair occupied two small houses at the back of a garden courtyard at 16 Rue Jean-Baptiste Pigalle (9th). Though long gone an impression of how the houses might have appeared is provided by the former garden home of the 19th century Romantic artist Ary Scheffer (1795–1858) at nearby 16 Rue Chaptal. It is preserved today as the Musée de la Vie Romantique.

Almost hidden from the road, the house is approached along a shady tree-lined driveway. At the end it opens out to reveal a flower-

The Musée de la Vie Romantique and its lovely garden

filled cobblestoned courtyard containing a charming Italianate villa flanked by a pair of studios. To this little oasis gravitated Romanticists such as Liszt, Rossini, and Lamartine, as well as Chopin and Sand. A tearoom open during the summer months is a lovely place to sit back and imagine them all.

In a reconstructed drawing room inside the villa are many memories of Sand, including pieces of her jewellery, a lock of her hair, a monogrammed cigar box (of course!), and a plaster cast of her arm reaching out towards another of Chopin's long-fingered left hand. There are also Sand's letters and manuscripts, and her family tree showing her aristocratic roots. Despite this she called herself a socialist, speaking out for women's rights during the 1848 Revolution but stopping short of supporting the Communards.

Before separating, Sand and Chopin lived respectively at numbers 5 and 9 Square d'Orléans off Rue Taitbout, an elegant enclave dubbed La Nouvelles Athènes. Thereafter Sand withdrew to the country, and poor Chopin succumbed to tuberculosis.

A different testimony to love is the so-called *Mur des Je t'Aime* on Place des Abbesses (18th). Inaugurated in 2000 it is inscribed with the phrase "I love you" in 311 different languages!

Other places of interest nearby: 60, 61

52 Wonders from the East

16th Arrondissement, the Musée National des Arts Asiatiques
Guimet at 6 Place d'Iéna
Métro 6 Trocadéro, 9 Iéna, Trocadéro

Paris is well endowed when it comes to collections of art and artefacts from the Asian world. Three significant museums grace the city centre, each with its own unique exhibits and atmosphere.

The Musée National des Arts Asiatiques Guimet at 6 Place d'Iéna (16th) is the city's foremost repository for Asian art, and contains sculptures, paintings, and religious and household objects from across Central and Southeast Asia. The collection owes its existence to Émile Guimet (1836–1918), an industrialist from Lyons, who was fascinated by Asian art and religion from an early age. He used his wealth to amass a huge collection of artefacts, which he brought to Paris in 1885. The variety of exhibits is astonishing, from Khmer carved dancers and Tibetan banners painted with Mandalas to the Bagram Treasure from Afghanistan, which betrays Greek influence on Indian art during the 1th and 2nd centuries BC. Look out, too, for the 16th century painted screen depicting the arrival of a Portuguese ship in Japan, the artist caricaturing the visitors with their ballooning Elizabethan-style trousers and dainty lace handkerchiefs!

It is worth noting that one of the museum's galleries is named after Paul Pelliott (1878–1945), a leading sinologist in his day, who in 1906 led an expedition to the Silk Road oasis of Dunhuang. Many of the ancient Chinese and Tibetan manuscripts he discovered there are now housed in the old Bibliothèque Nationale de France at 5 Rue Vivienne (2nd), which boasts a glorious 19th century oval reading room. As such it differs greatly from its ultra-modern successor on (and for eleven storeys below) Quai François-Mauriac (15th), commissioned by President François Mitterand in 1988.

A few doors away from the museum at 19 Avenue d'Iéna there is a surprising annex in the form of the Panthéon Bouddhique, which contains a collection of Buddhas seated in rows like the members of a choir. It is an extraordinary sight. To the rear of the building, and hidden behind a wall of bamboo, there is a small Japanese water garden containing a pavilion in which traditional tea ceremonies are performed.

Also in the 16th Arrondissement is the Musée d'Ennery at 59 Avenue Foch, which can be visited by appointment. This collection of Chinese

and Japanese art was put together by Clémence d'Ennery and housed in the Second Empire villa she shared with her husband, the playwright Adolphe Philippe d'Ennery (1811–1899). After his death both the villa and the collection were bequeathed to the state, and in 1908 opened to the public as a museum. The 7,000 objects on display illustrate daily life in China and Japan from the 12th-19th centuries. Much of the collection, which includes *Netsuke*, lacquerwork, and East India Company porcelain, is displayed in a series of exquisite wooden cabinets inlaid with mother of pearl.

The third collection of Asian art in Paris is the Musée Cernuschi at 7 Avenue Vélasquez (8th). Assembled in the early 1870s by the banker and philanthropist Henri Cernuschi (1821–1896) during a world tour, the focus here is

An 18th century suit of Japanese armour in the Musée National des Arts Asiatiques Guimet

set squarely on Chinese art, including Han, Tang and Song dynasty bronzes and ceramics. Like the Musée d'Ennery the collection is housed in its founder's former home, in this case a grand town house, which provides a suitably dramatic backdrop for many of the objects displayed. A highlight is the large 18th century Buddha of Meguro from Japan.

Other places of interest nearby: 42, 43, 44, 45

53 The Home of Art Nouveau

16th Arrondissement, the Hôtel Guimard at 122 Avenue Mozart
Métro 9 Jasmin, Michel-Ange – Auteuil,
10 Michel-Ange – Auteuil (Note: the interior
of the building is not open to the public)

In 1895 the German art dealer Siegfried Bing (1838–1905) opened a shop in Paris called Maison de l'Art Nouveau where he showcased works in *Le Style Moderne*. This new decorative style took its aesthetic cue from nature, and fostered many innovative industrial processes. More than that, however, it stood for artistic, religious, and sexual liberation in a city undergoing rapid social and economic change. By 1914 Bing's shop had lent its name to the style, and *Art Nouveau* had spawned conterparts from Budapest to Barcelona.

The best known proponent of French *Art Nouveau* was Hector Guimard (1867–1942). Although remembered chiefly for his distinctive Métro station entrances he designed many equally striking buildings. In the late 1890s he conjured up what many consider to be his masterpiece. Castel Béranger at 14 Rue La Fontaine (16th) is an astounding apartment building embodying all the artistic and technological principles of *Art Nouveau*. Notably it displays a tension between the static, medieval sense of geometrical volume and the writhing, sensuous decoration that is such a defining feature of *Art Nouveau*. In pursuit of total harmony Guimard also designed the doorknobs, carpets, and wallpaper. Despite some onlookers branding the building Castel Dérangé (!) it won an architectural competition and made Guimard a

The former home of architect Hector Guimard on Avenue Mozart

star. As if to please his detractors a more restrained effort stands at number 60 on the same street.

With commissions aplenty Guimard continued working in the *Art Nouveau* idiom. In 1909 he designed the Hôtel Guimard at 122 Avenue Mozart, a wedding gift for his wealthy American wife, Adeline Oppenheim. The couple lived there from 1913 until 1930, moving from floor to floor in a mirrored lift. Guimard operated his architectural practice from the ground floor, while his wife had an artist's studio up on the third. The first floor comprised an oval living room and dining room. It was typical of Guimard's talent for innovation that each floor plan was different so as not to overload the exterior walls on what was an awkward triangular plot.

The fact that so few of Guimard's Métro station entrances remain is a sad reminder of how quickly *Art Nouveau* fell from favour (the only complete example is at the Porte Dauphine Métro station on Line 2). Guimard's best creations remained unaffordable to the general public, and his attempts at facilitating mass production (an original tenet of *Art Nouveau*) failed to keep pace with his rapid stylistic evolution. In a post-war world where affordable social housing was paramount there was little room for *Art Nouveau*.

By the time Guimard died in New York in 1942 he was largely forgotten. His wife offered the Hôtel Guimard to the French State but the gift was refused, and the building auctioned instead. Fortunately Guimard's extraordinary dining room was salvaged in its entirety and is today displayed in the Musée des Beaux-Arts de la Ville de Paris in the Petit Palais on Avenue Winston Churchill (8th). Only in the 1960s was his work eventually reappraised and *Art Nouveau* reinstated as the defining artistic feature of the Parisian *Belle Époque*.

Another star *Art Nouveau* architect was Jules Lavirotte (1864–1924). He was responsible for a stunning doorway at 29 Avenue Rapp (7th) and the lustrous Hôtel Céramic at 34 Avenue de Wagram (8th). More *Art Nouveau* can be found at the Musée Art Nouveau, assembled by the fashion designer Pierre Cardin, in a recreated *Belle Époque* apartment above the restaurant Maxim's at 3 Rue Royale (8th), as well as in the Musée des Arts Décoratifs at 107 Rue de Rivoli (1st). Cardin's own fashion museum, the Musée Pierre Cardin, can be found at 5 Rue Saint-Merri (4th).

Other places of interest nearby: 54

Guimard's *Art Nouveau* Métro entrance at Porte Dauphine

54 Monsieur Hulot and Modernism

16th Arrondissement, the Maison La Roche
at 10 Square du Docteur-Blanche
Métro 9 Jasmin

In 1958 the film *Mon Oncle* starring French comedian and filmmaker Jacques Tati (1907–1982) won the Oscar for Best Foreign Film. The plot centres on the hapless Monsieur Hulot and his quixotic struggle with his country's postwar infatuation with modernism. Like Charlie Chaplin before him Tati infuses his slapstick brand of humour with some serious social comment.

One of the stars of *Mon Oncle* is Maison Arpel, the technology-driven suburban home of Hulot's well-to-do brother-in-law, to where Hulot must go to visit his nephew. This preposterous residence is a status symbol designed only to impress, whilst making slaves of its gullible owners. By deliberate contrast Hulot lives in impoverished contentment in a broken-down part of old Paris.

Whilst most audiences were satisfied with the humour arising from

Inside Le Corbusier's Maison La Roche

A Modernist street by
Robert Mallet-Stevens

Hulot's battles with kitchen gadgetry, and the playful affection shared with his nephew, there was a deeper message on offer. The design of Maison Arpel was not in fact from the 1950s at all but rather a pastiche of the International Style dating from the 1920s and 30s. This was Tati's clever way of pointing out how classical Modernism had been reduced from avant-garde statement to petit-bourgeois fashion accessory. One viewer so missed the point that she commissioned a full-size replica of the house including its oversized fountain in the shape of a fish!

Set designer Jacques Lagrange did not have to look far when conjuring up Tati's 'Arpel Style'. During the first decades of the 20th century Paris was the cradle of Modernism, spearheaded by the architect Charles-Édouard Jeanneret-Gris, better known as Le Corbusier (1887–1965). In 1923–25 he designed a pair of conjoined private homes on Square du Docteur-Blanche, a cul-de-sac tucked away in the 16th Arrondissement.

Maison La Roche at number 10 was commissioned by Le Corbusier's friend Raoul La Roche as a combined house and art gallery. With its concrete stilts, strip windows, roof garden, and experimental polychromy it sets out Le Corbusier's ideals for a radically new architectural aesthetic. Next door at number 8 is the Maison Jeanneret designed for Le Corbusier's brother and his family, and now home to the Fondation Le Corbusier (not open to the public). Both structures had a profound influence on Parisian architecture and still appear modern today. (The same, incidentally, can be said of Marcel Breuers's contemporary B3 steel-tube armchair displayed in the Centre Georges Pompidou (4th).)

The architectural experiment continues not far away at Rue Mallet-Stevens, where an entire street was constructed in the Modernist idiom in the mid-1920s by its namesake architect Robert Mallet-Stevens (1886–1945). Meanwhile, Le Corbusier's own apartment and studio, which of course he designed, stands a little to the southwest in the Immeuble Molitor at 24 Rue Nungesser et Coli. He occupied this light-filled space (made possible by using glass bricks) from 1934 until his death, and it still contains his personal effects.

Fascinating architectural walking tours of the 16th Arrondissement taking in all the above locations are available by visiting www.ga-paris.fr.

And don't forget the 17th Arrondissement, where recent architectural gems include Cardinet Quintessence at 155 Rue Cardinet and the Flower Tower at 23 Rue Albert Roussel, both innovatively-designed residential buildings. Nor has the historic city centre missed out on modern architecture, notably I. M. Pei's controversial pyramid inside the Louve, and not far away, Francis Soler's Ministry of Culture at 182 Rue Saint-Honoré, in which the architect unifies a 19th century building with a more recent extension by enveloping the whole with a glowing metallic lattice screen.

Another architectural pioneer in Paris was Joseph Monier (1823–1906), the father of reinforced concrete. A gardener by profession he first used concrete strengthened with iron mesh in 1849 to manufacture garden pots. He promoted his invention at the *Exposition Universelle de Paris de 1889*, where it was seen by the engineer François Hennebique (1842–1921), who in turn patented the world's first reinforced concrete building system in 1892. Hennebique's company premises at 1 Rue Danton (6th) are built from the patented material.

Other places of interest nearby: 53

55 Monet's Impression of Sunrise

16ᵗʰ Arrondissement, the Musée Marmottan at 2 Rue Louis Boilly
Métro 9 La Muette

The father of French Impressionism Claude Monet (1840–1926) was born at 45 Rue Laffitte (9ᵗʰ). One of the world's most recognised artists his works grace several famous Paris galleries, including the Musée d'Orsay at 1 Rue de la Légion d'Honneur (7ᵗʰ) and the Musée de l'Orangerie in the Jardin des Tuileries (1ˢᵗ). It is less well known that the most important collection of Monet's works is located in a small private museum on the western edge of the city.

The Musée Marmottan Monet stands at 2 Rue Louis-Boilly (16ᵗʰ) on the far side of the Jardin du Ranelagh, which was created in 1860 as part of Napoleon III's policy of beautifying Paris. Before being purchased by art collector Jules Marmottan (1829–1883) the museum building was a ducal hunting lodge on the edge of the Bois de Bou-

Monet's *Impression, Soleil Levant* in the Musée Marmottan

logne. Thereafter Marmottan's son Paul displayed his collection of First Empire art here. On his death in 1932 both building and paintings were bequeathed to the Académie des Beaux-Arts, which opened the museum in the premises shortly afterwards.

The museum's interest in Impressionism came about in 1957 when it accepted the private collection of Victorine Donop de Monchy, whose father Georges de Bellio was a great admirer of the genre. As a medical doctor he numbered amongst his patients not only Monet but also Manet, Renoir, Pissaro, and Sisley. Then in 1966 Michel Monet bequeathed his father Claude's famous home and garden in Giverny to the academy, and his paintings to the museum. Suddenly the little museum on Rue Louis-Boilly was home to the largest Monet collection in the world!

Pride of place goes to *Impression, Soleil Levant* (Impression, Sunrise). Painted in 1872 it depicts a port landscape in Le Havre, to where Monet's family relocated when he was a child. The painting was included in the first Impressionist exhibition staged in 1874 in the studio of the photographer Gaspard-Félix Tournachon ('Nadar') (1820–1910) at 35 Boulevard des Capucines (2nd). Prompted by the painting's title the art critic Louis Leroy coined the perjorative term "Impressionism" to describe a style he didn't care for. Despite this the Impressionists soon appropriated the name for themselves. The painting, incidentally, was stolen during an armed raid in 1985 and not seen again until it was retrieved by police in 1990.

A nice counterpart to Monet's Sunrise is his *Soleil Couchant sur la Seine a Lavacourt* (Sunset on the Seine at Lavacourt) in the Musée des Beaux-Arts de la Ville de Paris in the Petit Palais on Avenue Winston Churchill (8th). The painting hangs in a small room at the end of the main hall.

Although Monet spent most of his life away from Paris, it was in the city that he met fellow artists such as Renoir, and where together they experimented with new techniques in painting. Rejecting the strict traditions laid down earlier by the École des Beaux-Arts they instead rendered the effects of light *en plein air* with broken color and rapid brushstrokes, two of the most recognisable characteristics of what became Impressionism.

The Jardin du Ranelagh contains a bronze statue of the French fabulist Jean de la Fontaine (1621–1695). At Fontaine's feet is a crow with a cheese in its beak watched eagerly by a fox. The scene alludes to one of Aesop's fables dating back to ancient Greece, and is used as a warning against listening to flattery.

56 Two Thousand Years of Fakery

16th Arrondissement, the Musée de la Contrefaçon
at 16 Rue de la Faisanderie
Métro 2 Porte Dauphine

One of the most compelling of the many specialist museums in Paris is the Musée de la Contrefaçon at 16 Rue de la Faisanderie (16th). Housed inside a private mansion this museum of counterfeiting may at first glance appear novel but the message it conveys is a serious one. Fakery has been a profitable business for almost 2,000 years, and in the digital age it looks set to become even more widespread.

The museum was established in 1951 by the Union des Fabricants (Unifab), the first body in France to commence the fight against counterfeit goods. At the time counterfeiting was relatively small-scale, unlike today when almost every international brand is copied and then passed off at a price cheaper than the original. The extent of modern counterfeiting is shocking, from clothes, sunglasses, car parts and electrical goods to fountain pens, cigarettes, wristwatches, and banknotes.

The fun part of this museum is trying to ascertain what is real and what is not. Legitimate Levi's jeans, Bic razors, Tabasco sauce, Hermès scarves, and Barbie dolls are displayed alongside pirated ones – and it's sometimes difficult to tell the difference between them. In

True or false in the Musée de la Contrefaçon
on Rue de la Faisanderie

other cases there are tell-tale signs, including Lacoste crocodile logos that are just that little bit too big! Fake French goods are particularly in evidence and include all the usual suspects: Dior wallets, Louis Vuitton handbags, Givenchy perfume, and bottles of Cointreau.

The world of counterfeit drinks is particularly amusing with Dom Perignon faked as Dom Popignon, Suze as Buze, Pernod as Perrenod, and Byrrh as Pire. Other similar-sounding fake brands include Minolux for Moulinex, Babie instead of Barbie, and Game Child in imitation of Game Boy. The ingenuity of the counterfeiter seems to be inexhaustible!

Most surprising are the examples of counterfeiting from the ancient world. Inside a small cabinet near the entrance to the museum are some wine amphorae plugs made by the Gauls in third century France in imitation of those used by their Roman overlords. It is a 2,000 year old take on the current craze for pirating DVDs and computer games.

On a serious note the museum looks at the way counterfeit goods are today disseminated and sold, and the resultant impact on national and international economies. The importance of intellectual property is covered, too, as are the various sanctions and punishments that can be imposed if required. The story of the Union des Fabricants itself is also told, which was created in the late 19th century by several French pharmaceutical manufacturers, after they became aware that their products were being counterfeited in Germany. Over time they began working towards the international protection of industrial property, and helped draft various ground-breaking industrial protection and trademark conventions. Bilateral treaties followed with the aim of protecting property between France and its industrial partners around the world. In 1901 they recommended the creation of the first register of trademarks, out of which grew today's Institut National de la Propriété Industrielle.

In the heart of the nearby Bois de Boulogne is the Fondation Louis Vuitton at 8 Avenue du Mahatma Gandhi (16th). Unveiled in 2014 it hoves into view like a glass galleon in full sail. Designed by American architect Frank Gehry (b. 1929) the building's 6,000 square metres of curving glass are attached to a steel frame in revolutionary ways that necessitated the lodging of several new patents. It houses the foundation's collection of contemporary works of art and hosts temporary exhibitions and musical events.

57 Along Flower-Filled Lanes

17th Arrondissement, the Cité des Fleurs
at 154 Avenue de Clichy
Métro 13 Brochant (Note: this private lane closes daily
at 7.30pm)

Every now and then one encounters in Paris a flower-filled and cobble-stoned lane with the name *Cité* or *Villa*. Often hidden from the street these residential estates and former worker's enclaves were constructed predominantly during the 19th century for people in search of peace, rusticity, and affordable rents. Those located in the city's outer Arrondissements escaped Baron Haussmann's wholesale remodelling of the city during the 1860s, and are today a joy to discover.

A delightful example is the Cité des Fleurs at 154 Avenue de Clichy, deep in the 17th Arrondissement. This private residential lane close to a busy main street was laid out in 1847, and from the outset the planners had uniformity in mind. Whilst not identical the houses are all compatible in style and size. Each was given a front garden demarcated by matching iron gates and railings, and the owner instructed to plant three ornamental trees. The iron vases on top of the gateposts add further to the corporate feel, and initially could only be used to grow ap-

The Cité des Fleurs is a leafy enclave off Avenue de Clichy

proved species. The passage of time, however, has served to soften the original design, the trees have matured, and the gardens now reflect the individual tastes of their owners.

It is not surprising that such leafy seclusion appealed to artists, including the Impressionist Alfred Sisley (1839–1899) who lived at number 27. Peace did not always reign here though, as a plaque at number 25 reveals. Like artists' colonies elsewhere in Paris the Cité des Fleurs was a once a bastion of anti-Fascism, and during the German occupation members of the French Resistance forged papers here. When the Gestapo eventually tracked them down they executed one person and deported the rest to concentration camps.

After leaving the Cité des Fleurs visit the equally charming Cité Lemercier at 28 Rue Lemercier, where at number 11 the Belgian singer-songwriter Jacques Brel (1929–1978) rented a room during the 1950s.

More modest are the 60 or more cottages of the Villas Dietz-Monin, Émile-Meyer and Cheysson at 86 Rue Boileau (16th), built in the late nineteenth as low-cost housing for factory workers. The factories are long gone now, and the sleepy lanes draped with wisteria have become desirable places to live (although the enclave is private it can be appreciated from Rue Parent-de-Rosan). Equally lovely is the well-hidden Villa Poisonnière built in 1840 at 42 Rue de la Goutte-d'Or (18th) and the Cité du Palais-Royal-de-Belleville at 151 Rue de Belleville (19th) (both of which are also gated).

Of the numerous examples in the 20th Arrondissement a typical late 19th century cluster is the Cité Leroy, Villa de l'Ermitage, and Cité de l'Ermitage. Also worth exploring are the verdant Villas Georgina and du Borrégo, and the more workaday Cité Aubry and Villa Riberolle. Noteworth, too, are the low-cost homes built for the poor in the 1920s along the cobblestoned Rues Jules-Siegfried, Irénée-Blanc and Paul-Strauss. Known collectively as Campagne à Paris they were financed by a housing association on land rendered unstable by gypsum mining, which for a while afterwards had been used by Baron Haussmann to dump his waste.

Petite Alsace at 10 Rue Daviel (13th) on the Left Bank is a subsidised housing estate built in the Alsatian style around 1912. The Villa Daniel, a leafy working class enclave, stands opposite at number 7. The Villa Santos off Rue Santos (15th), with its 1920s red-brick houses clad in greenery, still appeals to artists as it did when first built.

58 Cabaret at Gill's Rabbit

18th Arrondissement, the cabaret Au Lapin Agile
at 22 Rue des Saules
Métro 12 Lamarck – Caulaincourt

Most people visit Montmartre to recapture the mood of a century ago, when the area was a lively centre for the arts. Many are drawn initially to Place du Tertre, with its cafés and street artists. More authentic by far, however, is Au Lapin Agile at 22 Rue des Saules (18th), which has played host to French cabaret for more than a century. Its rustic setting and roster of real performers make it a *bona fide* piece of old Montmartre (see no. 59).

Au Lapin Agile was known originally as Cabaret des Assassins, it is said because of the pictures of various killers that once adorned its walls. Its name was changed in 1872 after the artist André Gill painted a new sign for the establishment showing a rabbit escaping from a cooking pot. Inevitably Le Lapin à Gill, meaning Gill's Rabbit, became known as the nimble rabbit, hence Au Lapin Agile.

Montmartre's venerable cabaret Au Lapin Agile

The artists of Montmartre based themselves initially on Place Pigalle and only began moving up the hill after the area became a part of Paris in 1860. Painters and poets, singers and dancers were all drawn by the easy-going village life on *La Butte* (as Montmartre is known). They began frequenting Au Lapin Agile after it was bought by the singer and nightclub owner Aristide Bruand in 1905, who handed the tenancy to a suitably eccentric potter called Frédéric Gérard. From then on until the First World

War the cabaret served as the pulsating heart of Bohemian life in *Belle Époque* Paris.

Many of Montmartre's artists, including Renoir, Van Gogh, Dufy, and Utrillo, lived in squalor in Bel Air House at 12 Rue Cortot, which today contains the ever-popular Musée de Montmartre, with its lovely sloping gardens. Utrillo's paintings show how little the fabric of Montmartre has changed, including the famous *boulangerie* on Rue Norvins. He painted Au Lapin Agile, too, but only from outside leaving the animated interiors to be captured in a series of posters by Toulouse-Lautrec. Utrillo's own favourite watering hole was the more sedate Café de l'Abreuvoir, which has since been reconstructed in the museum.

In 1905 Picasso painted himself as a harlequin drinking at the bar of Au Lapin Agile, with Frédéric Gérard in the background. Together with Braque and Gris he created Cubism in studios several streets away at 13 Place Emile-Goudeau (see no. 2). There they were supported by poets such as Guillaume Apollinaire and Max Jacob, who dubbed the ramshackle building the Bateau-Lavoir or Laundry Boat. Artists including Modigliani and Brancusi lived and worked at the studios, and Picasso painted his ground-breaking *Les Demoiselles d'Avignon* there in 1907. Not everyone was impressed though. The writer Roland Dorgelès expressed his distaste for such art by tying a paintbrush to the tail of Gérard's donkey, and exhibited the haphazard results at the Salon des Indépendents under the spoof title *Sunset over the Adriatic*. It sold for 400 francs!

Today, Au Lapin Agile still has atmosphere, with young poets giving readings and budding singers climbing the stage to reinvent songs dating back centuries. Open into the wee hours it is a lively reminder of how Montmartre was before the artists crossed the river to Montparnasse in the 1920s.

Other popular Montmartre meeting places are the Café des Deux Moulins at 15 Rue Lepic (18th), which featured in the film *Le Fabuleux Destine d'Amélie Poulain* (2001), and the restaurant Moulin de la Galette at number 88. Housed in a former windmill-cum-dance hall it was depicted by Renoir in his boisterous *Bal du Moulin de la Galette* (1876).

Other places of interest nearby: 51, 59, 60, 61

59 New Vines for Old Montmartre

18th Arrondissement, the Clos Montmartre
at 14–18 Rue des Saules
Métro 12 Lamarck – Caulaincourt (Note: access to the
vineyard is only possible on the first Sunday in October
although it can be viewed easily from outside)

The famous artists may have long since departed *La Butte* (as the hill of Montmartre is known) but something of the village atmosphere that attracted them still remains. The winding streets and stairways, the rustic appeal of the cabaret Au Lapin Agile on Rue des Saules, and the unexpected presence of the Clos Montmartre, a walled vineyard across the road (see no. 58).

But the Clos Montmartre is not all it seems. In fact it only dates back to 1933, when a group of lesser known artists were permitted to plant 2,000 vines here to preserve the tradition of wine production started in the Île de France by the Romans. It's worth noting that until the mid-19th century vineyards stretched from the slopes of Montmartre all the

Vines enjoying summer sun in the Clos Montmartre

way to Ménilmontant. By the early 20th century, however, barely a plant was left, in part a result of the devastating Siege of Paris (1870), as well as disease and urban development.

That the artists knew little about viticulture is immediately apparent since the vineyard is north facing (it is usual practice in the northern hemisphere for vineyards to face south, so as to receive as much sun as possible). Furthermore, they were unaware that it takes four years for a vine to bear useable fruit and organised a harvest festival (Fête des Vendanges) in the first year of planting! The festival has been staged on the first Saturday in October ever since and it's a lively event, with the mainly Pinot Noir and Gamay grapes being pressed in the basement of the local *Mairie*. The 1,500 bottles produced each

The vineyard adds to the romance of old Montmartre

year are auctioned for charity the following April, with labels designed by local artists.

Contrary to popular opinion the Clos Montmartre is not the only vineyard in Paris, although it is certainly the largest. One can be found at the bottom of Montmartre, for example, where since 1926 a handful of vines have been growing over the railings of the fire station at 22–28 Rue Blanche (9th). Fifty bottles of *Château Blanche* are produced here each year, the name recalling the Plaster of Paris once mined on the hill above.

Another vineyard exists in the Parc de Bercy at 41 Rue Paul Belmondo (12th). Located on the banks of the Seine it acts as a reminder that Bercy was once the world's largest staging post for wine. From the 18th century

A vine draped over the façade of the Rue Blanche fire station

onwards huge barrels of wine arrived here from the south by barge. At the time the *Commune* of Bercy lay outside the city walls, and taxes were only levied once the wine was bottled and shipped onwards into Paris. By the 1960s, however, the increasing demand for wine bottled at source, and the replacement of barges with trucks, brought an end to Bercy's monopoly over the Parisian wine trade. Alongside the vineyard can still be seen the brick warehouses known as *Chais* once used to store the barrels, as well as the tracks of the narrow gauge railway that serviced them. When the park was created in the 1990s, as part of a plan to reinvent this overlooked part of Paris, many *Chais* were converted for retail and leisure use, including the intriguing Pavillons de Bercy (see no. 71).

The story of winemaking in the Paris region is described fully in the Musée du Vin at 5 Rue des Eaux (16th). It is suitably located in the former 16th century wine cellars of the Abbaye de Passy, which were excavated 300 years earlier for the quarrying of limestone.

Other places of interest nearby: 51, 58, 60, 61

60 Paris on the Big Screen

18th Arrondissement, the Cinéma Studio 28
at 10 Rue Tholozé
Métro 2 Blanche

In 1957 the children's fantasy film *Le Ballon Rouge* garnered a well-deserved Oscar for its director Albert Lamorisse (1922–1970). The deceptively simple tale, which follows the adventures of a young boy who discovers a stray but sentient balloon, has enchanted the young at heart ever since. As with many films set in Paris one of the main characters is the city itself. Lamorisse used the backstreets of Belleville to great effect, unwittingly recording for posterity places that would soon be lost to redevelopment (including the Passage Julien Lacroix, where the film begins).

France's place in film history was guaranteed in 1895 when Auguste and Louis Lumière organised the world's first paid public film screening – a two-minute clip of a train arriving in a station – at the Grand Café on Boulevard des Capucines 14 (2nd). Since then the country has played a significant role in the development of cinema from the *avant-garde* movement of the 1920s and 30s through *La Nouvelle Vague* of the late 1950s – and beyond. Through it all the French capital has supplied memorable cinematic backdrops and all of them are archived in the Forum des Images at 2 Rue du Cinéma (1st).

France is the world's third largest film market after America and India, and the capital contains over a hundred cinemas. The oldest still in operation is Cinéma Studio 28 at 10 Rue Tholozé (18th). It opened in 1928 as the first *avant-garde* cinema in France and in 1930 hosted the premiere of Luis Buñuel's surrealist classic *L'Age d'Or*. Jean Cocteau (1889–1963), who designed the light fittings in the main auditorium, became one of the cinema's patrons in 1950 together with Abel Gance (1889–1981), the director of the monumental *Napoléon* (1927). The cinema still screens art house films, hosts film-related exhibitions in the foyer, and even has its own garden replete with a bar.

The most unusual cinema in Paris is undoubtedly La Pagode at 57 Rue de Babylone (7th). This Japanese-style pagoda was built in 1895 by the owner of the Bon Marché department store, as a gift for his wife. Situated next to the couple's home it originally served as a ballroom and banquet hall. After the couple separated the pagoda was sold, and in 1931 it was converted into a cinema. Fittingly the film director Louis Malle (1932–1995) helped save it from demolition.

The La Pagode cinema on Rue Babylone was originally a private ballroom

Studio 28 on Rue Tholozé was the first *avant-garde* cinema in France

Equally exotic is Le Louxor at 170 Boulevard Magenta (10th). This enormous cinema from the 1920s boasts a façade decorated in the style of an ancient Egyptian temple. For a while during the 1980s it was transformed into a nightclub and when that closed it too faced demolition. Saved by the City of Paris it has now been restored to its former magnificence.

The largest cinema in Paris is Le Grand Rex at 1 Boulevard Poissonière (2nd). Built in 1934 and inspired by Radio City Music Hall in New York this *Art Deco* colossus was originally designed to hold 3,300 people. Backstage tours of what is still the largest cinema in Europe are available by appointment.

A wall plaque at 29 Boulevard Saint-Martin marks the birthplace of the French film-maker Georges Méliès (1861–1938), who is credited with pioneering special effects such as slow motion, dissolve, hand-colouring, and fade-out. His most famous film, *Le Voyage dans la Lune* (1902), features the celebrated scene in which a rocket hits the Man in the Moon in the eye! Props from the film are displayed in the Musée de la Cinémathèque Française at 51 Rue de Bercy (12th).

Other places of interest nearby: 51, 58, 59, 61

61 On the Mount of Martyrs

18th Arrondissement, the Martyrium Saint-Denis
at 9 Rue Yvonne-le-Tac
Métro 12 Abbesses, Pigalle, 2 Pigalle

The desire of most tourists to reach the top of Montmartre is understandable. As one of the highest points in Paris it provides a superb view, and the Sacré-Cœur, despite being dubbed "the basilica of the ridiculous" by Émile Zola, defines this part of the city's skyline (see no. 75). The real history of the place, however, dates back much farther, and begins with the bloody execution of a saint lower down the hill.

According to ancient sources Saint Denis was sent from Italy to convert Gaul to Christianity in the 3rd century AD. This was after the Roman Emperor Decius (201–251) had all but eliminated the Christian minority in Lutetia, as Roman Paris was known (see

A headless Saint Denis carved on the outside of Notre-Dame

no. 30). Together with his loyal companions Rusticus and Eleutherius, Denis settled on the Île de la Cité. There they set about converting the locals, much to the irritation of the local pagan priests. It was not long before all three were rounded up and taken to Montmartre, where they were beheaded. Although it is often said that the name 'Montmartre' is derived from the Latin *Mons Martyrium* (meaning Martyr's Mountain) it now seems more likely to be derived from *Mons Mercurei et Mons Martis* (Hill of Mercury and Mars), reflecting the likelihood that a temple to these Roman gods once stood on top of the hill.

After his execution, legend relates how Denis picked up his severed head and walked northwards, preaching all the way. At the place where he eventually stopped talking and died he was buried, and a shrine established there. This was replaced in the 12th century by the Abbaye de Saint-Denis (today a cathedral), a gem of Gothic architecture that became the traditional burial place for French kings.

Meanwhile, back on the lower slopes of Montmartre, in 475 a martyrium was erected on the site of the execution. It is thought to have been instigated by Saint Geneviève, the patron saint of Paris, and paid for by the people. Initially only Parisians came here, especially in times of war, to seek guidance from Saint Denis. But by the 8th century the veneration of the saint had spread beyond France, and pilgrims from across Europe began making their way to Montmartre.

In 1133 a Benedictine abbey was established on the summit of Montmartre by Louis VI (1108–1137) and his wife, Adelaide of Savoy, who became its first abbess. It too became a pilgrimage destination and its remains now form the vaulted choir of the 17th century Église Saint-Pierre-de-Montmartre at 2 Rue du Mont-Cenis (the church also contains columns said to have been part of the original Roman temple).

Returning to the martyrium it was there in 1534 that Ignatius of Loyola (1491–1556) took his vows of poverty and chastity. The event heralded the birth of the Society of Jesus, known later as the Jesuits, who fought to save the Catholic Church from the Protestant Reformation.

In 1611 during renovation work at the abbey a mysterious vault was unearthed. Whatever its original purpose it sparked renewed interest in Montmartre and a further 60,000 pilgrims visited, including Marie de Médicis. To help cater for them a convent dependent on the abbey was erected around the martyrium in 1622. The martyrium and convent both still exist at 9 Rue Yvonne-le-Tac (18th), and although badly damaged during the Revolution they have been rebuilt. Located underground the Martyrium Saint-Denis provides a welcome spiritual retreat from the bustle of modern Montmartre.

Other places of interest nearby: 51, 58, 59, 60

62 A Visit to a Hindu Temple

18th Arrondissement, the Sri Manicka Vinayakar Alayam
Hindu Temple at 17 Rue Pajol
Métro 2 La Chapelle, 12 Marx Dormoy

The French have a name for multicultural Paris: *Paris Mondial*. To experience this vibrant world inhabited by immigrants from former French colonies and their descendants, as well as exiles and refugees, visit the area north of the Gare du Nord. Here is a Maghrebi enclave centred on the Rue de la Goutte d'Or, with Afro-Caribbean stores along Rue des Poissoniers, a bustling African market on Rue Dejean and another beneath the Métro tracks at Barbès Rochechouart, and the Mosquée Al-Fath at 55–57 Rue Polonceau. The area is also home to the Sri Manicka Vinayakar Alayam, the first Hindu temple in Paris.

The temple is located at 17 Rue Pajol (18th), and was founded in 1985 by its president, the Sri Lankan Tamil M. Sanderasekaram. Like many

Pooja ceremony in the Sri Manicka Vinayakar Alayam Hindu Temple on Rue Pajol

Tamils he was forced to exchange his homeland for Europe because of civil war. Upon arriving, however, he realised that the country's scattered Hindu community were only able to worship at household altars. By constructing a temple in Paris Mr. Sanderasekaram created an important focal point for the Tamil Hindu community, which today has around 9,000 members. It seems that temple-building runs in Mr. Sanderasekaram's family, since his father built a temple in the Sri Lankan city of Jaffna, and other members of his family have built temples in London and Australia.

The Sri Manika Vinayakar Alayam is dedicated to the elephant-headed god Ganesh, son of Shiva the destroyer, who, together with Brahma the Creator and Vishnu the Preserver, makes up the Hindu Trinity *(Trimurti)*. Outsiders are most welcome at the temple, and it is an enlightening experience to witness Hindu religious practices taking place there. Three times a day, for example, at 10am, noon, and 7pm so-called *Poojas* are performed. This is a ritual that all Hindus perform (usually in the morning after dressing but before eating) and consists of chanting a sacred *Mantra*, and offering food and drink to statues of deities known as *Murtis*. These statues are displayed in the temple's prayer hall.

Another important ritual is a bathing ceremony called *Abhishekam*, in which the *Murtis* are undressed and then cleansed with water, milk, honey, rose water, and curdled milk. After the robes have been replaced a floral garland is placed over the statues, while priests *(Pujaris)* chant more *Mantras*. At weekends vegetarian food is served to anyone attending the temple ceremonies.

A highlight of the temple's year is the Fête de Ganesh in late August/early September. During the celebration a chariot carrying a five-faced statue of Ganesh is drawn through the streets surrounding the temple by barefooted devotees. The way is prepared for them by dousing it with saffron-infused water.

The core beliefs of Hinduism are based on traditional scriptures such as the *Bhagavad-gītā* and the *Śrīmad Bhāgavatam*, both of which date back more than 5,000 years. At its heart is the devotional worship *(Bhakti)* of Krishna and his lover Radha (both avatars of Vishnu), which is realised by singing their holy names in the form of the well-known *Hare Krishna* mantra. The focus is set squarely on universal respect, tolerance, and freedom: the goal is to encourage non-Hindus to open themselves to the worship of Krishna, and to incorporate it into their daily life and work. Some go as far as giving up their previous lives entirely.

For a taste of India visit the Passage Brady at 43 Rue du Faubourg-Saint-Martin (10th), a former 19th century *Passage Couvert* now filled with curry houses, spice shops, and fabric bazaars (see no. 4).

Other places of interest nearby: 63, 74

63 A Litany of Liturgies

18th Arrondissement, the Église Notre-Dame-de-Chaldée
at 13–15 Rue Pajol
Métro 2 La Chapelle

Freedom of worship has been guaranteed in France since the passing
of the Déclaration des Droits de l'Homme et du Citoyen (Declaration
of the Rights of Man and the Citizen) during the French Revolution.
Despite the subsequent emergence of many non-Christian immigrant
communities – Buddhists, Hindus, Jews, and Muslims – the majority
of the country's worshippers remain Roman Catholic, as they were
when Catholicism was the state religion (see nos. 29, 62, 72). Within
the broader Christian community numerous rites are practised, including Russian and Armenian Eastern Orthodoxy (see nos. 50, 95). Here
are some less well-known ones.

The anonymous-looking Église Notre-Dame de Chaldée at 13–15
Rue Pajol (18th) pales next to its famous namesake in the city centre, and yet it offers something very special. Every Sunday morning at
11am a mass is given in Aramaic, the language thought to have been
spoken by Jesus Christ. Once used widely in the Middle East the Aramaic language is today considered endangered, although it is retained
as a liturgical language by members of the Eastern Christian Church.
One of these is the Chaldean Catholic Church, which comprises ethnic

The Assyro-Chaldean rite is celebrated in the Église Notre-Dame-de-Chaldée on Rue Pajol

Assyrians whose origins lie in the Sumero-Akkadian civilisation that emerged in Mesopotamia around 4000 BC. The Chaldeans have often been suppressed, notably in Syria and Mesopotamia by the Ottoman Turks, and more recently by Islamic extremists in Iraq. This explains why the congregation celebrating the Assyro-Chaldean rite at the Église Notre-Dame de Chaldée includes ethnic Assyrians who have fled those countries.

A different rite is observed at the Église Saint-Julien-le-Pauvre at 79 Rue Galande (5th). Dating to the 12th century this is one of the city's oldest churches, and was once the official seat of the Sorbonne. Thereafter it was neglected and following the Revolution it became a storehouse and granary. By 1889 it was abandoned and given over to the Melchites, a mixed Greek and Eastern Mediterranean Catholic community that traces its origins back to the early Christians of Antioch in the 1st century AD. This explains the presence of an *Iconostasis* and the performance each Sunday morning of the Eastern Orthodox Byzantine rite, sung beautifully in Greek, French, and Arabic.

Representing the western branch of the early Catholic Church is the Gallican Rite, which developed out of the Aramaic/Greek rites and was translated into Latin by the Romans. It was well established in Gaul by the 5th century AD and used across Western Christendom before being abolished by Charlemagne. The rite was reintroduced during the 20th century and could be witnessed in an extraordinary mass for living animals dedicated to their patron saint, Francis of Assisi. Unfortunately the church where it was held, the Église Sainte-Rita at 27 Rue François-Bonvin (15th), has recently been sold to property developers and at the time of writing no alternative venue has been found. It is a great loss.

Also unusual is the Église Saint-Eugène-Sainte-Cécile at 6 Rue Sainte-Cécile (9th), which boasts not only two patron saints but also two Catholic rites. The Pauline Mass, in which the priest faces the audience and speaks French, has been normal since it was introduced by Pope Paul VI in 1969. The older Tridentine Mass is given in Latin, the priest turning his back to the congregation. The building itself, which is made of brightly painted cast iron, provided the perfect backdrop for the wedding of science fiction author Jules Verne in 1857 (see no. 27).

Scarcely any rite at all is observed in the Temple Antoiniste at 34 Rue Vergniaud (13th). Founded in Belgium in 1910 this Christian-oriented movement is focussed on healing through daily prayers (*L'Opération Générale*) and readings (*La Lecture*).

Other places of interest nearby: 62, 74

64 Concealed Courtyards and Secret Squares

10th Arrondissement, a tour of concealed courtyards including the Cour de l'Hôpital Saint-Louis at 2 Place du Docteur-Alfred-Fournier
Métro 5 Jacques Bonsergent, 11 Goncourt
(Note: the courtyard is closed at weekends)

Courtyards can be secretive places, visited by those privileged to know of their existence or else just happened upon by the fortunate stroller. In Paris they come in all sizes, each with a particular atmosphere and a story to tell.

The city's large courtyards are generally the more frequented ones, the most famous being the Place des Vosges (4th). This sublime ensemble of public square surrounded by aristocratic *Hôtels* was commissioned by Henry IV (1589–1610) and completed in 1612. Very popular today with visitors it still retains a few secrets, including the hidden garden of the Hôtel de Sully at number 7, with its original *Orangerie* (the layout of the *Hôtel* reflects the aristocratic penchant for setting one's home back from the street – in this case Rue Saint-Antoine – so as to provide a suitably grand entrance).

The Cour du Rohan can be glimpsed at from the end of Rue du Jardinet

Other large city centre courtyards include the immense Cour Carrée du Louvre on Rue de l'Amiral-de-Coligny (1st), with its myriad Classical sculptures, and the Cour d'Honneur des Invalides on Place des Invalides (7th), a former parade ground which boasts a first floor arcade lined with upended cannons. Les Invalides, incidentally, was founded by Louis XIV (1643–1715) as

Peace reigns in the Cour de l'Hôpital Saint-Louis on Place du Docteur-Alfred-Fournier

a hospital for wounded soldiers and is still home to the Musée de l'Armée.

Contemporary with the Place des Vosges – but without the crowds – is the impressive Cour de l'Hôpital Saint-Louis at 2 Place du Docteur-Alfred-Fournier (10th). This peaceful and leafy quadrangle was also commissioned by Henry IV but for a very different reason. Located on land which at the time lay outside the city walls, the hospital was built in response to the plague of 1562, which resulted in the death of 68,000 Parisians. The city's oldest hospital, the Hôtel-Dieu on the Île de la Cité, had not been able to cope with the disaster, and so a new one was required, where victims could be quarantined and the spread of contagion minimised. The fortress-style appearance of the Hôpital Saint-Louis was to ensure infected patients didn't escape!

Modest by comparison is the Cour du Rohan, which can be glimpsed at from the end of Rue du Jardinet (6th) (like many old Paris courtyards it is now usually kept locked). The series of three inter-connected courtyards was originally part of the 15th century townhouse of the archbishops of Rouen (hence the corruption to Rohan). The middle courtyard is of particular interest since it contains a rare wrought-iron *Pas-de-Mule* once used by the elderly to climb into their carriages.

Many more modest courtyards can be found on either side of the Rue du Faubourg Saint-Antoine (11th/12th), where they originally gave access to workshops and artists' studios. The most attractive is the cobblestoned Cour du Bel-Air at number 56, its low-rise premises now draped with climbing plants. Other courtyards awaiting discovery on the same street can be found at numbers 66, 71, 74, 75, 81, 89, and 95.

The small public squares of Paris, so beloved by its citizens as a place to rest, can also prove revelatory to the uninitiated city stroller. Square Barye, for example, at the eastern tip of Île Saint-Louis (3rd) offers a less usual view of Notre-Dame. Its counterpart, Square du Vert-Galant at the westernmost tip of the Île de la Cité, is like the prow of a ship. Tiny Square Récamier at 7 Rue Récamier (7th) is hard by the busy Rue de Sèvres and yet manages to offer plant life galore and even a waterfall! Equally bucolic is Square Denys-Bühler at 147 Rue de Grenelle (7th).

Other places of interest nearby: 65, 75

65 Illuminating the City of Light

**10th Arrondissement, the electricity sub-station Temple
at 36 Rue Jacques-Louvel-Tessier
Métro 11 Goncourt**

Why is Paris called *La Ville-Lumière*? Some say it reflects the importance of the city as a centre for ideas during the Age of Enlightenment. Others cite the second half of the 19th century, when Baron Haussmann tore down the dingy medieval city and replaced it with open boulevards and buildings of light-coloured limestone. Or perhaps it dates from the 1820s, when Paris became one of the first European cities to adopt gas street lighting? Whether or not the latter explanation is true, the history of the city's illumination is worth retelling.

The earliest record of street lighting comes from the city of Antioch during the 4th century AD, followed by Cordoba in the 10th, and eventually London in 1417. Louis XIV (1643–1715) first introduced lanterns to the streets of Paris in the mid-17th century. To learn more about the history of French lighting technology visit the tiny Musée des Éclairages Anciens inside the shop Lumière de l'Oeil at 4 Rue Flatters (5th). This fascinating private collection contains many bygone forms of illumination, the oldest of which dates from the late 18th century. It features a flat wick, a technological innovation introduced in the wake of the discovery in 1775 of the importance of oxygen in combustion by chemist Antoine Lavoisier (1743–1794). His laboratory has been reconstructed in the Musée des Arts et Métiers at 60 Rue de Réaumur (3rd).

Europe's first gas street lighting was installed on London's Pall Mall in 1807. Although one Philippe Lebon used gas to illuminate his Paris home in 1801 it was not until 1817 that gas lighting appeared in the Passage des Panoramas (2nd), and not until the 1820s that the Champs-Elysées was lit by gas. Electric lighting followed in 1841, when carbon-arc lamps were installed on Quai de Conti (6th) and Place de la Concorde (8th), followed by Avenue de l'Opéra (2nd) in 1878.

During the late 19th century Paris experienced a rapid increase in demand for electricity for street lighting, as well as for industry. Power stations were required across the city, and with the opening of the Métro, sub-stations were needed, too. Many of these were designed by the Alsatian architect and civil engineer Paul Friésé (1851–1917), and are still extant.

Friésé's first power station was constructed in 1890 in imposing neo-Classical style on Rue des Dames (17th). Thereafter he adopted

An elegant former electricity sub-station on Rue Jacques-Louvel-Tessier

a lighter brick construction on a visible steel frame, as seen in his power station for the Paris Compressed Air Company at 130–134 Quai de Jemmapes (10th). Compressed air technology was popular in Paris, where it was used for lifts, ventilation, the postal system, and even the city's public clocks! Friésé's Temple sub-station not far away at 36 Rue Jacques-Louvel-Tessier is of a similar construction, its elegant façade pierced by huge arched windows of the sort used in his other facilities at 18 Rue de la Cerisaie (4th), 6 Rue Récamier (7th), and 2bis Rue Michel-Ange (16th). The style is shared by a former lithography works across the road at number 27bis.

Little heavy industry exists in central Paris today, and many old factories (including Friésé's power plants) have found new uses or else been demolished (see no. 68). The former Citroën plant in Javel (15th), for example, is today the ultra-modern Parc André-Citroën. A novel example of reuse is a former 19th century railway viaduct between Place de Bastille and Vincennes (12th), which now supports an elevated garden (the 4.5km long Promenade Plantée) with a series of shops (Viaduc des Arts) beneath it.

Other places of interest nearby: 64, 75

66 In the Sparrow's Nest

11th Arrondisement, the Musée Édith Piaf
at 5 Rue Crespin-du-Gast
Métro 2 Ménilmontant (Note: visits strictly
by appointment only)

The story of Édith Piaf (1915–1963) is linked inextricably to Belleville in the 20th Arrondissement, a former hilltop village absorbed into Paris in 1860. It was here that the chanteuse was born into poverty, and where she was laid to rest just 47 years later. During her short life she conquered France and the world with her torch song ballads, sung in the *Accent de Belleville* without a hint of self-pity.

A must-see for fans is the Musée Édith Piaf at 5 Rue Crespin-du-Gast (11th). This private collection occupies a two-room apartment occupied by Piaf in 1933, and was created by Bernard Marchois, an acquaintance during her final years. Not only photographs, posters, and records are displayed but also personal effects, including Piaf's porcelain collection and the trademark black dress she wore on stage. Amongst the souvenirs given by family and friends is an over-sized teddy bear almost the same size as the singer, who was only 1.42m high.

Despite claims that she was born on a pavement at 72 Rue de Belleville, Piaf's birth certificate states clearly she was born Édith Giovanna Gassion in the Hôpital Tenon in Belleville. The area had gained a tough reputation after Baron Haussmann levelled the inner city slums in the 1860s prompting workers to move here *en masse*. During the workers' uprising of the Paris Commune in 1871 the barricades of Belleville were the last to fall.

Aged just two months Piaf was abandoned by her mother, an Italian café singer, and given to her alcoholic maternal grandmother. Her father, a travelling acrobat, then sent her to live with his own mother, a madam in a Normandy brothel, while he went to war. Upon his return he took young Édith with him on tour around France, where she sang in public for the first time.

Aged fifteen Édith left her father and returned to Paris, earning a living by singing on the streets of Pigalle and Ménilmontant. She soon fell in love with a delivery man and gave birth to her only child, Marcelle, who shortly afterwards succumbed to meningitis. Then in 1935 she was spotted by the impresario Louis Leplée and persuaded to sing professionally in his club Le Gerny's. He billed her as *La Môme Piaf*

– Parisian slang for 'The Little Sparrow' – which suited her frail build and tremulous voice that wrung every drop of emotion out of her songs. Leplée also suggested she wear the famous black dress.

After Leplée was murdered by gangsters in 1936 Piaf took a new manager, the composer Raymond Asso, who promoted her successfully as Édith Piaf. Whilst treading the boards at the Folies Belleville at 8 Rue de Belleville she befriended Maurice Chevalier, whose own career was launched at the more famous Folies Bergère (9th). By the time the Second World War was over Piaf was known internationally and she appeared twice at Carnegie Hall. Her signature song *La Vie en Rose* was recorded in 1946, whilst the equally recognisable *Non, Je Ne Regrette Rien* was premiered at the Paris Olympia music hall in 1961.

The legend lives on in the Musée Édith Piaf

Aside from the music Piaf's great love was the former world middleweight boxing champion Marcel Cerdan, who died in a plane crash in 1949, while flying to meet her. His battered boxing gloves can be seen in the museum. Piaf herself was badly injured in a car accident in 1951, and slid into addiction before dying from liver cancer. Around 40,000 admirers accompanied her coffin to the Cimetière du Père-Lachaise (see no. 78).

Other places of interest nearby: 67, 78

67 Like an Army of Shadows

11th Arrondissement, some Second World War sites
including the the former Petite Roquette prison
at 147 Rue de la Roquette
Métro 2 Philippe Auguste, 9 Voltaire

On 18th June 1940 General Charles de Gaulle (1890–1970) made a radio broadcast from London to the French people. He encouraged them to join forces with the Allies in resisting the German occupation that had just begun. Since most could not reach Allied territory they instead formed *La Résistance Française*. Like an army of shadows they set about sabotaging the actions of the Nazi regime and its Vichy collaborators. Eventually in 1944 the Resistance turned on its oppressors, effectively launching the liberation of Paris several days before the arrival of Allied troops. Their heroism is recorded discreetly by inscribed wall plaques across the city.

One such location is 28 Rue de la Huchette (5th), where a simple wall plaque records the death on 17th May 1944 of one Jean Albert Vouillard, a member of a resistance cell codenamed *Arc en Ciel*. By this time the Resistance had already liberated the Préfecture de Police on the Île de la Cité, and they were now using the Rue de la Huchette as a base from which to further harass the enemy. The narrow part of the street, which Vouillard and his companions had barricaded, was precisely that part left unwidened by the city planner Baron Haussmann, when he left his job in 1870. Haussmann's intention had been to widen the full length of the street to prevent disgruntled citizens from barricading it as they had done during the Revolution. That this part of the 5th Arrondissement was a focus of wartime resistance is witnessed by other memorial plaques at 27 Rue Saint-Jacques and on Place du Petit Pont. It is likely, too, that *Arc en Ciel* members held clandestine meetings in cellars at 5 Rue de la Huchette (see no. 24).

Whilst many Resistance fighters were executed, including 30 at the Gare du Nord (10th), many more were incarcerated in the city's prisons (see no. 85). One was La Petite Roquette at 147 Rue de la Roquette (11th), where 4,000 members of the Resistance were held captive. Demolished in 1974 and replaced by a park, only the prison's gateway with its barred windows remains. On it hangs a plaque recording the prisoners' contribution to the eventual liberation of France.

In August 1944, with the Allied liberation of Paris only days away, the Resistance led by Colonel Henri Rol-Tanguy (1908–2002) co-

DE L'APPEL DU
GENERAL DE GAULLE
LE 18 JUIN 1940
A LA LIBERATION DE PARIS
LE 25 AOUT 1944
DANS CES LIEUX
4000 RESISTANTES
ONT ETE EMPRISONNEES POUR
AVOIR LUTTE CONTRE L'OCCUPANT
ELLES ONT CONTRIBUE A LA
LIBERATION DE LA FRANCE

All that remains of the Petite Roquette prison is its gateway

ordinated its efforts from an air raid shelter beneath Place Denfert-Rochereau (14th). So as not to be discovered the colonel entered it by means of an old quarry tunnel accessed via a secret staircase in Rue Schoelcher. Such tunnels provided a useful way for the Resistance to move around this part of the city without being detected (see no. 87).

On 25th August 1944 the German military governor of Paris surrendered to Rol-Tanguy and General Philippe Leclerc (1902–1947) at the Gare Montparnasse. Later when the station was rebuilt farther down the line a superb museum commemorating Leclerc, as well as the Resistance hero Jean Moulin (1899–1943), was installed there. It is called the Mémorial du Maréchal Leclerc de Hauteclocque et de la Libération de Paris – Musée Jean Moulin and is located at 23 Allée de la 2ème Division Blindée (15th).

To discover more about Paris in the Second World War visit the Musée de la Préfecture de Police at 4 Rue de la Montagne-Sainte-Geneviève (5th). It is also possible to explore an intact air raid shelter beneath the Gare de l'Est in Place du 11-Novembre-1918 (10th) (visit www.parisfacecachee.fr).

Other places of interest nearby: 66, 78, 79

68 Paris at Work

**11th Arrondissement, a tour of historic work places finishing
with the Cour de l'Industrie at 37bis Rue de Montreuil
Métro 8 Faidherbe – Chaligny**

Until the 1970s a certain amount of industrial activity was still being pursued in the City of Paris. Much of this has subsequently relocated to purpose-built factories beyond the *Périphérique*. What remains is a fascinating mix of former factories, converted workers' enclaves, and reused workshops.

The building at 39 Rue de Francs-Bourgeois (4th) is a prime example. Over its door is the curious name Societé des Cendres, a reminder that here was once a works where gold was extracted from jewellers' waste. Established in 1867 the operation has since moved to the suburbs, where metals are extracted from dental and other prosthetics. Other former factories include the Meccano construction kit factory at 78–80 Rue Rébeval and the Bornibus mustard company at 58 Boulevard de la Villette (both 19th), as well as the Loebnitz faience factory at 4 Rue de la Pierre-Levée (11th).

The 11th Arrondissement is especially rich in industrial-era remains, with many traditional workers' courtyards still in evidence. Some have been transformed into offices and homes, including the smart enclave at 186 Rue de la Roquette, and the Passage du Cheval-Blanc farther along at number 2. Others have been taken over by contemporary artists thereby continuing their original function as is the case with the Passage Lhomme at 26 Rue de Charonne, and the nearby Passage du Chantier. Rue des Immeubles-Industriels is of particular interest. It was built in 1873 to provide modern workshops on the ground floor with comfortable accommodation for workers' families above. The surprisingly elegant street façade features neo-Classical columns made from cast iron. By 1900 around 2,000 people lived here, their premises powered by a steam engine installed beneath the street.

Craftsmen have been in the area since the founding of the Abbaye Saint-Antoine in the 12th century. However, they only came into their own after Louis XI (1461–1483) freed them from supervision by the city's municipal corporation. Allowed to develop independently they took advantage of the fact that building timber was brought into Paris at the nearby river port of La Rapée and they became expert woodworkers. By 1700 there were almost a thousand of them, includ-

The Cour de l'Industrie on Rue de Montreuil has known generations of craftspeople

ing Andre-Charles Boulle, the preferred cabinetmaker of Louis XIV (1643–1715).

The king's army, meanwhile, was kept in munitions by Maximilien Titon, who built a factory and a grand home for himself on Rue Titon. In 1763 a wallpaper factory was installed in the garden, where in 1783 the Montgolfier brothers launched the first manned hot air balloon using materials from the factory. Poor working conditions, however, and the fact that most of the factory's output was for the aristocracy brought rioters here in the early years of the Revolution, and the factory was destroyed.

In the mid-19th century the factory was replaced by the Cour de l'Industrie at 37bis Rue de Montreuil, to where woodworkers once again gravitated. Escaping demolition in 1991 the trio of courtyards with their timber-framed workshops are now protected and administered by a

Sculptress Aline Christine Putot in her studio in the Cour de l'Industrie

workers' association. Crafts including carving, gilding, and furniture restoration are all represented by artists who source their materials from the long-established family firm Laverdure at 58 Rue Traversière (12th).

The oldest journeymen's guild building in Europe is in Paris at the back of the Restaurant Aux Arts et Science Réunis at 161 Avenue Jean-Jaurès (19th). One of four craftsmen's guilds in the city it contains the Musée des Compagnons Charpentiers, which includes numerous masterpieces demonstrating the skills of budding guild members, presented at the end of their travelling apprenticeship. Further details about the guilds can be found in the Musée du Compagnonnage de Paris at 10 Rue Mabillion (6th).

69 Peace amongst the Gravestones

12th Arrondissement, three peaceful cemeteries
including the Cimetière de Picpus at 35 Rue de Picpus
Métro 6 Picpus

Not without reason is the Cimetière du Père Lachaise the most visited cemetery in the world. The list of those buried reads like a who's who of modern times. But when the sheer size of the place gets too much, there is respite at hand. Just around the corner at 111 Rue de Bagnolet (20th) is the more intimate Cimetière de Charonne.

The former village of Charonne was absorbed into the City of Paris along with ten other villages (including Belleville and Ménilmontant) in 1860 but only Charonne has retained its village feel. The cobbled Rue Saint Blaise, still the village high street, leads gently upwards towards the sturdy 12th century Église de Saint-Germaine-de-Charonne as it has for centuries. Surrounding the church is the peaceful cemetery, which is unusual in being one of only two burial grounds in Paris with medieval churches attached; the other is the Cimetière du Calvaire, which serves the Église Saint-Pierre-de-Montmartre at 2 Rue du Mont-Cenis (18th). There are few celebrities buried here but one is François Bègue, nicknamed Père Magloire, a house painter who claimed to have been secretary to the revolutionary Robespierre. The grave is marked by an iron statue of Bègue clutching a cane in one hand and a rose in the other.

Another village absorbed into Paris in 1860 was Picpus, and its peaceful cemetery can be found at 35 Rue de Picpus (12th). It contains the remains of the 1,306 people beheaded on Place du Trône-Renversé (now Place de la Nation) during *La Terreur*, the bloodiest chapter of the French Revolution (1789–1799), which only halted when Robespierre himself was beheaded (see no. 48). The corpses of aristocrats, nuns, soldiers, and shopkeepers were all dumped here in two common pits in a former convent garden (protected today behind a fence).

Since 1803 the cemetery has been owned by an association of families of the victims making it the only private cemetery in Paris. They continue to bury their dead in a distinct part of the cemetery, which explains the presence of the grave of the Marquis de La Fayette (1757–1834), a leader in the Garde Nationale during the Revolution and a hero of the American War of Independence, whose wife's sister and

The Cimetière de Charonne with its statue of Père Magloire

mother were amongst those beheaded. His grave was the only place in Paris where an American flag flew throughout the Second World War.

A third peaceful burial ground is the Cimetière de Passy at 2 Rue du Commandant-Schloesing (16th), which was one of several new burial grounds commissioned in the suburbs by Napoleon (1804–1815) (see no. 89). Once the aristocratic necropolis of Paris it was the city's only cemetery to boast a heated waiting room! Aside from big names such as Claude Debussy (1862–1918), the cemetery also contains the oft-overlooked co-founder of Impressionism Berthe Morisot (1841–1895), the French volcanologist Haroun Tazieff (1914–1998), the last Emperor of Vietnam Bảo Đại (1913–1997), and the young Ukrainian-born artist Marie Bashkirtseff (1858–1884). Her extravagant domed mausoleum is a life-sized reconstruction of her studio replete with *Chaise Longue* and paintings on easels!

Inside the entrance to the nearby Charonne Métro station is a memorial from the time of the Algerian War of Independence (1954–1962). Nine people died here when police dispersed a demonstration organised by the Left to denounce not only the war but also those opposing independence. During the police curfew that followed many more Algerians suffered as recalled in a discreet plaque on the Pont Saint-Michel (6th).

70 Hagia Sophia in Miniature

12th Arrondissement, the Église Saint-Esprit
at 186 Avenue Daumesnil
Métro 6, 8 Daumesnil

Turks have been arriving in France ever since a bilateral labour recruitment agreement was signed between the two countries in 1965. In Paris the community has made a home for itself along the southern stretch of the Rue du Faubourg Saint Denis (10th), where halal butchers, kebab shops, and fancy goods' bazaars jostle for space with French bistros and florists. There are mosques here, too, but they're well concealed.

Turkish influence extends to other parts of Paris, too, and in some cases it is much older. A stunning example is the Église Saint-Esprit at 186 Avenue Daumesnil (12th), which is a replica in miniature of Hagia Sophia in Istanbul. Although the latter served as a mosque for almost five centuries it was built originally as an Orthodox Christian basilica, and is considered the highpoint of Byzantine architecture. That its style has been mimicked not only in Paris but elsewhere is evidence of the originality of its structure.

The Église Saint-Esprit was built between 1928 and 1935 to a design by the French architect Paul Tournon (1881–1964). He was a member of the Académie des Beaux-Arts and known for his religious buildings built from reinforced concrete. A good example is the Cathédrale Sacré-Cœur de Casablanca in Morocco. The outward appearance of both churches is somewhat similar, with the architect using *Art Deco*-

The Église Saint-Esprit on Avenue Daumesnil is inspired by Hagia Sofia

The concrete cupola of the
Église Saint-Esprit

style columns and pilasters. Inside, however, is a very different story. Whereas the Morrocan church is light and airy neo-Gothic, its Paris counterpart is dark and mysterious neo-Byzantine. Concrete vaults and arches give the appearance of a perspective-defying M.C. Escher drawing, with the use of bricks adding a deep red glow. The wall surfaces are enlivened by the addition of murals, as well as engraved and gilded Latin texts. Most impressive is its 33 metre-high concrete cupola, which is a reference to Christ's age at the time of his crucifixion (similarly the crypt is 33 metres long). Despite its dimensions, however, it pales next to the far older dome of Hagia Sophia, which towers more than 50 metres high and is made only from bricks and mortar!

The influence of Hagia Sophia and Byzantine architecture can be found in several other churches in Paris. The Chapelle des Sœurs Auxiliatrices du Purgatoire, for example, at 14 Rue Saint-Jean-Baptiste-de-la-Salle (6th) is a 19th century building topped off with a lovely turquoise and ochre tiled cupola. There is also a pair of churches constructed during the 1930s at the behest of Cardinal Jean Verdier (1864–1940), as part of his initiative to promote Christianity anew in Paris. Both the Église Sainte-Jeanne-de-Chantal on the Place de la Porte de Saint-Cloud (16th) and the Église Sainte-Odile at 2 Avenue Stéphane-Mallarmé (17th) feature imposing cupolas like those of Hagia Sophia. There is even an electricity sub-station at 1 Rue de la Cerisaie (4th) built in neo-Byzantine style (see no.65). Only in Paris!

The first church in Paris to be made from reinforced concrete was the Église Saint-Jean-de-Montmartre at 19 Rue des Abbesses (18th). Completed in 1904 it displays an eclectic mix of styles from *Art Nouveau* to Moorish, and is known locally as Église Saint-Jean-de-Briques because much of its structure is masked with that material. In 1926 the Église Saint-Christophe-de-Javel at 28 Rue de la Convention (15th) became the world's first church to be built from prefabricated concrete.

71 All the Fun of the Fair

**12ᵗʰ Arrondissement, the Pavillons de Bercy
at 53 Avenue des Terroirs-de-France
Métro 14 Cour Saint-Émilion
(Note: visits normally by appointment only)**

Until the 1960s there was only one reason to visit Bercy (12ᵗʰ) in the southeast of Paris, and that was for wine. From the 18ᵗʰ century onwards this former *Commune* beyond the city walls was a tax-free inland port used for the transhipment of wine into Paris. Parisians flocked here at the weekends to drink cheaply at the many *Guinguettes* lining the river. So much so in fact that having 'Bercy Fever' was once a popular Parisian euphemism for being drunk! As tastes and technology changed, however, so the old wine warehouses *(Chais)* were abandoned. Then in 1996 the area was transformed into the Parc de Bercy, and the *Chais* adapted for retail and leisure use (see no. 59). Some became part of the aptly-named Cour Saint-Émilion, a popular shopping complex. More intriguing, however, are those known as the Pavillons de Bercy at 53 Avenue des Terroirs-de-France (12ᵗʰ), since they now contain one of the world's finest fairground museums.

The private museum is the work of actor and antiques dealer Jean-Paul Favand, who for the last 30 years has acquired and preserved historic fairground equipment from across Europe. Encompassing the fairground's golden age from 1850–1950 the collection is vast. It is divided into three sections spread across three separate warehouses: the Théâtre du Merveilleux (Theatre of Marvels), the Musée des Arts Forains (Museum of Fairground Art), and the Salons Vénitiens (Venetian Rooms). The magic of the place is further enhanced by it normally being open by appointment or invitation only (as well as during Journées du Patrimoine on the third weekend in September and at the end of December during the Festival du Merveilleux).

An antique carousel in the Musée des Arts Forains

The whimsical art adorning the exterior of the museum gives only a hint of what lies within. Passing through the door is like entering another world. And it's not only to be viewed at a distance. Many of the rides and sideshows have been lovingly restored for use by the visitor – and few will be able to resist!

First stop is the Théâtre du Merveilleux, which recreates a form of spectacle popular in the Tivolis and other public pleasure gardens during the second half of the 19th century. Using technological wizardry made possible by the Industrial Revolution the marvels and mysteries of the natural world are vividly brought to life, in an updated version of the Renaissance 'Cabinet of Curiosities'.

The second area, the Musée des Arts Forains, is the heart of the historical collection. This magnificent tribute to 19th century fairground attractions includes several thrilling rides and other attractions. There are German swing boats here, Japanese billiards, a noisy Parisian racing waiters' game, and a Hooghuys pipe organ blasting out its classic fairground melodies. Best of all is a bicycle merry-go-round from 1875, which featured in a memorable scene in Woody Allen's *Midnight in Paris* (2011). An estimated 20,000 hours were spent on the ride's restoration. Climb aboard and pedal as hard as possible to enjoy the full effect!

The last part is the Salons Vénitiens, which is a colourful homage to Venice and its carnival. The gondolas that so inspired the fairground showmen of the 19th century are inevitably much in evidence here. There is also an Italian opera in full swing performed entirely by mechanical automatons.

Should one be fortunate enough to visit the Pavillons de Bercy for a special event then the atmosphere will be intensified by the presence of fire eaters and contortionists, jugglers and magicians, and trapeze artists swinging through the air. Truly all the fun of the fair!

Carousels have long been popular in Paris. On an ancient, hand-cranked example in the Jardin du Luxembourg baton-wielding children still play *Jeu de Bagues*, a juvenile version of medieval tournaments in which galloping knights spear rings with lances. Like the old wine warehouses at Bercy, the former barge depots at 34 Quai d'Austerlitz (13th) on the Left Bank have also been converted to a new use. As Les Docks they contain the Cité de la Mode et du Design, as well as shops, bars and restaurants.

72 On Colonialism and Immigration

12th Arrondissement, the Centre Bouddique du Bois
de Vincennes at 40 Route de Ceinture du Lac Daumesnil
(Note: visits available during festivals and by appointment)
Métro 8 Porte Dorée

"Le Tour du Monde en un Jour" stated a poster advertising the *Exposition Coloniale Internationale Paris*, an exhibition staged in 1931 to celebrate French colonial achievements. The setting was the Bois de Vincennes (12th) on the eastern edge of the city, a former royal hunting preserve which had been turned into a public park in 1860. The exhibition inevitably had its detractors and its fragmentary remains still provide timely reminders regarding the country's colonial past.

The outward aim of the six-month long exhibition was to display the diverse cultures and rich traditions of French colonial possessions, from West Africa to Indochina. That more than thirty million people from around the world attended confirms there was enormous public interest. But there was a political goal, too. France wished to depict its colonial arrangements in a positive and mutually beneficial light, and to negate German criticism that it was only interested in exploiting the immense resources of its empire. By highlighting the indigenous aspects of its colonies, and downplaying efforts to spread its own language and culture abroad, the exhibition hoped to advance the notion that France associated rather than assimilated the societies it colonised.

The scale of the exhibition was enormous. At its heart were a number of grandly-scaled pavilions, each built in the native style of a particular colony. The French government brought in people from these colonies to occupy the pavilions and demonstrate their various

Buddhist Lent in the Centre Bouddique du Bois de Vincennes

crafts and traditions there. Even at the time the nomadic Senegalese village must have appeared somewhat reminiscent of the degrading Negro human zoos that had been a feature of the Paris expositions of 1878 and 1889. Not surprisingly the French Communist Party took the opportunity to mount a counter-exhibition entitled *La Vérité sur les Colonies* highlighting abuses made in the name of "imperialist colonialism". It attracted barely 5,000 visitors.

Of the structures remaining from the exhibition two are of particular interest since their current usage keeps the subject of colonialism and its legacy alive. One is the Palais de la Porte Dorée at 293 Avenue Daumesnil, which was built as a permanent museum of colonialism. For many years it contained the city's African and Oceanic holdings until they were transferred to the Musée du Quai Branly (see no. 43). Now in its place is the more pertinent Cité Nationale de l'Histoire de l'Immigration, which details the history of immigration in France from the 19th century onwards (don't miss the *Art Deco* reliefs outside).

The second important structure surviving from the exhibition is the former pavilion of Cameroon at 40 Route de Ceinture du Lac Daumesnil (12th). Restored in 1977 the building is today the Centre Bouddique du Bois de Vincennes, where Southeast Asian Buddhists pray before the largest Buddha in Europe (including its seat it is nine metres high and covered in gold leaf). The city's Cambodians celebrate several festivals here – including Khmer New Year in April and the start of Buddhist Lent at the end of July – to which outsiders are made very welcome. In front of the temple there is a newly-constructed Tibetan Buddhist temple opened in 1985. Plans are also afoot to convert the nearby former Togo pavilion into a Buddhist library.

Several sculptural fragments from the Exposition Colonial Internationale Paris, including a telling one depicting an African looking up at a European, can be found in a corner of the Jardin d'Agronomie Tropicale at Nogent-sur-Marne, where another colonial exhibition was staged in 1907. People from French colonies including Tunisia, Morocco, Congo, Madagascar, Dahomey and the Sudan were set up in replica villages like a living curiosity cabinet. Many of the buildings and associated monuments are still standing albeit abandoned amidst rampant vegetation.

Another survival from the *Exposition Colonial Internationale Paris* is the Église Notre-Dame des Missions, which was rebuilt in Épinay-sur-Seine north of Paris in 1932. The pagoda-like porch, African decorative motifs, and minaret-style spire were designed to recall the work undertaken by French missionaries around the world.

73 The Curse of Vincennes

Vincennes, the Château de Vincennes on Avenue de Paris
Métro 1 Château de Vincennes

Located just outside the *Périphérique*, the Château de Vincennes warrants inclusion here because it has long been at the heart of French history – and its walls conceal a curse!

Like many other French châteaux, Vincennes originated as a hunting lodge, erected in 1164 for Louis VII (1131–1180). During the 13th century, Philippe Auguste (1180–1223), the last King of the Franks and first King of France, erected a more substantial structure. It was his successor but one, the gentle monarch Louis IX (1226–1270), who temporarily housed the True Crown of Thorns here, while the Sainte-Chapelle was under construction on the Île de la Cité (see no. 23). It was from Vincennes in 1270 that Louis departed on the last crusade, dying of plague shortly after his arrival in Tunis. And it was to Vincennes that his successor, Philippe III (1270–1285), returned with his body.

Both Philippe and his successor married at Vincennes. Louis X (1314–1316), however, died there, from pneumonia after drinking chilled wine following a game of tennis. Philippe V (1316–1322) and Charles IV (1322–1328) died there, too, giving credence to a curse placed on Vincennes after Louis executed his father's former minister on false charges, in a bid to seize his assets.

The mighty keep of Château de Vincennes

The story of Vincennes continues with the accession of Philippe VI (1328–1350) of the House of Valois. In 1337 he commissioned a 52 metre-high keep *(donjon)*, at the time the tallest medieval fortified structure in Europe. It served as a royal residence and later contained the library of Charles V, the Learned (1364–1380). During Charles's reign much of France was reconquered from the English, only to be torn apart again in the struggle between Burgundians and Armagnacs under Charles VI, the Mad (1380–1422). Following the English victory at Agincourt in 1415 Henry V was set to take the French throne but died of dysentery at Vincennes. Instead, Charles VII (1422–1461) acceded with the support of Joan of Arc. Vincennes thereafter fell out of favour and became a state prison.

A century later royalty returned to Vincennes – but the curse was still in place. Charles IX (1560–1574) is remembered for the Saint Bartholomew Day's Massacre during which many Huguenots were murdered. He died a broken man at Vincennes, haunted by scenes of the slaughter. In 1650 Vincennes was again used as a prison, this time for the Fronde, a group determined to exert control over the young Louis XIV (1643–1715), and to oust Cardinal Mazarin, who ruled as coregent. After coming of age Louis imprisoned his minister of finance, Nicolas Fouquet, at Vincennes, and built himself a new home at Versailles based on Fouquet's Château Vaux-le-Vicomte.

By the 18th century Vincennes was again abandoned and after a stint as a porcelain factory it became a prison once more, counting the Marquis de Sade amongst its inmates. During the Revolution an unsuccessful attempt was made by the mob to demolish it, after rumours circulated it was to be used to imprison political activists. In 1804 the Duc d'Enghien was executed at Vincennes for allegedly conspiring against Napoleon, and in 1917 the Dutch exotic dancer Mata Hari (1876–1917) was executed there on a charge of spying for Germany. Only after the Second World War (during which 30 hostages were murdered at Vincennes by the Nazis) did peace finally return to this accursed castle.

East of the château stands the 19th century Fort Neuf de Vincennes, where the conspirators in the 1962 attempt on the life of President Charles de Gaulle were tried.

74 Navigating Saint Martin's Canal

19th Arrondissement, a walk along the Canal Saint-Martin
beginning at the Pont Crimée
Métro 7 Crimée

The Canal Saint-Martin is a 4.5 kilometre long waterway connecting the Seine in Paris with the surrounding countryside. Completed in 1825 it was commissioned by Napoleon (1804–1815) not only to bring fresh water into the city but also to transport grain and building materials. The canal later became an important industrial corridor, and an unofficial border between the city's middle- and working-class neighbourhoods. To walk its banks today is to walk through history.

The starting point is the Pont Crimée (19th), the last remaining lift bridge in Paris, constructed in 1855 by the same company that installed the Eiffel Tower lifts. North is the Canal de l'Ourcq, which connects the Canal Saint-Martin with the Ourcq river, providing half the water required by the city's sewers and parks. A second waterway, the Canal

The Pont Crimée on the Canal Saint-Martin

Saint-Denis, branches off it and rejoins the Seine to the northwest, fulfilling Napoleon's desire of diverting shipping away from the city and providing a navigational shortcut.

South is the Bassin de la Villette, from where drinking water was once sent by acqueduct as far as Monceau, and where barges docked before passing through the Tax Farmers' Wall (Enceinte des Fermiers Généraux). Constructed in the 1780s the wall allowed taxes to be levied on goods entering the city, in what for a time was the fourth busiest port in France. One of the former tollhouses is the Rotonde de la Villette, overlooking the point where the *Bassin* joins the Canal Saint-Martin (see no. 21).

Work commenced on the Canal Saint-Martin in 1805. Stretching from Place de la Bataille Stalingrad down to Quai de la Rapée on the Seine it scribes an S-shape, turning first westwards to avoid the 17th century Hôpital Saint-Louis, and then eastwards to take advantage of the old moat of the city wall of Charles V (1364–1380). Along the way there are nine locks used to accomodate the 29-metre difference in altitude between one end of the canal and the other. At 130–134 Quai de Jemmapes is one of the many industrial-era buildings that once lined the canal, and at number 101 is the Hôtel du Nord, made famous in Marcel Carné's 1938 film of the same name (see no. 65). In the Jardin Villemin opposite there once stood a military hospital, where soldiers wounded during the Franco-Prussian War were treated after arriving at the nearby Gare de l'Est.

At the Rue du Faubourg du Temple the canal changes its appearance. The chestnut-lined towpaths and graceful iron *Passerelles* are exchanged for a tunnel extending all the way to Place de la Bastille. Passing through the 2.5 kilometre long tunnel on an organised boat trip is a memorable experience, the ventilation shafts in the roof throwing down columns of light from the Boulevard Richard Lenoir above. The tunnel dates to the 1860s, when the Prèfet de la Seine, Georges-Eugène Haussmann (1809–1891), created the Rue Voltaire. Rather than installing a lift bridge where the road met the canal he used locks to lower the water level instead. Quaysides robbed of their usefulness were replaced by the tunnel, and the new boulevard above made the so-called 'Red Suburbs' easier to police.

Where the canal reappears it enters the Bassin de l'Arsenal, which is today a marina for pleasure boats. It is difficult to imagine that not long ago the craft here would have been barges, laden not with tourists but sugar, cereals and blocks of stone, and that the quaysides would have been lined not with cafés but with factories, warehouses, and mills.

Other places of interest nearby: 75

75 The Little Hills of Paris

19th Arrondissement, the Parc des Buttes-Chaumont
on Rue Botzaris
Métro 7bis Buttes Chaumont

Paris is a predominantly flat city punctuated by numerous conspicuous hills known as *Buttes*. Whilst the lowest point of the city is undisputed – around 20 metres above sea level on the Seine at the city's western edge – debate still surrounds its highest point. This is commonly misstated as being the summit of Montmartre at 130 metres above sea level, whereas in reality it is Rue du Télégraphe (148m) in Belleville (20th). The confusion stems from a wall plaque outside the Cimetière de Belleville giving a height of 128m. It should be remembered, however, that this only represents the difference between the lowest and highest points.

The street name itself recalls the fact that in 1792 the French engineer Claude Chappe (1763–1805) chose this lofty location to build a signal station as part of the world's first optical telegraph system (see no. 93). Other

A Classical temple marks the highest point in the Parc des Buttes-Chaumont

highpoints on the Right Bank include the aptly-named Ménilmontant (108m), as well as Passy (71m) and Chaillot (67m), whilst on the Left Bank is the less-than-mountainous Montparnasse (66m), the Butte-aux-Cailles (63m), and the Montagne-Sainte-Geneviève (61m) on which stands the Panthéon.

Returning to the Right Bank, one of the most interesting little hills of Paris is the Buttes-Chaumont (103m). Like Montmartre it is an out-crop of gypsum and both were once quarried for plaster (hence Plaster of Paris). By the mid-19th century, however, the Buttes-Chaumont had become a a shanty town and rubbish dump, and so in 1864 Napoleon III (1852–1870) commissioned his Prèfet de la Seine, Georges-Eugène Haussmann (1809–1891), together with his engineer Jean-Charles Adolphe Alphand (1817–1891), to transform the brutalised area into a public garden.

The Parc des Buttes-Chaumont on Rue Botzaris is today a paean to 19th century Romanticism, the former quarry metamorphosed into a patch of rolling countryside. At its heart is a lake with a craggy island reached by a suspension bridge. Near the top of the island is a grotto with artificial stalactites, and at its highest point a neo-Classical belvedere. A copy of the Temple of Sibyl in Tivoli it offers fine views over the park and surroundings. A surreal description of the park is given in Louis Aragon's *Le Paysan de Paris (Paris Peasant)* (1926).

Immediately west of the park is the Butte Bergeyre, a peaceful hill-top enclave built in the 1920s and consisting of just five short streets: Rues Georges-Lardennois, Rémy-de-Gourmont, Edgar-Poë, Philippe-Hecht, and Barrelet-de-Ricou. On its west slope there is a vineyard with a splendid view of Montmartre beyond. East of the park is the so-called Quartier de la Mouzaïa centred on Rues de la Mouzaïa, David-d'Angers, and Miguel-Hidalgo. Because the former gypsum quarries beneath it cannot bear much weight (mining continued until 1872) the area boasts the largest concentration of low-rise dwellings in Paris, strung out along a series of narrow leafy lanes.

The Butte aux Cailles on Rue de la Butte-aux-Cailles (13th) is another characterful hilltop community with low-rise buildings. During the 1800s it was home to local factory work-ers and covered with windmills. Annexed to Paris in 1860 it is remembered as one of the strongholds of the Paris Commune of 1871, when a workers' movement took control of the city. It is therefore fitting that the Association des Amis de la Commune de Paris is located here today. It was also here that the first manned balloon flight touched down in 1783 on Square Henri-Rousselle.

Other places of interest nearby: 64, 65, 74, 77

76 Remembering Georges Brassens

19th Arrondissement, in the footsteps of Georges Brassens
finishing at the Porte des Lilas Métro station
Métro 11 Porte des Lilas

The modern French troubadour Georges Brassens (1921–1981) achieved fame throughout France with his anarchic songs and complex mingling of voice and guitar. Although he rarely toured abroad, and his work is notoriously difficult to translate, artists from Spain to Japan have interpreted his work, and he has been the subject of more than 50 doctoral dissertations. So who was Georges Brassens, and how is he remembered in Paris today?

Brassens was born in Sète, near Montpellier in southern France. His family members were always singing at home, while he listened avidly to the likes of Charles Trenet and Tino Rossi. Despite not being able to attend music school he was determined from an early to pursue poetry and music as a career. Alongside such lofty ambitions, however, he also succumbed to the temptations of youth, and was expelled from school for petty theft.

In 1940 Brassens moved to Paris, where he lived with his aunt in the 14th Arrondissement. He worked at the Renault car factory, which

Singer-songwriter
Georges Brassens
commemorated in the
Porte des Lilas Métro
station

in May 1940 was bombed prior to the German invasion of France. Brassens was subsequently sent to work in an aircraft factory near Berlin. Whilst on leave in Paris in 1944 he took refuge in a slum on Impasse Florimont (14th) where he was befriended by his landlady. He wrote his first collection of poems there, *Des Coups d'Épée dans l'Eau*, and would remain at the same address until 1966.

A self-confessed anarchist, Brassens was urged by friends in Paris to try out his poems in front of a live audience. His first performance occurred in 1948 in a Montmartre cabaret, when the songstress Patachou invited him to join her on stage. Accompanying himself on acoustic guitar, and armed with a clutch of clever songs decrying hypocrisy and self-righteousness, Brassens quickly conquered the hearts of his listeners. Word spread and more concerts followed although he never conquered his shyness on stage. Instead he let his songs speak, with their lyrics targeting the pious, the well-to-do, and those in law enforcement.

Brassens is recalled today in several locations across Paris. A wall plaque marks his longtime home at the end of Impasse Floriment (14th), and a park built in the 1980s on the site of the former Vaugirard abattoir on Rue des Morillons (15th) is named after him. A bust of Brassens adorns the park, as do a pair of bronze bulls marking the old abattoir gateway (a sculpture of a butcher carrying a carcass stands in front of the former animal pens on Rue Briançon, which today play host to secondhand book fairs). The tram stop on the nearby T3, the first modern tramway in Paris, is also named Georges Brassens.

Best of all is the memorial to Brassens at the Porte des Lilas Métro station (19th). On the platform is a tiled portrait of the singer puffing away on his trademark pipe. It is accompanied by a quote from his song *La Porte des Lilas*, reminding the onlooker that Brassens wrote it for the 1957 film of the same name in which he has a supporting role.

Hidden from view there is another platform at the Porte des Lilas Métro station that has been closed to the public since 1939. The platform is now used occasionally for location filming.

Many of the ceramic tiles in the Paris Métro were supplied by the company Hippolyte Boulanger de Choisy-le-Roi. Their company headquarters at 18 Rue de Paradis (10th) are still faced with the lustrous tiles for which they became famous.

Other places of interest nearby: 77

77   The Waters of Belleville

20th Arrondissement, the *Regards* of Belleville
around Rue des Cascades
Métro 11 Jourdain

For Parisians today it's a given that fresh water is easily and readily available. Behind the scenes, however, there lies a vast and complex network of springs, rivers, and artesian wells that have been martialled for their use over the last 2,000 years.

The Romans were the first to address the problem of providing fresh water in Paris (see no. 30). Having settled on the Left Bank after conquering the area in 52BC they supplied their homes and baths with spring water brought from Rungis, 16 kilometres to the south. By the Middle Ages, however, the Roman acqueduct had long since been abandoned. Most Parisians now drank river water, which was polluted not only with domestic waste but also that of the many tanners, dyers, and butchers operating along the riverbanks.

From the 12th century onwards the situation prompted wealthy Right Bank abbeys to set about exploiting the springs of the Belleville plateau. They dug trenches *(Pierrées)* to channel the water into stone-built conduit rooms known as *Regards*, where the flow could be monitored and protected. From here the water ran by means of gravity-fed pipes to its final destination in the city.

Although the springs have long since dried up several *Regards* remain. A cluster of them can be found on and around the aptly-named Rue des Cascades (20th). Two carry the names of their builders: the Regard Saint-Martin at 42

The Regard Saint-Martin on Rue des Cascades

Rue des Cascades once supplied the Abbaye Saint-Martin-des-Champs (today the Musée des Arts et Métiers) at 60 Rue de Réaumur (3rd), and the Regard de la Roquette at nearby 36–38 Rue de la Mare supplied the Couvent de la Roquette on Rue de la Roquette (11th). Also on Rue des Cascades at number 17 is the Regard des Messiers, a name derived from an Old French word for those involved in harvesting. Farther north on Rue Compans, the Regard de la Lanterne is so-named because of the decorative stone lantern on its roof (the interior can be visited by appointment and during Journées du Patrimoine).

By 1700 there were still only 15 public fountains to supply the city's half million residents. Napoleon (1804–1815) tried to alleviate the problem by constructing the Canal de l'Ourcq to provide fresh water to the northern part of Paris, which was distributed between La Villette and Monceau by means of an acqueduct (see no. 74). He also constructed several kilometres of sewers but it did little to prevent outbreaks of cholera. New sources of water were again sought, and consequently a handful of deep artesian wells were dug. A couple of them, on Place Paul-Verlaine (13th) and Square Lamartine (16th), are still used today by locals convinced of their curative properties.

Eventually in 1852 Napoleon III (1852–1870) commissioned his Prèfet de la Seine, Georges-Eugène Haussmann (1809–1891), together with his waterworks engineer Eugène Belgrand, to construct a citywide network of tunnels for both fresh water delivery *and* waste removal (sewage would flow along the tunnels while drinking water would be distributed through smaller pipes attached to the walls of the tunnels). It is a testament to the men's vision that the system they installed still lies at the heart of the city's water facilities (see no. 44).

Half the water used in Paris today still comes from springs, whilst the rest is taken from the Seine and Marne rivers. It is delivered to a handful of reservoirs by means of six acqueducts, of which the Arcueil acqueduct is noteworthy in so much as it still follows the course of its Roman predecessor.

Other places of interest nearby: 75, 76

78 "To Live, to Die, to be Reborn"

20th Arrondissement, the Cimetière du Père Lachaise
on Avenue du Père Lachaise
Métro 3 Gambetta
(Note: using the entrance on Avenue du Père Lachaise
enables the visitor to navigate the cemetery from top to
bottom; a map of the cemetery is essential)

Jim Morrison, Modigliani, Maria Callas, Proust, Édith Piaf, Chopin, Oscar Wilde, Colette, Simone Signoret. What a party it would make if they could be raised from their eternal slumbers in the Cimetière du Père Lachaise! Covering more than 40 hectares of undulating ground east of Boulevard de Ménilmontant (20th) the cemetery contains a million burials, and is visited by more than that number annually. The chestnuts dictate the best time to come: either in May, when they blossom, or else October, when their leaves turn yellow. On All Saints Day (*Toussaint*, 1st November) the French flock here with bunches of chrysanthemums.

The cemetery is named after a priest, François de la Chaise (1624–1709), the confessor of Louis XIV (1643–1715). Indeed, the cemetery is located on the site of the Jesuit retreat where the priest lived. It was from here that the young king observed the skirmishes of the Fronde, a civil war that encouraged him to establish an absolute monarchy.

At Napoleon's bidding in 1804 the property was purchased for use as a cemetery, one of several designed to replace the city centre's medieval burial grounds (see no. 89). It opened the same year and the first person to be buried was the five-year-old daughter of a humble doorman. This fulfilled Napoleon's declaration that the cemetery should be open to all citizens irrespective of their background.

Initially the cemetery was considered remote and attracted few burials.

Many tombs in Père Lachaise feature stained glass

The grave of Allan Kardec in the Cimetière du Père Lachaise attracts visitors from around the world

This changed after the remains of Molière and La Fontaine were relocated here, followed in 1817 by those of star-crossed lovers Abélard and Héloïse (their hard-to-find grave in the southwest corner of the cemetery highlights the importance of bringing along a map). Soon Parisians clamoured to be buried at Père Lachaise and by 1850 it had been expanded five times. A funerary chapel was erected on the site of the former Jesuit retreat, followed in 1894 by a Columbarium for the remains of those wishing to be cremated. Another feature is the so-called Federalists' Wall (Mur des Fédérés) in the southeast corner of the cemetery, against which the last defenders of the Paris Commune were shot on 28th May 1871.

The range of tombs in the cemetery is extraordinary, from simple headstones to extravagant mausoleums. A standard 30-year lease is issued on most burial plots, although they can also be bought. If the grave is not attended after this period the remains are removed to an ossuary secreted behind the dramatic *Aux Morts* monument.

The devotion expressed at the graves of Wilde and Morrison is well documented but it can be witnessed elsewhere, too. Take, for instance, Allan Kardec (1804–1869), the founder of Spiritism. Visitors from all over the world bring flowers to his grave, especially from Brazil, where his doctrine of reincarnation retains many followers. Along the top of the tomb is inscribed his famous phrase: "To be born, to live, to die, to be reborn and to keep progressing". Don't be surprised to see his devotees in a trance-like state.

Venerated for a very different reason is the grave of Victor Noir (1848–1870), a young journalist and opponent of Napoleon III (1852–1870), who was murdered by the king's nephew. Initially the grave was visited for political reasons but later it became a symbol of fertility. Only a visit to the grave will reveal why!

Another much-decorated grave is that of Jacob the Zouave in the Cimetière de Gentilly at 7 Rue de Sainte-Hélène (13th). This 19th century French infantryman of Berber origin was a renowned faith healer.

Those enamoured by tales of the undead might like to take a vampire tour of Père Lachaise with expert Jacques Sergent. Not only has he published a French translation of *Dracula* but he also runs the little-known Museum of Vampires and Legendary Creatures at 14 Rue Jules David (open by appointment only). Perfect for those in need of a vampire killing kit!

Other places of interest nearby: 66, 67, 79

79 Exploring Urban Jungles

20th Arrondissement, the Jardin Naturel
at 120 Rue de la Réunion
Métro 2 Alexandre Dumas

Not without reason could it be said that Paris is one vast formal garden. Certainly great swathes of the city centre have been planned with far reaching vistas in mind, an effect irresistible to both the city's planners and the country's rulers. But when the floral symmetry and tree-lined boulevards get too much there are alternatives at hand. Far from the city centre there are two wild public gardens just waiting to be explored.

The first of these urban jungles is the aptly named Jardin Naturel at 120 Rue de la Réunion (20th), located just beyond a side entrance to the Cimetière de Père Lachaise. Created in 1994–1996 it covers an area of just 6,000 square metres within which Mother Nature has been allowed to roam free. The idea behind the garden is to give an impression of how Paris would look if it had never been built. Thus the untamed garden falls naturally into three zones: a meadow dotted with wild flowers, a thicket of bird-filled trees casting dappled shade, and a lily-strewn pond alive with dragonflies, frogs, and newts. It is not permitted to use pesticides or herbicides on any of the garden's 200 plant species, which are left to seed themselves naturally. Even artificial watering is strictly forbidden. It is little wonder that this city Eden is often used as a venue for workshops on biodiversity. A slow walk through the garden can be a delight – but only if one takes the time to really look at what's going on here. The pleasure really is in the detail.

The second jungle in the city is even smaller. The Jardin Sauvage Saint-Vincent was established in 1985 at 17 Rue Saint-Vincent (18th) and covers just 1,500 square metres. Despite this it is no less of a wilderness. Once an unloved patch of wasteland it was earmarked by the Paris City Council as the perfect place to encourage the indigenous wildlife of Montmartre to make a home for itself. Again chemicals and artificial watering are banned. The garden has subsequently become a haven for birds and insects drawn here by plants such as white nettles, artemisias, and wild blackberries. The intervention of man has been limited only to the the consolidation of the natural slope, the excavation of a pond, and the creation of a footpath for use by visitors on the twice-monthly open days.

Plants grow wild in the Jardin Naturel on Rue de la Réunion

The humble allotment has long been popular in Paris, where local residents and workers can sow their own seeds and enjoy the fruits of their labours. Increasingly popular are the city's so-called *Jardins Partagé* or Shared Gardens. A delightful example is the charmingly-named Potager des Oiseaux alongside the Marché des Enfants-Rouges at 9 Rue de Beauce (3rd). Such gardens are proving especially popular in the 19th Arrondissement, where they are managed and promoted by a local association called Espace 19. Others are rented out by Paris City Council, including those down one side of the Musée d'Art Moderne de la Ville de Paris on Rue de la Manutention (16th).

Other places of interest nearby: 66, 67, 78

80 Tapestries for the Sun King

13th Arrondissement, the Manufacture des Gobelins
at 42 Avenue des Gobelins
Métro 7 Les Gobelins (Note: the factory is open
for guided tours only)

Voltaire called the 17th century *Le Grand Siècle*, a period epitomised by Louis XIV (1643–1715), the longest reigning king in Europe. Louis was an absolutist, who chose the sun for his emblem, and called himself *Le Roi-Soleil*. Inspired by Apollo, he cast himself as a warrior hero, who brought peace to his people and promoted the arts. Historians are still divided about his legacy but few can deny that his court was one of history's most dazzling.

Louis's extensive patronage of the arts undoubtedly encouraged the growth of French industry. One company to benefit was the dye works of Jean Gobelin, founded in 1440 on the banks of the Bièvre in the Faubourg Saint-Marcel, where the minerals in the river were ideal for fixing dyes. In 1602 Henry IV (1589–1610) had rented factory space at the works for his Flemish tapestry makers. Later in 1662 the works were purchased for Louis by his finance minister, Jean-Baptiste Colbert (1619–1683), who had been tasked with assembling the country's best artisans to furnish the king's new palace at Versailles. The acquisition of the works meant that Colbert could create a royal workshop under one roof, not only for dyers and weavers but also furniture makers, sculptors, metalworkers, and mural painters.

Between 1663 and 1690 the workshop director was the court painter Charles Le Brun (1619–1690). As chief designer he made all the design decisions, creating what became known as the Louis Quatorze Style. As a result Louis lauded him as "the greatest French artist of all time". Under Le Brun's watchful eye 250 Flemish weavers were employed to create tapestries for the palace.

Le Brun began work on the interiors of the state apartments at Versailles in 1671. Commencing with the Salon d'Hercule, each room is dedicated to an Olympian deity, and everywhere are references to Apollo. The climax is the famous Hall of Mirrors, with its 17 great arched mirrors facing identically-sized windows. Louis moved his court there in 1682, where he became an arbiter of taste and his court etiquette found many admirers.

Financial problems saw the workshop closed between 1694 and 1697, after which it specialised once again in tapestry, chiefly for royal use, until work was again suspended by the Revolution. The Bourbons revived the factory during the Restoration, by which time there were several dye works and tanneries along the Bièvre, and the heavily polluted river had to be culverted beneath the Rue Berbier-du-Mets (see no. 81). In 1871 the main building was set ablaze by the Communards, and not rebuilt until 1912.

Today the Manufacture des Gobelins at 42 Avenue des Gobelins (13th) is administered by the French Ministry of Culture, and can be visited on a guided tour. Participants will see Le Brun's residence, the workshops where the bronze statues in the gardens at Versailles were cast, and the traditional looms on which *Haute Lisse* (high warp) and *Basse Lisse* (low warp) tapestries are still woven using 17th century techniques.

Weaving on a traditional loom in the Manufacture des Gobelins

Around the corner at 18bis Rue Berbier-du-Mets is the Château de la Reine Blanche, the 16th century home of the Gobelin family, which they purchased with the proceeds of their dye works.

Tapestries aside, the 13th Arrondissement is also home to more contemporary art forms, notably street murals. A stunning example called *Rise Above Rebel Woman* by Shepard Fairey (b. 1970) adorns an apartment block at the junction of Boulevard Vincent Auriol and Rue Jeanne d'Arc.

81 Looking for a Lost River

**13th Arrondissement, a walk along the course
of the River Bièvre beginning in Parc Kellermann
Métro 7 Porte d'Italie; T3 Poterne des Peupliers**

Everyone knows the Seine but who remembers the Bièvre? Until its disappearance underground in the early 20th century this river (named after the beavers that inhabited its waters) had for centuries been the life blood of what is today the 13th Arrondissement. This walk follows the river's course, revealing its hidden history along the way.

Start in Parc Kellermann near the Porte d'Italie Métro station (13th). This is where the Bièvre, which rises in Guyancourt, near Versailles, originally meandered into Paris, and where it was split artificially in two, so as to power as many watermills and irrigate as many gardens as possible. Since 1910 the upper (eastern) arm *(Bras Vif)* has been culverted, while the lower (western) arm *(Bras Mort)* has run dry.

Parc Kellermann was created in the 1930s on land released by the demolition of the Thiers Wall (see no. 21). Its poplar trees, like those along Rue de la Poterne des Peupliers, mark the Bièvre's former banks. From here the river flowed northwards along Rue des Peupliers to Place de l'Abbé-Georges-Henocque, its course identified in the pavement by circular brass medallions. A watermill operated at what is now 98 Rue du Moulin-des-Prés, albeit on land 20 metres below the present pavement level.

The river then turned south-west to avoid the Butte-aux-Cailles. The lower arm followed the Rue de la Fontaine-à-Mulard to Place de Rungis, and then onwards along Rues Brillat-Savarin and Wurtz, the curving streets following exactly the river's course. The practice of taking winter ice from the water meadows here and storing it in ice-houses is recalled in the name Rue de la Glacière. After the meadows were drained in the 1920s the Cité Florale was built, an enclave of low-rise housing popular with writers and artists in search of charm and low rents.

On Boulevard Auguste-Blanqui the two arms of the Bièvre rejoined briefly to pass through the 18th century Tax Farmers' Wall (Enceinte des Fermiers Généraux), and then divided once more (see no. 21). The upper arm followed Rue Edmond-Godinet (where it powered a water-mill at the corner with Rue Corvisart); the lower arm followed Rue Paul-Gervais. Beyond they enclosed an island of vegetable gardens occupied today by Square René-le-Gall. Madame Grégoire's riverside cabaret at 41 Rue de Croulebarbe was frequented by Victor Hugo (1802–1885). The upper arm continued northwards along Rue Berbier-du-Mets, where the Gobelins dyeworks were established in 1440 to exploit the Bièvre's mineral-rich waters in fixing their dyes (see no. 80). By the 18th century the banks were lined with similar works, and the resulting pollution explains why the river was eventually covered over.

Both arms crossed Boulevard Arago near Rue Pascal then rejoined at the foot of Rue Mouffetard, where in the Middle Ages the fertile riverbank became the well-to-do village of Bourg Saint-Marcel (a pair of medieval flour mills once operated here). From here the river skirted around the Montagne Sainte-Geneviève, and headed eastwards between Rues Buffon and Poliveau, to empty eventually into the Seine near the Pont d'Austerlitz.

Poplars mark the former course of the River Bièvre in Parc Kellermann

In 1151 the monks of the Abbaye Saint-Victor de Paris re-routed the Bièvre to irrigate their gardens and turn a waterwheel. The long vanished canal ran along Rues Jussieu, Saint-Victor, and de Bièvre. When the city wall of Philippe Auguste (1180–1223) was constructed 50 years later it included a stone arch to accommodate the canal (see no. 21). Revealed in 1991 at 30 Rue du Cardinal-Lemoine the Arche de la Bièvre can be visited each first Wednesday of the month (except August) at 2.30pm.

82 An Experiment in International Living

14ᵗʰ Arrondissement, the Cité Internationale Universitaire
de Paris at 19 Boulevard Jourdan
T3 Cité Universitaire

Europe in the 1920s and early 30s was a time of both diplomatic idealism and economic crisis. It was the era of Woodrow Wilson and the League of Nations, as well as a chronic housing shortage that prompted the construction of social housing. The extraordinary Cité Internationale Universitaire de Paris at 19 Boulevard Jourdan (14ᵗʰ) combines all these themes.

The idea for the university came about when the French industrialist Emile Deutsch de la Meurthe (1847–1924) decided to bequeath a tangible legacy to the city. He contacted the rector of the Université de Paris, Paul Appel, who at the time was grappling with a post-war dearth of student housing. Together with the politician André Honnorat, they conjured up a *Cité Universitaire*, a campus of residence halls for students from around the world. Living and studying together would engender dialogue, overcome differences, and promote international peace.

The Cité Internationale Universitaire is located just inside the *Périphérique*, on a strip of land made available when the Thiers Wall was torn down after the First World War (see no. 21). Upon entry the first building encountered is the Maison Internationale, gifted in 1936 by the oil baron and philanthropist John D. Rockefeller (1839–1937). In the style of a French château it contains a library, theatre, pool, and restaurant, and is where the students congregate.

Ranged either side and beyond are 37 residence halls erected between 1925 and 1969, each realised in a style reflecting the nationality of their inhabitants. Turn right, past the charming Fondation Deutsch de la Meurthe (the first building opened in 1925) and cross Avenue André Rivoire. Here there is a fascinating group of buildings commencing with the Résidence Lucien Paye (1949), built to house for students from French Colonial Africa. Next is the Fondation Hellénique (1932), with its neo-Classical porch, and then the Fondation Rosa-Abreu-de-la-Grancher (1932). Financed by Rosa Abreu, the owner of a sugar cane plantation in Cuba, and her husband, the doctor Joseph Grancher, it is realised in the Spanish colonial style, and is still used by medical students today. In the far corner is the Maison des Étudiants de l'Asie du Sud-Est (1930) (formerly Indochina), which incorporates Asian-style columned balconies. Alongside it and in complete contrast the Collège Néerlandais (1926) is the work of the Dutch modernist Willem Marinus Dudok (1884–1974). Despite being one of the oldest buildings on the campus it still appears contemporary.

Returning to the Maison Internationale, notice on the far side of the lawn the Maison du Cambodge (1957), its entrance guarded by a pair of stone lions. To the right is the Fondation Avicenne, formerly the Pavillon de l'Iran (1969), designed by the Persian architect Heydar Ghiai. The last hall to be built it consists of two units daringly suspended from a steel frame. On the other side of the Maison Internationale, past the reliably sturdy Fondation des États-Unis (1930), are more interesting halls: the pagoda-like Maison du Japon (1927);

The Maison des Étudiants de l'Asie du Sud-Est in the Cité Internationale Universitaire

Le Corbusier's Fondation Suisse (1930) held aloft by a series of pillars; the Maison du Maroc (1953), with its mosaic fountain courtyard; and at the far end Lucio Costa and Le Corbusier's Maison du Brésil (1954), considered an icon of modern architecture.

The Cité Internationale Universitaire is today home to around 5,500 students from more than 130 countries. Many still live in the halls designated to their home countries, although each hall now reserves a third of its rooms for students from other lands to further this experiment in international living.

Other places of interest nearby: 83

83 Dinner Chez Jim

14th Arrondissement, Jim Haynes' Sunday dinner club
in Atelier A-2 at 83 Rue de la Tombe Issoire
Métro 4 Alésia, 6 Saint-Jacques (Note: dinner available
only by advance reservation at www.jim-haynes.com)

Long before the advent of social media the American expatriate Jim Haynes (b. 1933) was connecting people the old-fashioned way. For more than 30 years he has provided Sunday dinner at his Paris atelier to thousands of complete strangers, resulting in enduring friendships, marriages, and even children!

To understand Haynes' motivations one need look no further than his colourful Curriculum Vitae. Born in Louisiana, from an early age he developed a taste for travel and literature. By the age of four he was wandering his local neighbourhood making friends and talking to shopkeepers. Whilst at university during the 1950s he spent his free time in Venezuela, deep sea fishing, frequenting bordellos, listening to Édith Piaf, and reading Henry Miller's *Tropic of Capricorn*. Then, after dropping out of university he joined the air force, and requested he be sent to Edinburgh (a listening base where his knowledge of Russian would come in useful). Simultaneously he studied at Edinburgh University, opened a paperback bookshop, and hosted literary festivals.

Following a move to London in the late 1960s Haynes founded the Arts Laboratory, an art space and cinema where he staged Steven Berkoff's first production and a sculptural exhibition by John Lennon and Yoko Ono. A move to Paris followed in 1969 to teach media studies and sexual politics, and for the next decade his list of acquaintances reads like a Who's Who of the period.

In 1978 Haynes hosted the first of his now legendary Sunday dinner parties in his Atelier A-2, a former sculptor's studio at 83 Rue de la Tombe Issoire (14th) (during the 1930s his hero Henry Miller had lived around the corner at 18 Villa Seurat, where he liaised with erotic authoress Anaïs Nin). The guest list was limited initially to just friends and colleagues but was soon expanded to include anyone, regardless of their nationality, age, or profession. The dinner parties have continued ever since, except for August when Haynes religiously attends the Edinburgh Festival.

In 1980 he founded a kitchen table publishing house, Handshake Editions, and in 1984 his autobiography *Thanks for Coming!* was published. Then in 1989 he created the first of his unique *People to People*

Jim Haynes (seated) supervises dinner on Rue de la Tombe Issoire

travel guides, in which he listed people in different cities willing to host travellers. Additionally, he hosts art exhibitions and makes a habit out of travelling and taking in house guests whenever possible.

To attend one of Haynes' Sunday dinner parties it is necessary to make a reservation well in advance, either online or in writing. The parties are now something of an institution, and, while no-one is ever turned away, the waiting time can be lengthy. But it's worth the wait. The first 50 people to apply for each event are accepted, with twice that number when the garden can be used. The proceedings commence at 8pm prompt and run for three hours, with a different volunteer cooking each week. With no organised seating the opportunity for mingling is maximised, which greatly pleases Haynes who says he loves the randomness. Haynes endeavours to remember the names of his guests so that he can introduce them personally. Inevitably his idea has been imitated but rarely bettered, and there are few people who can say that they've had 130,000 people to dinner – and still counting!

Those wishing to entertain their own crowd at home should buy the book *Throw a Great Party* written by three of Haynes' chefs, Mary Bartlett, Catherine Monnet and Antonia Hoogewerf. All the recipes are inspired by Sunday evenings Chez Jim.

Other places of interest nearby: 82, 84

84 Entering the Empire of Death

14th Arrondissement, the Catacombes de Paris
at 1 Avenue du Colonel Henri Rol-Tanguy
(formerly Place Denfert-Rochereau)
Métro 4, 6 Denfert-Rochereau (Note: queuing times
can be lengthy; last admission 4pm)

Anyone with a sense of adventure and a taste for the macabre will want to visit the Catacombes de Paris. Occupying a labyrinth of tunnels beneath the Left Bank they form one of the most extraordinary manmade subterannean spaces in the world.

Until the Revolution burials in Paris took place in long-established parish cemeteries in the heart of the city. Consisting of little more than communal pits, in which bodies were tipped and sprinkled with quick-lime to accelerate decomposition, the health hazards to those living nearby were enormous. Attempts by Louis XVI (1774–1792) to relocate the cemeteries beyond the city walls were resisted by the Church, which profited from burial fees. In 1780, however, after a prolonged period of rain, the situation (and the smell!) became intolerable, and further burials in the city were forbidden. In the case of the Cimetière des Innocents, the city's oldest and largest burial ground on what is today Place Joachim-du-Bellay (1st), the site became part of the Les Halles wholesale food market.

It would eventually fall to Napoleon (1804–1815) to replace the abandoned cemeteries with new ones – but not before a massive clearance operation was undertaken to remove the existing human remains (see no. 89). The question of where to put them was solved by the presence of abandoned tunnels beneath Montparnasse, which had been previously used for the extraction of limestone (see no. 87). It must have been a curious scene from 1786 onwards as priests escorted black-veiled carts from the cemeteries to the tunnels under cover of the night. The fat from bodies still only partially decomposed was collected and turned into candles and soap.

To visit the catacombs today is a memorable experience. The entrance is at 1 Avenue du Colonel Henri Rol-Tanguy (14th), where a spiral staircase gives access to the two kilometres of quarry tunnels set aside for use as an ossuary. Beyond a doorway inscribed "Arrête! C'est ici l'Empire de la Mort" are the mortal remains of more than six million people. The countless skulls, femurs, tibias and other bones are stacked from floor to ceiling on either side of the narrow tunnels.

Skulls and other bones piled high in the Catacombes de Paris

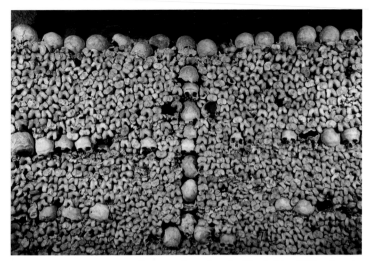
The bones of more than six million Parisians fill the catacombs

Sometimes this has been done in an artistic fashion, creating symbols such as hearts and crosses. This reflects the fact that since 1804 the catacombs have been accessible to the public. Indeed as early as 1787 the future Charles X (1824–1830) escorted ladies from the Bourbon court to see the bones. The catacombs reached a much wider audience after they were photographed by Gaspard-Félix Tournachon ('Nadar') (1820–1910), who is credited as being the first photographer to use artificial light.

During a tour of the catacombs the visitor will encounter numerous curiosities, including the Fontaine de la Samaritaine, which once contained blind carp, a quarryman's stone model of the Minorcan fortress of Fort Mahon, and the Crypte de la Passion, where members of the Paris Opera gave a clandestine performance in 1897. The cryptic numbers and letters inscribed on the walls were added to aid navigation in the gloom, as well as provide details of the cemeteries whence the various groups of bones originated.

Note, too, the iron bars that block several passages. They prevent visitors from wandering off and getting lost, as happened to one Philibert Aspairt, doorkeeper of the nearby Hôpital Val-de-Grâce during the Revolution. Not until eleven years later were his remains recovered, gnawed to the bone by rats, and identifiable only by his bunch of keys!

Other places of interest nearby: 83, 85, 86, 87, 88

85   The Last Prison in Paris

**14ᵗʰ Arrondissement, the Maison d'Arrêt de la Santé
at 42 Rue de la Santé
Métro 6 Glacière, Saint-Jacques**

Flying over Paris using Google Earth is a great way of viewing places hidden from the street. There is one pocket of land, however, at the corner of Rue de la Santé and Boulevard Arago (14ᵗʰ) that even Google won't reveal – and with good reason. It is the Maison d'Arrêt de la Santé, the last city prison in Paris.

Opened in 1867, when green fields still surrounded it, La Santé was built to a design by the French architect Joseph Vaudremer (1829–1914), who is more usually associated with churches and *Lycées*. For La Santé he came up with a hub-and-spoke design inspired by prison and asylum architecture in late 18ᵗʰ century England. Such buildings consisted of wings radiating outwards from a central tower, from where the complex could be kept under constant supervision.

The grim aspect of La Santé was designed to intimidate those incarcerated and to remind passers-by of what awaits the lawbreaker. Few get to see inside but it's safe to say it was not designed as a place to linger. The cells will be small with only a bed, a wash basin, and toilet. In the wall there will be a hole through which food is passed, and in the door a peephole used by the guards. Alleged issues of overcrowding, disease, and suicide at La Santé were addressed in a controversial book published in 2000 by the then prison's doctor.

A walk along the streets surrounding La Santé is a sobering experience. The gloomy visitors' entrance on Rue Messier has a battered bench for those waiting to enter. Around the corner on Boulevard Arago the trees lighten the mood a little, and there can be found the last remaining example of a traditional pavement urinal (see no. 86). At the far end a wall plaque marks where the guillotine stood between 1900 and 1940 and recalls the 40 prisoners executed here in public. The machine was afterwards moved inside and last used in 1972 (see no. 48).

Around the corner on Rue de la Santé is the imposing entrance used by staff and those visiting prisoners held in the VIP wing. At the next corner another plaque recalls those executed for opposing the German occupation of Paris during the Second World War. On Bastille Day 1944, with the Allies fast approaching the city, the prisoners revolted but were bloodily suppressed by Vichy militia.

The Maison d'Arrêt de la Santé is a prison in the heart of Paris

Coming full circle the long unbroken wall along Rue Jean Dolent is a reminder of the prison's proximity to the modern apartment blocks now surrounding it, a narrow corridor between freedom and captivity.

Many villains have done time at La Santé. They include the Russian émigré Paul Gorguloff (1895–1932), who murdered French President Paul Doumer, and the serial killer Doctor Marcel Petiot (1897–1946). The rope he used to lower the bodies of his victims into a furnace in his cellar can be seen in the Musée de la Préfecture de Police at 4 Rue de la Montagne-Sainte-Geneviève (5th). Also here was the Gaullist politician Maurice Papon (1910–2007), convicted of crimes against humanity for his part in deporting Jews during the Second World War, and the bank robber Jacques Mesrine (1936–1979), who became the first successful escapee in 1978. The deposed military dictator of Panama Manuel Noriega (b. 1934) and Ilich Ramírez Sánchez (b. 1949), better known as Carlos the Jackal, passed through, too. One prisoner proved innocent was the writer Guillaume Apollinaire (1880–1918), who was wrongly accused of stealing the *Mona Lisa*!

Other places of interest nearby: 83, 84, 86, 87, 88

86 Paris at your Convenience

14th Arrondissement, the last *Vespasienne* public urinal
opposite 86 Boulevard Arago
Métro 6 Glacière, Saint-Jacques

"Pecunia non olet" (Money doesn't stink) is a Latin saying attributed to the Roman Emperor Vespasian in the 1st century AD. It finds its origin in a tax he imposed on the collection of urine from public latrines, which at the time was used for tanning leather, as a mordant in dyeing, and for whitening woollen togas. According to the Roman historian Suetonius, when Vespasian's son Titus objected to the odiferous nature of his father's tax, the emperor held up a gold coin and asked if that offended his son's nose. Titus, of course, said not, and Vespasian coined his famous expression.

In deference to the emperor and his tax, public urinals in Italy were called *Vespasiani*. Some other countries using Romance languages followed suit, notably France, where urinals were dubbed *Vespasiennes*. Cylindrical in shape they first appeared in Paris in 1834, when Comte Rambuteau, the Préfet de la Seine at the time, ordered their erection to replace the sawdust-filled barrels used previously by gentlemen in need. They were certainly a little more discreet! By 1914 there were

Detail of the Art Nouveau toilet facility beneath Place de la Madeleine

The last *Vespasienne* on Boulevard Arago

around 4,000 *Vespasiennes* in service making them as much a part of the Parisian scene street as the similarly-shaped advertising columns known as *Colonnes Morris*.

Not until 1959 was it decided for reasons of hygiene to remove *Vespasiennes* from streets of Paris. The process was a slow but thorough one, and today only a solitary example remains opposite 86 Boulevard Arago (14th). In their place are more than 400 automated *Sanisettes* invented by the company JCDecaux (the same company pioneered the

Vélib shared bicycle scheme in return for city-wide advertising space). What the new facilities lack in old world charm they make up for in being unisex and self-cleaning.

At the other end of the scale as far as public conveniences are concerned is the magnificent example beneath Place de la Madeleine (8th). Reached by a pair of crumbling tiled staircases this magnificent *Art Nouveau* facility was built by the company Porcher in 1905. Unlike the *Vespasiennes*, with their simple metal screens to provide the standing user with some privacy, customers here are offered their own wood-panelled cubicle with mirror and sink, finished off with floral frescoes and a stained glass window in the door. In the centre of the facility, which is illuminated by a skylight and adorned with decorative tiles and brass fittings, there is an old fashioned shoe shine stand. (Note: opening hours can be irregular).

Most people visit Place de la Madeleine for its enormous namesake church, La Madeleine, designed originally as a neo-Classical temple to the glory of Napoleon's army. There are plenty of distinctive shopping opportunities here, too, including venerable institutions such as Hédiard and Fauchon (see no. 91), a good flower market, and, not far away at 3 Boulevard de la Madeleine, Lavinia, the largest wine shop in France. Also very much worth exploring is the Galerie de la Madeleine at 9 Place de la Madeleine, a fine example of the city's charming *Passages Couverts* (see no. 4).

> The public wash houses and communal baths of Paris also claim a venerable past. Of the former there were once around 300 but only the modest façade of a single example now remains, the Grand Lavoir du Marché Lenoir constructed in 1830 on Rue de Cotte (12th). Bath buildings have fared better, although none of the 26 steam baths recorded in the city during the 13th century have survived. The first indoor pool in Paris was the Piscine Château-Landon built in 1884 at 31 Rue du Château Landon (10th), and it is still in use. However, it was not until the construction in 1924 of the Piscine de la Buttes-aux-Cailles at 5 Place Paul Verlaine (13th) that personal washing and swimming for leisure were separated into two distinct areas of the building. *Art Nouveau* in design with a vaulted roof and galleries down each side, the pool finds a counterpart in the equally appealing Piscine Pointoise at 19 Rue de Pontoise (5th). Definitely worth a visit is the Piscine Molitor in Porte Molitor (16th), an *Art Deco* pool built in 1929 and recently restored after a period of abandonment. It featured in the film *The Life of Pi* (2012).

Other places of interest nearby: 83, 84, 85, 87, 88

87 Descent into the Capuchin Quarries

14th Arrondissement, the Anciennes Carrières des Capucins beneath the Hôpital Cochin at 27 Rue du Faubourg-Saint-Jacques
Métro 6 Saint-Jacques (Note: visits by appointment only)

Subterannean Paris takes many forms, including sewers, cellars, catacombs, and railway tunnels (see nos. 17, 44, 84, 98). Perhaps the most surprising – and least visited – are the city's abandoned quarries (Carrières), which form a vast 300 kilometre-long network of subterannean galleries either side of the Seine.

The Romans were the first to extract the area's hard, fine-grained limestone for building purposes, and they did so in the open. It was not until the building boom of the late 1100s that demand for limestone drove quarrying underground. The activity was focussed on the Left Bank beyond the city wall around Montparnasse. Much of the limestone used for the construction of Notre-Dame de Paris came from here, as did material for the Église Saint-Séverin (5th).

By the time the Order of Capuchins took possession of the area in the 1613 the ground was riddled with tunnels. For reasons of safety the monks strengthened these in 1653 before extracting further stone to build their own convent (demolished in the 1920s). Similar precautions were taken by the architect François Mansart prior to the construction of the Église du Val-de-Grâce (5th), and by Claude Perrault at the Observatoire de Paris (6th).

By the 18th century Paris had grown considerably, and much of the newly occupied land inevitably had pre-existing quarry tunnels beneath it. In 1774 a tunnel collapse on Avenue Denfert-Rochereau took numerous houses and people with it. This prompted Louis XVI (1774–1791) to create the Inspection Général des Carrières (IGC) to map and further reinforce the tunnels, a task it is still pursuing today.

Quarrying was banned within the new city walls in 1813 by which time some of the abandoned tunnels were being used to store bones exhumed when the city's medieval cemeteries were cleared (see no. 84). Others were later used to cultivate mushrooms and as a refuge for the Communards and the French Resistance. Today some are the domain of thrill-seeking clandestine explorers known as Cataphiles.

An exciting descent into the Anciennes Carrières des Capucins can

In the Anciennes Carrières des Capucins beneath the Hôpital Cochin

be made by prior arrangement with S.E.A.D.A.C.C. (Société d'Études et d'Aménagement des Anciennes Carrières des Capucins). Eighteen metres beneath the Hôpital Cochin at 27 Rue du Faubourg-Saint-Jacques (14th) the society has preserved over a kilometre of former quarry tunnels. It is no coincidence that a hospital is located here since it finds its origins in an infirmary established to treat injured quarry workers.

The quarry is reached by means of a staircase in an underground car park to the rear of the hospital. As it spirals down it passes through rock laid down 45 million years ago when Paris was a tropical sea. At the bottom a tunnel leads to a spacious gallery, illuminated by orange lights designed to suppress the growth of fungus on the damp walls. Accompanied by an experienced guide the visitor will now spend an hour or more exploring the old quarries. A highlight is a superbly-carved well called the Fontaine des Capucins used to monitor the quarry's phreatic water level. There are also numbers carved on the walls accompanied by the royal Fleur-de-Lys, placed there by the king's inspectors to identify buildings on the surface directly above.

Gypsum was quarried beneath Montmartre until 1873, when the 12 metre-high galleries were sealed off (they are not open to the public). As Plaster of Paris gypsum had been used to fireproof buildings since medieval times. The white dust kicked up as it was transported down the hill explains the name of the Blanche Métro station.

Other places of interest nearby: 84, 85, 86, 88

88   Putting Paris on the Map

14th Arrondissement, the Observatoire de Paris
at 61 Avenue de l'Observatoire Métro 4, 6 Denfert-Rochereau
(Note: visits by appointment only)

Scientists have long viewed the surface of the Earth like the segments of an orange, divided by invisible lines of longitude known as meridians. Running between the North and South Poles they link those places where at noon the sun is at its zenith. To make use of meridians in navigation a zero meridian is required, one from which all measurements can be made. For almost two centuries this so-called Prime Meridian was not in Greenwich but in Paris.

The story of the Paris Prime Meridian began in 1634, when Louis XIII (1610–1643) decreed that Ferro in the Canary Islands be used as a reference point on maps. It was the most westerly known point in the Old World and believed to lie exactly 20 degrees west of Paris. This made it easy for the king to decree that the Prime Meridian ran through the French capital – and from now on through all French-made maps.

It was intended that the improvement in navigation resulting from the establishment of the Paris Prime Meridian would strengthen French maritime power and international trade. With this in mind Louis XIV (1643–1715) and his finance minister Jean-Baptist Colbert approved the construction of the Observatoire de Paris, where further research could take place. Designed by Claude Perrault and completed in 1671 it straddles perfectly the meridian at 61 Avenue de l'Observatoire (14th). In 1679 the observatory published the world's first almanac to aid seafarers in establishing longitude.

A fascinating guided tour can be made of the observatory beginning on the ground floor with a collection of speaking clocks, including the first one ever built in 1933. On the first floor is a superb collection of scientific instruments used by French astronomers and cartographers, and on the roof is the observatory's telescope. Of greatest importance, however, is the Cassini Hall on the second floor, named after Giovanni Cassini (1625–1712), astronomer to the king and the observatory's first director. Embedded in its floor is a brass strip marking the exact line of the Paris Prime Meridian, across which a beam of sunlight moves at noon. For those experiments needing a sight line beyond the observatory a stone obelisk was erected directly south near the entrance to Parc Montsouris on Boulevard Jourdan (14th).

A shaft of sunlight illuminates the Paris Meridian in the Observatoire de Paris

In the 1790s the Paris Prime Meridian was recalculated to serve as the basis for determining the length of a Metre (see no. 37). It was further refined in the early 19th century by the astronomer François Arago (1786–1853), whose name now appears on a series of bronze pavement medallions tracing the line of the meridian all the way across Paris. The line is continued by trees across the entire country as part of a project called the Méridienne Verte.

In 1884 at the International Meridian Conference held in Washington DC the Greenwich Meridian was adopted over its Paris counterpart as the world's Prime Meridian. France did not attend the conference and instead clung onto its own meridian for timekeeping purposes until 1911 and for navigation until as late as 1914.

The Église Saint-Sulpice on Place Sulpice (6th) contains a curious stone on one of its walls. It is an 18th century *Gnomon* used to cast a shadow to determine how high the sun is over the horizon, and hence indicate noon. It is one of three such indicators on the line of the Paris Prime Meridian, the others being in the Hôtel des Monnaies at 11 Quai de Conti (6th) and the Palais Royal on Place du Palais Royal (1st).

Other places of interest nearby: 84, 85, 86, 87

89 Heroes of the Polar Seas

14th Arrondisement, the grave of Jules Dumont d'Urville
in the Cimetière du Montparnasse at 3 Boulevard
Edgar-Quinet
Métro 4 Raspail, Vavin, 6 Raspail, Edgar Quinet

The Cimetière du Montparnasse at 3 Boulevard Edgar-Quinet (14th) opened in 1824 on former arable land, which accounts for the 17th century windmill standing in its midst. Known originally as Le Cimetière du Sud it was one of several new suburban cemeteries established by Napoleon (1804–1815) after he closed the old ones in the city centre on health grounds (the others included Montmartre in the north, Père Lachaise in the east, and later Passy in the west) (see nos. 69, 78). The numerous Left Bank celebrities buried here always attract attention – Charles Baudelaire, Guy de Maupassant, Simone de Beauvoir, Jean Paul Sartre, Serge Gainsbourg – but there are many other lives worth remembering. One of them is the French explorer Jules Dumont d'Urville (1790–1842).

Fascinated by travel from an early age Dumont became an ensign in the French navy in 1812. In 1820 he joined a survey ship heading to the eastern Mediterranean, and it was there off the Greek island of Milos that his life changed forever. He saw and sketched a recently excavated ancient statue, and urged his captain to buy it. After his suggestion was refused he instead showed his sketches to the French ambassador in Constantinople, from where a French vessel was dispatched immediately to collect the statue. For his part in acquiring for France what became known as the *Venus de Milo* Dumont was awarded the Légion d'Honneur and promoted to Lieutenant. The statue is today one of the most popular exhibits in the Musée du Louvre.

Dumont spent the next 17 years circumnavigating the globe, mapping areas of interest to his country, and coining the names Micronesia and Melanesia along the way. In 1837 he headed to Antarctica in an attempt to secure the South Magnetic Pole for Louis Philippe I (1830–1848). Difficult conditions in the Weddell Sea forced his ice-strengthened ship *Astrolabe* to retreat but he returned in 1840 and this time made landfall, naming the new territory (and the penguins he found there) after his wife, Adélie. It was the first step made by man on the Antarctic continent. Promoted to Rear Admiral and awarded the gold medal of the French Société de Géographie, Dumont and Adélie were killed less than two years later in a train crash between Versailles

Jules Dumont d'Urville encounters penguins on his journey south

and Paris. Their obelisk-shaped tombstone against the west wall of the Cimetière du Montparnasse is suitably adorned with bas-reliefs of the *Venus de Milo* and the *Astrolabe* – as well as a couple of penguins!

Another French polar hero is Jean-Baptiste Charcot (1867–1936), who is buried in a family mausoleum in the Cimetière de Montmartre at 20 Avenue Rachel (18th). Occupying a former quarry the high-walled cemetery is known chiefly for its writers, artists, and composers, including Berlioz, Degas, Delibes, Fragonard, Offenbach, Heine, Nijinsky, Stendhal, and Truffaut.

After inheriting a small fortune from his father, Charcot financed the construction of the schooner *Français* and in 1903 headed south. Avoiding the Ross Sea, with its potential for international rivalry, he instead investigated the coastline of the Antarctic Peninsula, a selfless act for which the British explorer Captain Scott called him "the gentleman of the Pole". After striking a rock Charcot returned home to a hero's welcome. He headed south again in 1908 to resume his work, this time in the *Pourquoi Pas?* The highpoint of this expedition was the discovery of Charcot Island, which he named after his father the renowned neurologist Jean-Martin Charcot (1825–1893). Twenty six years later Charcot and most of his crew were lost in a storm off Iceland.

Other places of interest nearby: 38, 84, 88, 90, 92, 93

90 Some Hidden Church Treasures

14th Arrondissement, a tour of church treasures finishing with the Église Notre-Dame-du-Travail at 59 Rue Vercingétorix Métro 13 Gaîté, Pernety

All too often Paris is defined by its museums and galleries. For a change why not explore the city's history through its many Catholic churches? Here are some starting points.

From the medieval period the Église Saint-Gervais-Saint-Protais on Place Saint-Gervais (4th) is unique in preserving a series of *Misericords* beneath the folding seats in its choir. These carved shelves afforded a place to lean during long services. Beneath a gargoyle at the Église Saint-Germain-l'Auxerrois at 2 Place du Louvre (1st) is a medieval *Boule aux Rats* (Ball of Rats). Surmounted by a Cross it represents the Church's power to redeem a corrupt world. Equally unusual is the Gothic column in the form of a palm tree supporting the vaulted ambulatory of the Église Saint-Séverin on Rue des Prêtres-Saint-Séverin (5th). The Église Saint-Médard at 141 Rue Mouffetard (5th) also has a magnificent ambulatory, as well a tapestry depicting the martyr Saint Etienne made at the nearby Manufacture des Gobelins (see no. 80).

The Chapelle de la Sorbonne on Place de la Sorbonne (5th) was erected in 1622 when Cardinal Richelieu (1585–1642) appointed himself university chancellor. His familiar red hat hangs over his tomb and will remain there, so it is said, until his soul is released from Purgatory. His sin was supporting the Protestants during the Thirty Years' War. The Sorbonne remained vigorously anti-Protestant until the Revolution, when a wave of violent anti-clericalism saw the city's churches secularised and their contents removed or destroyed. One of them was the Église Saint-Étienne-du-Mont at 1 Place Sainte-Geneviève (5th) but fortunately its remarkable rood screen (or *Jube*) was spared. This ornately carved gallery separating the choir from the nave supports the Crucifix and is now unique in Paris (the remaining relics of Saint Genevieve, patroness of Paris, reside in a chapel nearby, the rest having been burnt publically by the revolutionaries). At the same time the Église Saint-Joseph-des-Carmes at 70 Rue de Vaugirard (6th) was turned into a prison for clerics who refused allegiance to the new Republic. In 1792 they were executed in the garden, where bloodied paving stones can still be seen.

The interior of the Église Notre-Dame-du-Travail on Rue Vercingétorix resembles a factory!

Conch shell stoups for holy water donated by Victor Hugo

When Napoleon (1804–1815) rehabilitated the Catholic Church many paintings previously hidden went back on display. Amongst these unexpected masterpieces is Tintoretto's *Last Supper* in the Église Saint-François-Xavier at 12 Place du Président-Mithouard (7th). And don't miss the superb mural depicting *The Transfiguration* above the altar in the Église Saint-Thomas-d'Aquin at 3 Place Saint-Thomas-d'Aquin (7th), which was the only decoration in the church to survive the Revolution.

During the 19th century new artworks were installed in some churches, including several by Eugène Delacroix (1798–1863). His *Christ in the Garden of Olives* hangs in the Église Saint-Paul-Saint-Louis at 99 Rue Saint-Antoine (4th), which also contains a pair of conch shell stoups given by Victor Hugo on the occasion of his daughter's wedding there. During the same century believers flocked to the early 17th century Église Notre Dame des Victoires on Place des Petits-Pères (2nd) to donate ex-votos engraved on small marble plaques, which now cover the walls.

Modern church art in Paris is represented by a bronze triptych by American artist Keith Haring (1958–1990) in the Église Saint-Eustache at 2 Impasse Saint-Eustache (1st). It was donated to the church by Haring's foundation in gratitude for its work with AIDS victims. This part of the church also contains a colourful depiction of the exodus of market traders from nearby Les Halles, when it closed in 1969. The market's former presence explains the presence of a stained glass window depicting a pig, the symbol of the Corporation des Charcutiers.

This tour concludes with perhaps the most extraordinary church in Paris. The Église Notre-Dame-du-Travail at 59 Rue Vercingétorix (14th) appears unexceptional until one enters it. Built in 1901 and influenced by the work of Gustave Eiffel its nave is supported on a visible iron framework, installed it is said to make factory workers in the congregation feel at home!

The curious Église Notre-Dame-de-Compassion at 2 Boulevard Aurelle-de-Paladines (17th) is a memorial to Prince Ferdinand-Philippe d'Orléans (1810–1842), who died here in a carriage accident.

Other places of interest nearby: 89, 91, 92, 93, 94

91 Paris for the Bon Viveur

14th Arrondissement, a tour of specialist food shops
including the bakery Moulin de la Vierge
at 105 Rue Vercingétorix
Métro 13 Gaîté, Pernety

For the person who likes to live well – the *Bon Viveur* – Paris has much to offer. The city contains hundreds of specialist food shops, some of which are historic institutions in themselves. Here is just a taster.

For a one-stop shop, Paris boasts several *Grande Dame* department stores, each of which contains a delicatessen. La Grande Épicerie at 38 Rue de Sèvres (7th), for example, is the food hall of Le Bon Marché next door. Established in 1838 it offers a cosier shopping experience than the bustling Galeries Lafayette and Au Printemps on Boulevard Haussmann (9th) (although the latter do boast magnificent Second Empire coloured glass ceilings). Equally venerable is Hédiard, famous for its fruit jellies, at 21 Place de la Madeleine (8th), and Fauchon nearby at 24–26, with its pink-packaged jams.

Bread making is a serious business in Paris. Poilâne at 8 Rue du Cherche-Midi (6th) bakes its bread in antique, wood-fired ovens, including a large sourdough loaf known as a *Miche*. For plump golden

The bakery Moulin de la Vierge on Rue Vercingétorix is a Belle Époque jewel

Croissants try Eric Kayser, an artisanal baker at 14 Rue Monge (5th), and for the classic *Baguette* visit Gosselin at 123 Rue Saint-Honoré (1st). The best *Pain au Raisins* come from Moulin de la Vierge at 105 Rue Vercingétorix (14th). Surprisingly for this normal-looking street the tiny premises are an astonishing *Belle Époque* jewel, with mirrored walls and a glorious painted ceiling. Another historic bakery is Du Pain et des Idées at 34 Rue Yves Toudic (10th), home of the best crusty loaf!

For those with a savoury tooth there is much on offer. Androuët at 37 Rue de Verneuil (7th) is where Hemingway and Callas bought their raw milk cheeses, and despite its name Fromagerie Quatrehomme at 62 Rue de Sèvres (7th) is home to an award-winning female *Fromagère*. Maison Pou at 16 Avenue des Ternes (17th) has supplied *Charcuterie* since 1830, whilst Maison de la Truffe at 19 Place de la Madeleine (8th) has done the same with truffles since 1932; for those in need of *Foie Gras* there is Pierre Champion at 110 Rue Mouffetard (5th). Pescatarians will appreciate La Sablaisse Poissonerie at 28 Rue Cler (7th), where fish, oysters, and crustaceans are displayed on ice.

The *Bon Viveur* might also consider quality oils and vinegars from TOMAT's Épicerie Fine at 12 Rue Jacob (6th), with perhaps a jar of honey from La Maison du Miel at 24 Rue Vignon (9th). And he or she will undoubtedly appreciate a bottle or two of wine from the *Caviste* La Maison des Millesimes at 137 Boulevard St Germain (6th), or perhaps even a vintage Armagnac from Ryst Dupeyron at 79 Rue du Bac (7th) and Champagne from the family firm Arlaux at 29 Rue Censier (5th).

Paris caters equally well for those with a sweet tooth. The city's oldest confectioner is À la Mère de Famille at 33–35 Rue du Faubourg-Montmartre (9th). Established in 1761 it looks like something from a children's story book. The city's oldest patisserie established in 1730 is Stohrer at 51 Rue Montorgeuil (2nd), with its majestic frescoes, where a century later the *Baba au Rhum* was invented (it is also renowned for its mouth-watering *Éclair au Chocolat* the name of which, meaning 'flash of lightning', reflects how quickly it is usually devoured!). Debauve & Gallais, meanwhile, at 30 Rue des Saint-Pères (7th) have been supplying chocolate to the rich and famous for two centuries, whilst the exciting young chocolatier Patrick Roger is relatively new on the scene at 45 Avenue Victor Hugo (16th). For the original double-decker *Macaron* visit Ladurée at 16 Rue Royale (8th), with daring new flavours courtesy of Pierre Hermé at 72 Rue Bonaparte (6th). And let's not forget ice cream. Parisians and tourists alike are always happy to queue at Glacier Berthillon at 29–31 Rue Saint-Louis-en-l'Île (4th).

Other places of interest nearby: 89, 90, 92, 93, 94

92 The Spirit of Montparnasse

15th Arrondissement, a walk through Montparnasse
finishing at the Cité des Arts at 21 Avenue du Maine
Métro 4 Vavin

Montparnasse may lack the scenic attractions of its Right Bank counterpart Montmartre but its history is no less fascinating. Since the 12th century, when theologian and philosopher Peter Abelard led a student exodus from Notre-Dame to the Église Saint-Julien-le-Pauvre (creating the Quartier Latin in the process), scholars and creatives have been drawn to the Left Bank. Later during the 17th century, when the area around Pont Neuf became too noisy, and the proximity of Henry IV's debauched ex-wife too worrisome, poets and students moved out to Montparnasse. It was never a mountain though but rather a spoil heap for the area's medieval quarries (see no. 87). Only after the First World War did the artists of Montmartre follow, attracted by the area's cafés, cabarets, and art schools (see no. 2).

Life in Montparnasse has inevitably changed since Ernest Hemingway described it in *A Moveable Feast* – but with a little imagination the old atmosphere can be recreated. This journey begins on Boulevard du Montparnasse, which was laid out when the area was reimagined by Baron Haussmann (1809–1891) during the 1860s. At number 171 is La Closerie des Lilas, Hemingway's favourite café, where he penned *The Sun Also Rises* (1926). Baudelaire, Strindberg, and Wilde were there before him, and when Montparnasse eclipsed Montmartre so Picasso, Braque, and Modigliani

A corner of the Cité des Arts in Montparnasse

took their place; they too had drifted away by the time Hemingway arrived in the early 1920s, accompanied by the likes of Jean Paul Sartre, Simone de Beauvoir, Samuel Beckett, and André Gide.

Whilst strolling leisurely westwards in the footsteps of Hemingway it's worth recalling his illustrious contemporaries in Montparnasse: the artists Kandinsky, Klee, and Matisse; the writers Scott Fitzgerald, Henry Miller, and Jean Cocteau; and the composers Stravinsky, Satie, and de Falla.

Soon the Place Pablo Picasso is reached. This busy crossroads is overlooked by the venerable Dôme and Rotonde cafés, where the artist Modigliani hawked his paintings from table to table. Just around the corner at 14 Rue de la Grande Chaumière is a private art school that hasn't changed in a century.

Then come two more Montparnasse cafés with artistic connections: Le Select at 99 Boulevard du Montparnasse and La Coupole opposite at number 102, the latter retaining its glorious *Art Deco* interior with columns decorated by Chagall amongst others. There are cabarets, theatres, and clubs, too, along the aptly-named Rue de la Gaîté at the southern end of Rue du Montparnasse.

Much of it, of course, trades on past glories but there are two locations that retain the true spirit of Montparnasse. One is the artists' colony La Ruche on Passage de Dantzig (15th), which attracted the likes of Chagall, Zadkine, and Modigliani (see no. 2). The other is the Cité des Arts at 21 Avenue du Maine (15th), a leafy, cobblestoned cul-de-sac once the site of a 19th century coaching inn. Thirty artists' studios were later installed here using material salvaged from the *Exposition Universelle de Paris de 1900*. One of them was rented by the Russian painter Marie Vassilieff (1884–1957), who ran a canteen for impoverished artists here. The studios are still in use today.

Art devotees will also want to visit the Cartier Fondation and the Fondation Henri-Cartier Bresson alongside the nearby Cimetière du Montparnasse.

The sculptor Antoine Bourdelle (1861–1929) also lived and worked in Montparnasse, and his former studio at 18 Rue Antoine Bourdelle is now a museum. Amongst the plaster casts for his monumental neo-Classical works are those created for the Théâtre des Champs-Elysées at 15 Avenue Montaigne (8th).

Other places of interest nearby: 89, 90, 91, 93, 94

93 The French Art of Communication

15th Arrondissement, L'Adresse – Musée de la Poste
at 34 Boulevard de Vaugirard
Métro 6 Montparnasse – Bienvenüe, Pasteur, 12 Falguière,
Montparnasse – Bienvenüe, Pasteur, 13 Montparnasse –
Bienvenüe

It's no easy feat to make the history of French communications technology appealing. But that's exactly what has been achieved by L'Adresse – Musée de la Poste at 34 Boulevard de Vaugirard (15th). Covering everything from carrier pigeons to satellites this is a surprisingly dynamic place, and one that will entertain and enlighten not only adults but children, too.

The museum is spread across several floors, each introducing a different theme. The pre-industrial display is particularly interesting, with its couriers on horseback, mail coaches, and balloon post. Here visitors will also be reminded that Rue du Télégraphe in Belleville (20th) – the highest point in Paris – is where French engineer Claude Chappe (1763–1805) pioneered the world's first optical telegraph (see no. 75). At the time France was in the throes of Revolution and surrounded

Padlocked envelopes for military dispatches in L'Adresse – Musée de la Poste

by foreign enemies, and so it was hoped the telegraph would provide better communications. In 1792 Chappe constructed a telegraph between Paris and Lille 230 kilometres away using a system of mechanical signal stations, including one in Belleville. Henceforth it only took 32 minutes to send a message, and the telegraph proved invaluable in relaying news of the war between France and Austria.

The optical telegraph transformed communications in France, and a network of telegraph stations soon criss-crossed the country. Napoleon (1804–1815) used it to coordinate both his empire and army and it remained operational until its replacement by the electric telegraph in the 1850s. Fittingly the gravestone of Chappe in the Cimetière du Père-Lachaise (20th) is surmounted by a scale model of his invention.

Amongst other old fashioned communication equipment displayed in the museum is a working Morse code station, an antique phone booth, and a traditional postal counter. There are also items relating to the pneumatic post, which operated in Paris between 1866 and 1983. Using compressed air a brass shuttle was propelled along special tubes running through the sewers, each shuttle carrying around 35 letters at an average speed of 700 metres per minute. In 1957 at its greatest extent the pneumatic network reached a length of 400 kilometres. The arrival of the fax machine and computer inevitably brought about its demise.

The museum also illustrates the French postal service, something very important in a highly centralised country such as France. One display case contains examples of secret military dispatches, or rather the padlocked metal envelopes in which they were sent. During the Franco-Prussian War pigeons were used to carry the post and they proved so useful that afterwards a huge *Pigeonnier* was erected in the Jardin d'Acclimation (16th) to house them (it is still there today). Another room is devoted to the development of the French airmail, with routes across Africa and South America pioneered from the 1920s onwards by heroic pilots such as Antoine de Saint-Exupéry (1900–1944).

Philatelists will delight in the many postage stamps displayed in the museum gallery, including those designed by Joan Miró (1893–1983). Like other countries the humble postage stamp has long been an excuse for expressing French national pride. Alongside them are displayed some distinctive French post boxes both ancient and modern.

All in all this unique museum provides a timely reminder, if one were needed, of the impact of communications technology on the modern world – and all the hard work that has gone into bringing it about!

Other places of interest nearby: 89, 90, 91, 92, 94

94 A Mausoleum for Louis Pasteur

15th Arrondissement, the Musée et Mausolée Pasteur
in the Institut Pasteur at at 25 Rue du Docteur-Roux
Métro 6, 12 Pasteur (Note: identificaton must be shown
at the hospital gate)

The 300 stations of the Paris Métro are not only named after significant geographical locations but also famous battles, historical figures, and talented artists. Without leaving the Métro a passenger can obtain a condensed if sometimes biased history of France. There are stations named after scientists, too, including Louis Pasteur (1822–1895). Near to his namesake station is the Institut Pasteur, which was established on his initiative in 1888. It is where he spent his last years and where surprisingly he is also buried.

Louis Pasteur was born into the family of a poor tanner in Dole in the Jura. Despite this he proved himself an able student, and in 1843 he entered the École Normale Supérieure at 45 Rue d'Ulm (5th), an elite Paris college also attended by Jean-Paul Sartre. In his late twenties Pasteur became Professor of Chemistry at the University of Strasbourg after presenting an impressive thesis on crystallography. There he met his wife and together they had five children, two of whom died from

A rabid dog features in the mosaic decoration of Louis Pasteur's mausoleum

typhoid. It was this tragedy in part that prompted him to commence pioneering work on the cause and prevention of human disease.

In 1856 Pasteur became head of science at his old college. His most important breakthrough during this period was his demonstration that fermentation is caused by the growth of micro-organisms. Not only could such germs form beer but they could also turn milk sour, and Pasteur's suggestion that wine and beer be heated before consumption resulted in the process that still carries his name: Pasteurisation. His subsequent identification of harmful bacteria such as staphylococcus and streptococcus led to the first vaccines against rabies and anthrax, as well as the development of antibiotics and hygienic surgical practices.

Much of the equipment used by Pasteur is now displayed in the Musée Pasteur at 25 Rue du Docteur-Roux (15th), which was established at the Institut Pasteur in 1935. The ground floor of the museum is given over to the rooms where Pasteur spent the last seven years of his life. The furniture and decorations they contain provide a unique insight not only into Pasteur's private life but also middle class living at the turn of the century. Among the personal effects are his letter opener decorated with the French flag, a glass vase etched with microbes by the ceramicist Gallé, and his wife Marie's unfinished knitting!

After his death and an elaborate funeral at Notre-Dame de Paris, Pasteur's body was laid to rest in a private mausoleum at the institute. It was designed in neo-Byzantine style by Charles-Louis Girault (1851–1932), the architect of the Petit Palais (8th), and is adorned with mosaics and paintings. There is much symbolism here alluding to Pasteur's achievements. The rabbits on the ceiling recall those used in his experiments, the dogs the source of the rabies he was trying to prevent. The boy depicted on the arch represents the first patient he cured of rabies. The sheep and cows recall his work with anthrax, while the decorative motifs of vines and hops represent his work with fermentation and pasteurisation.

The radiologists and Nobel Prize winners Pierre and Marie Curie are also honoured with a Métro station and a museum. The Musée Curie at 1 Rue Pierre-et-Marie-Curie (5th) contains Marie's laboratory, which required decontamination before being opened to the public in the 1990s. Pierre was the first to recognise the use of radiology in the treatment of cancer.

Other places of interest nearby: 90, 91, 92, 93, 95, 96

95 Russians in Paris

15th Arrondissement, the Église Saint-Séraphin-de-Sarov
at 91 Rue Lecourbe
Métro 12 Volontaires (Note: admission for Sunday Mass
by pressing the entry button on the main door keypad)

During the 1920s there were 25,000 Russian immigrants living in Paris. Amongst them were not only refugees from the tsarist regime – notably the Marxist revolutionaries Lenin and Trotsky – but also pro-Tsarist White Russians, many of them well-to-do aristocrats, fleeing the Bolshevik Revolution. The latter settled in the 15th and 16th Arrondissements, where, keen to maintain their culture and religion, they established several Orthodox churches. Russians are still worshipping there today.

One of the churches is concealed inside a courtyard at 91 Rue Lecourbe (15th), with only a discreet nameplate to identify it. Built in 1933 the Église Saint-Séraphin-de-Sarov is administered by the Patriarch of Constantinople, and is dedicated to one of the most venerated saints of the Russian Orthodox Church. Healed as a young boy by a miraculous icon, Saint Seraphim (1754–1853) took his vows in the ancient Monastery of Sarov. Thereafter he lived an ascetic life as a hermit in a log cabin, receiving pilgrims in search of healing and wisdom. Seraphim was canonized in 1903 and the little church bearing his name recalls his former home by being constructed around a tree trunk. Originally

The Cathédrale Saint-Alexandre-Newsky on Rue Daru

The distinctive onion-shaped dome of the Église Saint-Séraphin-de-Sarov on Rue Lecourbe

little more than a shack the church was enlarged during the 1970s but still retains its rustic aspect. Its blue onion-shaped dome topped with an Orthodox cross rises above the surrounding garden, while the simple wooden interior glows with the warmth of painted icons.

Elsewhere in the same area the Église des Trois-Saints-Docteurs at 5 Rue Petel is administered by the Patriarch of Moscow. By contrast, the discreetly-located Église de Tous-les-Saints-de-la-Terre-Russe at 19 Rue Claude-Lorrain (16th) comes under the sway of neither Moscow nor Constantinople but rather the patriarchate known as The Russian Church beyond the Frontiers. In common with all Russian Orthodox churches none contain stained glass, saintly statues, pews, or organs. The picture is rounded out by the Église Russe-Catholique-de-la-Très-Sainte-Trinité at 39 Rue François-Gérard, where the Slavic-Byzantine rite is observed.

Elsewhere in Paris the Église Saint-Serge at 93 Rue de Crimée (19th) is remarkable for its *Iconostasis*, whilst the most magnificent venue for Russian Orthodox worship is the Cathédrale Saint-Alexandre-Newsky at 12 Rue Daru (8th). Consecrated in 1861 and part-financed by Tsar Alexander II (1818–1881) the cathedral was placed under the jurisdiction of Constantinople in 1931, since when it has served as the archdiocesan seat of the Russian Orthodox Church in Western Europe. With five cupolas representing Christ and the Evangelists, it was here that Picasso married the Russian ballerina Olga Koklova in 1918. The celebrations afterwards were held at the Café à la Ville de Petrograd across the road.

Russian influence in Paris is not only restricted to places of worship. The Russian-style log cabins *(Izbas)* at 7 Boulevard de Beauséjour (16th) were built for the *Exposition Universelle de Paris de 1867*. The Pont Alexandre III, the most flamboyant of all the bridges spanning the Seine, is named after the penultimate tsar of Russia, who laid the foundation stone during a visit to Paris in 1896 (Avenue Franco-Russe (7th) nearby recalls the treaty between the two nations resulting from the visit). And the two rows of cottages at 22 Rue Barrault (13th) were built in 1912 for Russian aristocratic émigrés, many of whom were obliged to work as taxi drivers and parked their cars in the garages below.

For a taste of modern Russia visit Petrossian at 18 Boulevard La Tour-Maubourg (8th), which has been supplying fine caviar since it was founded in the 1920s.

Other places of interest nearby: 41, 92, 93, 94, 96

96 A Very French Ball Game

15th Arrondissement, the Union Bouliste du 15ème
in Square Blomet at 43 Rue Blomet
Métro 12 Volontaires

France is one of the fittest countries in Europe, with a quarter of the population playing regular sports (the European Union average is around 15%). In terms of sports club membership football tops the list, with tennis, cycling, and swimming not far behind. But also high on the list is *Pétanque*, a close relative of the distinctively French game of *Boules*.

Pétanque is a ball-throwing game which originated in 1907 in La Ciotat, near Marseille (simple tossing games had been introduced into Provence by the Romans). Unlike *Boules*, however, its players must remain in one spot. The inventor of *Pétanque*, Jules Lenoir, suffered from arthritis and was no longer able to play the more energetic *Boules*. This explains the origin of the name *Pétanque*, which comes from the Provencal dialect 'Pès tancats', meaning 'feet anchored'. It also explains why a *Pétanque* court is half the size of a *Boules* court.

Restricted mostly to the south of France, *Pétanque* also retains a healthy following in the backstreets of Paris, where it is played both socially and professionally. An example of a *Pétanque* court is in Square Blomet, a little-known corner of the 15th Arrondissement once popular with artists. The court is the headquarters of the Union Bouliste du 15ème, one of around fifty *Pétanque* associations in Paris. The letters F.F.P.P. over the entrance show it is part of the international *Pétanque* federation (Fédération Française de Pétanque et Jeu Provençal) founded in 1958 in Marseilles.

Boules and *Pétanque* are similar in that the aim is to throw a metal *Boule* so it lands as close as possible to a smaller wooden jack ball called a *Cochonnet*. Played by two, four, or six people in two teams, the starting team make a circle on the ground from where all players must throw their *Boules*. The first player throws the jack and then the first *Boule*. An opposing player then makes a throw, and play continues with the team farthest from the jack continuing to throw until they land nearer the jack than their opponents, or until they run out of *Boules*. Play continues with a player from the winning team making a new circle where the jack finished, and then throwing the jack for a new game. Play ends and points are scored when both teams have no more *Boules*, or when the jack is knocked out of play. The winning team receives a point for each *Boule* it has closer to the jack than the best-placed *Boule* of the opposition. If the jack is knocked out of play, no points are awarded unless one team has *Boules* left to play, in which case the team receives a point for each *Boule* left. The first team to reach 13 points wins.

Pétanque is played casually by about seventeen million people in France. It is also played in Southeast Asia as a result of French colonialism. Other *Pétanque* courts in Paris include Place Dauphine (1st), Square des Arènes-de-Lutèce (5th), Passage Bourgoin (13th), and Passage de la Sorcière at 23 Avenue Junot (18th).

Veteran Pétanque player Didier Vincent warms up in Square Blomet

Artist Paul Gauguin (1848–1903) once had a studio on Rue Blomet, whilst that of Joan Miró (1893–1983) was demolished to make way for Square Blomet. This explains the presence there of his bronze *L'Oiseau Lunaire*. Picasso meanwhile frequented the Bal Nègre dance hall at 33 Rue Blomet.
Billiards is also popular in Paris and the Académie de Billard at 84 Rue de Clichy (9th), with its wood panelling and glass skylight, is a living museum of the sport.

Other places of interest nearby: 41, 92, 93, 94, 95

97 The First 'Lost and Found'

15th Arrondissement, the Service des Objet Trouvés
at 36 Rue des Morillons
Métro 12 Convention; T3 Georges Brassens
(Note: bags are searched on entry)

During the Middle Ages and the subsequent years of the *Ancien Régime* objects lost on the streets of Paris were handed over to local landlords and rarely seen again. This state of affairs changed in 1804 when Napoleon (1804–1815) instructed his Préfet de Police to hold such objects until they were retrieved. In doing so he created the world's first lost property office.

From 1850 onwards the Service des Objets Trouves was located on Rue de Harlay, not far from the Préfecture de Police on the Île de la Cité (1st). Around 10,000 objects were deposited there each year, although it was not until 1893 that the préfet Louis Lépine coordinated efforts to locate the owners of the objects. Since 1939 the service has been based at 36 Rue des Morillons (15th), to where more than 150,000 objects are taken each year, around a quarter of which are subsequently reunited with their owners.

The office on Rue des Morillons could hardly be called a tourist attraction but the tales emanating from it are every bit as interesting. Visitors will only ever see the first floor reception area, where hopefuls queue to reclaim their lost valuables (the old photos and documents on the wall help pass the time). What few realise is that beneath their feet is a vast warehouse bursting with unclaimed objects, most of which have been found on the city's sprawling transport network.

Not surprisingly mobile telephones are the most common single item, with 40 lost each day. Cufflinks and ladies' hats were once common but are rarer now as fashions have changed. Other lost objects reflect the passing of the seasons, with sunglasses proliferating in the summer and skis in the winter. Inevitably the more mundane items include thousands of umbrellas, keys, bicycles, wallets, and handbags. Objects valued at less than 50 Euros are retained for three months and then disposed of, whereas more valuable items are held for a year and a day, and then auctioned.

Far more interesting are the objects that have passed through what the service calls its Cabinet of Curiosities. These have included several human skulls (probably left by medical students), a boxed collection of blue butterflies, a prosthetic leg, a pair of wedding dresses with

This way to the world's oldest lost property office

shoes to match, and even two chunks of masonry from the World Trade Centre! Historic items include a Napoleonic sabre, an antique English telescope, and a First World War helmet. A 110kg coil of copper wire was probably stolen from a building site and then dumped after it was deemed too heavy to carry. Perhaps not surprisingly many of these more curious items, including a funerary urn filled with ashes, have never been collected.

A few years ago the service received a bag containing a handful of cut diamonds together with a doctor's business card. The doctor was contacted and he identified a woman in New York as the rightful owner. The next day she flew to Paris to retrieve them. A 1kg gold bar handed in by an honest taxi driver, however, remains unclaimed to this day.

In 1804 Napoleon revived the fortunes of the Mont-de-Piété, the city pawnshop at 55 Rue des Francs-Bourgeois (4th). As Crédit Municipal de Paris it continues to grant loans to those in need with no limit on repayment, and like the Service des Objets Trouves its warehouse contains thousands of items.

98 The Story of a Forgotten Railway

15th Arrondissement, a walk along the *Petite Ceinture* from
Rue Balard to Rue Olivier de Serres
Métro 8 Balard; T3 Balard

The music club Flèche d'Or at 102bis Rue de Bagnolet (20th) is one of the liveliest in Paris. When a band is on stage it's easy to forget the club is housed inside a former railway station suspended above an abandoned railway line. Its name recalls the express train *La Flèche d'Or*, which between 1926 and 1972 ran from Paris's Gare du Nord to Calais, and onwards to London. For a while it was the fastest passenger train in the world.

The railway line beneath the music club was rather less glamorous. Commenced in 1852 it was devised initially as a means of deploying troops and ammunition around the Thiers Wall, which had encircled Paris since the 1840s (see no. 21). Another function of the line was to convey passengers and freight between the city's main Right Bank stations (including the Gare du Nord), which at the time were administered by different independent companies. Called the *Petite Ceinture* (meaning 'Little Belt') the railway was one of the world's first mass transit systems.

Whilst the government financed the rails, bridges, and tunnels, the rail companies paid for the stations and rolling stock. The first section of line to be built connected freight yards near the Gare Saint-Lazare with others at Villette and Ivry to the south, including a long tunnel in Charonne not far from the Flèche d'Or. Once the Right Bank stations were connected the track was continued westwards, which served the added function of connecting Paris with the town of Auteuil, enabling well-to-do Parisians to travel quickly to their country homes. Eventually, in 1867 the less profitable Left Bank rail terminals were also connected thereby completing the circular line all the way around the city.

An extension of the *Petite Ceinture* built to service the *Exposition Universelle de Paris de 1900* brought the line into direct competition with the newly-constructed Métro, which was inaugurated to coincide with the same event. As the Métro grew more popular – 16 lines now snake to virtually every corner of the city – so traffic on the *Petite Ceinture* diminished. The Thiers Wall was demolished in 1919, and the *Petite Ceinture* was itself abandoned in 1934. Ironically, to avoid competition with the railways the Métro has never linked Paris's mainline stations in the effective way that the *Petite Ceinture* once did.

Plans to reuse the old railway for the T3 tramway opened in 2006 came to nothing – it used the Boulevards des Maréchaux instead – and parts of the old track bed have since been obliterated. Despite this several associations are working hard to preserve what remains. To understand their motives take a stroll along a stretch of former line between Rues Balard and Olivier de Serres (15th), converted recently into a public footpath, and enjoy a unique piece of French railway history.

Only ghost trains run along the *Petite Ceinture*

For the miniature railway enthusiast there is much to enjoy in Paris. The narrow gauge *Petit Train*, which runs between Porte Maillot and the Jardin d'Acclimation in the Bois de Boulogne (16th), opened in 1878, and is the city's oldest regular rail service. Less well known is the 50cm gauge railway inside the Musée des Arts et Métiers at 60 Rue de Réaumur (3rd), once used to move heavy exhibits (the track is still visible on the ground and first floors). There is also a fine model railway run by the Association Française des Amis des Chemins de Fer beneath the Gare de l'Est at Place du 11-Novembre-1918 (10th).

*   *   *

Strolling along the *Petite Ceinture* on the southern edge of the city is as good a place as any to finish this French odyssey during which some of the unique, hidden, and unusual aspects of Paris have been revealed. Looking back across the city from this forgotten corner, once so important to the burgeoning metropolis, enables the satisfied explorer to appreciate the ebb and flow of history in this, one of the great capital cities of Europe.

Opening Times

Correct at time of going to press but may be subject to change.
Most shops in Paris except bakeries are closed Sunday; many museums and public attractions are closed on Monday or Tuesday; some shops, restaurants and other attractions close in the middle of the day, and in July and August.
Some places of interest not normally open to the public can be visited in September as part of the Journées du Patrimoine and Fête des Jardins.

59 Rivoli (1st), 59 Rue de Rivoli, Tue–Sun 1–8pm

À la Civette (1st), 157 Rue Saint-Honoré, Mon–Sat 10am–7pm

À la Mère de Famille (9th), 33–35 Rue du Faubourg-Montmartre, Mon–Sat 9.30am–8pm, Sun 10am–1pm

Académie de Billard (9th), 84 Rue de Clichy, daily 3pm–6am

Anciennes Carrières des Capucins (14th), Hôpital Cochin, 27 Rue du Faubourg-Saint-Jacques, visits by appointment only www.seadacc.com

Ancien Collège des Bernardins (5th), 18–24 Rue de Poissy, Mon–Sat 10am–6pm, Sun 2–6pm

Androuët (7th), 37 Rue de Verneuil, Mon 4–7.30pm, Tue–Sat 9.30am–1pm, 4–7.30pm

Appartement-Atelier Le Corbusier (16th), Immeuble Molitor, 24 Rue Nungesser et Coli, Sat 10am–1pm, 1.30–5pm

Arènes de Lutèce (5th), 49 Rue Monge, daily winter 8am–5.30pm, summer 9am–9.30pm

Arlaux (5th), 29 Rue Censier, Tue-Sat 10am–1pm, 2–7.30pm

Association Française des Amis des Chemins de Fer (10th), Gare de l'Est, Place du 11-Novembre-1918, visits by appointment only tel. +33 (0)1 40 38 20 92

Atelier Houdart (13th), 77 Rue Broca, Mon & Sat 10am–5pm, Tue–Fri 9.30am–5.30pm

Atelier Renault (8th), 53 Avenue des Champs-Elysées, Sun–Thu 10.30am–11.30pm, Fri & Sat 10.30am–1.30pm

Au Caïd (5th), 12 Rue de la Sorbonne, Tue–Sat 10am–1pm, 2–7pm

Au Lapin Agile (18th), 22 Rue des Saules, Tue–Sun 9pm–1am; reservations recommended tel. +33 (0)1 46 06 85 87

Au Petit Fer à Cheval (4th), 30 Rue Vieille-du-Temple, daily 9am–2am

Au Pied de Cochon (1st), 6 Rue Coquillière, daily 24 hours

Au Printemps (9th), 64 Boulevard Haussmann, Mon–Sat 9.35am–8pm (Thu 8.45pm)

Auberge Nicolas Flamel (3rd), 51 Rue de Montmorency, Mon–Sat 12am–2.30pm, 7–10.30pm

Aux Tonneau des Halles (1st), 28 Rue Montorgueil, Tue–Sat 12am–3pm, 7.30–10.30pm

Bibliothèque Forney (4th), Hôtel de Sens, 1 Rue du Figuier, Tue–Sat 1.30–7pm

Bibliothèque Nationale de France (2nd), 5 Rue Vivienne &, Quai François-Mauriac (15th), Tue–Sat 10am–8pm, Sun 1–7pm

Bibliothèque Nubar (16th), 11 Square Alboni, Mon & Tue, Thu & Fri 10–12am, 2–6pm (closed Aug)

Bibliothèque Polonaise (4th), 6 Quai d'Orléans, Tue–Fri 2.15–6pm

Bibliothèque Sainte Geneviève (5th), 10 Place du Panthéon, Mon–Sat 9–10am (identification for a reader's card required); closed during student holidays

Café à la Ville de Petrograd (8th), 13 Rue Daru, daily 12am–4pm, 7–12pm

Café de Flore (6th), 172 Boulevard Saint-Germain, daily 7am–1.30am; debates first Wed each month 7–9pm

Café des Deux Moulins (18th), 15 Rue Lepic, daily 7.30am–1am

Café des Phares (4th), 7 Place de la Bastille, Mon–Thu & Sun 7am–3am, Fri & Sat 7am–4am; debates Sun 10.30–12.15am

Café Procope (6th), 13 Rue de l'Ancienne Comédie, Sun–Wed 11.30am–12pm, Thu–Sat 11.30am–1am

Cassegrain (8th), 422 Rue Saint-Honoré, Mon–Fri 10am–6.30pm, Sat 11am–5.30pm

Catacombes de Paris (14th), 1 Avenue du Colonel Henri Rol-Tanguy, Tue–Sun 10am–8pm (last admission 7pm)

Cathédrale Saint-Alexandre-Newsky (8th), 12 Rue Daru, Tue, Fri & Sun 3–5pm

Cathédrale Saint-Jean-Baptiste (8th), 15 Rue Jean Goujon, Mass Sun 10.30am

Caveau de la Huchette (5th), 5 Rue de la Huchette, Thu–Thu 9.30pm–2.30am, Fri & Sat 9.30pm–4am

Caveau des Oubliettes (5th), 52 Rue Galande, daily 5pm–4am

Centre Bouddique du Bois de Vincennes (12th), 40 Route de Ceinture du Lac Daumesnil, visits by appointment only +33 (0)6 19 14 25 52, info@bouddhisme-france.org

Centre Georges Pompidou (4th), Place Georges Pompidou, Wed–Mon 11am–10pm

Chapelle de la Médaille-Miraculeuse (7th), 140 Rue du Bac, Tue 7.45am–7pm, Wed–Mon 7.45am–1pm, 2.30–7pm

Chapelle de la Sorbonne (5th), Place de la Sorbonne, guided tours only one Saturday each month, visites. sorbonne@ac-paris.fr

Chapelle Expiatoire (8th), Square Louis-XVI, Thu–Sat 1–5pm

Chapelle des Prêtres de la Mission Lazariste (6th), 95 Rue des Sèvres, Mon–Sat 7–11.30am, 1.30–6.30pm, Sun 8–12am, 1.30–3.15pm

Chapelle Saint-Aignan (4th), 5 Rue de la Colombe, only open during Journées du Patrimoine on the third weekend in Sep

Charvet (1st), 28 Place Vendôme, Mon–Sat 10am–7pm

Château de la Reine Blanche (13th), 18bis Rue Berbier-du-Mets, only open during Journées du Patrimoine on the third weekend in Sep

Château de Vincennes (Vincennes), Avenue de Paris, May–Sep daily 10am–6pm, Oct–Apr daily 10am–5pm

Cimetière de Charonne (20th), 111 Rue de Bagnolet, mid Mar–Oct Mon–Fri 8am–6pm, Sat 8.30am–6pm, Sun 9am–6pm, Nov–mid Mar Mon–Fri 8am–5.30pm, Sat 8.30am–5.30pm, Sun 9am–5.30pm

Cimetière de Gentilly (13th), 7 Rue de Sainte-Hélène, Feb–Oct daily 8am–5.45pm, Nov–Jan daily 8am–4.45pm

Cimetière des Juifs Portugais (19th), 44 Avenue de Flandre, visits by appointment only tel. +33 (0)1 40 82 26 90

Cimetière de Montmartre (18th), 20 Avenue Rachel, mid Mar–Oct Mon–Fri 8am–6pm, Sat 8.30am–6pm, Sun 9am–6pm, Nov–mid Mar Mon–Fri 8am–5.30pm, Sat 8.30am–5.30pm, Sun 9am–5.30pm

Cimetière du Montparnasse (14th), 3 Boulevard Edgar-Quinet, mid Mar–Oct Mon–Fri 8am–6pm, Sat 8.30am–6pm, Sun 9am–6pm, Nov–mid Mar Mon–Fri 8am–5.30pm, Sat 8.30am–5.30pm, Sun 9am–5.30pm

Cimetière de Passy (16th), 2 Rue du Commandant-Schloesing, mid Mar–Oct Mon–Fri 8am–6pm, Sat 8.30am–6pm, Sun 9am–6pm, Nov–mid Mar Mon–Fri 8am–5.30pm, Sat 8.30am–5.30pm, Sun 9am–5.30pm

Cimetière du Père-Lachaise (20th), Boulevard de Ménilmontant, mid Mar–Oct Mon–Fri 8am–6pm, Sat 8.30am–6pm, Sun 9am–6pm, Nov–mid Mar Mon–Fri 8am–5.30pm, Sat 8.30am–5.30pm, Sun 9am–5.30pm

Cimetière de Picpus (12th), 35 Rue de Picpus, Summer Tue–Sun 2–6pm, Winter Tue–Sat 2–4pm

Cire Trudon (6th), 78 Rue du Seine, Mon–Sat 10am–7pm

Cité de l'Architecture et du Patrimoine (16th), Palais de Chaillot, 1 Place du Trocadéro, Wed–Mon 11am–7pm (Thu 9pm)

Cité des Sciences et de l'Industrie (19th), 30 Avenue Corentin-Cariou, Tue–Sun 10am–6pm (Sun 7pm)

Cité Nationale de l'Histoire de l'Immigration (12th), 293 Avenue Daumesnil, Tue–Fri 10am–5.30pm, Sat & Sun 10am–7pm

Cité Internationale Universitaire de Paris (14th), 19 Boulevard Jourdan, daily 7am–10pm

Cloître des Billettes (4th), 24 Rue des Archives, daily 2–7pm, Mass Sun 10am

Cloître du Val-de-Grâce (5th), 1 Place Alphonse-Laveran, Tue, Wed, Sat & Sun 12–5pm

Clos des Blancs-Manteaux (4th), 21 Rue des Blancs-Manteaux, Sat & Sun only 9am–5pm

Clos Montmartre (18th), 14–18 Rue des Saules, first Sat in Oct

Cognacq-Jay Museum (3rd), 8 Rue Elzévir, Tue–Sun 10am–6pm

Collection de Minéraux de l'Université Pierre et Marie Curie (5th), 4 Place Jussieu, Campus Universitaire de Jussieu, Wed–Mon 1–6pm

Cour de l'Industrie (11th), 37bis Rue de Montreuil, Mon–Fri 9am–5pm; individual studios have no fixed operating hours

Couvent des Récollets (10th), 150 Rue du Faubourg-Saint-Martin, Mon–Fri 9.30am–12.30am, 2–7pm (Fri 6pm)

Debauve & Gallais (7th), 30 Rue des Saint-Pères, Mon–Sat 9am–7pm

Detaille 1905 (9th), 10 Rue Saint-Lazaire, visits by appointment only, www.detaille.com

Detrad (9th), 18 Rue Cadet, Mon–Fri 11–12am, 1–8pm, Sat 11–12am, 1–7pm

Deyrolle (7th), 46 Rue du Bac, Mon 10am–1pm, 2–7pm, Tue–Sat 10am–7pm

Duluc Détective (1st), 18 Rue du Louvre, the agency is open for official business only Mon–Sat 9–12am, 2–7pm

École des Beaux-Arts (6th), 14 Rue Bonaparte, guided tours by appointment only Mon–Fri from 10am, contact@cultival.fr

Église de la Madeleine (8th), Place de la Madeleine, daily 9.30am–7pm

Église de Tous-les-Saints-de-la-Terre-Russe (16th), 19 Rue Claude-Lorrain, mass daily 6pm and Sun 11am

Église des Trois-Saints-Docteurs (15th), 5 Rue Petel, Mass Mon–Sat 8am, Sun 10am

Église du Val-de-Grâce (5th), at 1 Place Alphonse-Laveran, Tue & Wed, Sat & Sun 12am–5pm

Église Notre-Dame-de-Chaldée (18th), 13–15 Rue Pajol, Mass Sun 11am

Église Notre-Dame-de-Compassion (17th), 2 Boulevard Aurelle-de-Paladines, daily 9am–6pm, Sun Mass 11am

Église Notre Dame des Victoires (2nd), Place des Petits-Pères, daily 7.30am–7.30pm

Église Notre-Dame-du-Travail (14th), 59 Rue Vercingétorix, Mon–Fri 7.30am–7.45pm, Sat 9am–7.30pm, Sun 8.30am–7.30pm

Église Russe-Catholique-de-la-Très-Sainte-Trinité (16th), 39 Rue François-Gérard, Mass Sun 9.15am

Église Saint-Christophe-de-Javel (15th), 28 Rue de la Convention, Mon 5–7.30pm, Tue–Sun 6am–7.30pm

Église Saint-Esprit (12th), 186 Avenue Daumesnil, daily 9.30am–7pm

Église Saint-Étienne-du-Mont (5th), 1 Place Sainte-Geneviève, Tue–Fri 8.45am–7.45pm, Sat 8.45am–12am, 2–7.45pm, Sun 8.45am–12.15am, 2–7.45pm

Église Saint-Eugène-Sainte-Cécile (9th), 6 Rue Sainte-Cécile, Mon 6.30–8pm, Tue 10am–1.15pm, 6.30–8pm, Wed 9.45am–8pm, Thu & Fri 10am–8pm, Sat 9.30am–1pm; Pauline Mass Sun 9.45am, Tridentine Mass Sun 11am

Église Saint-Eustache (1st), 2 Impasse Saint-Eustache, Mon–Fri 9.30am–7pm, Sat 10am–7pm, Sun 9am–7pm

Église Saint-François-Xavier (7th), 12 Rue du Président-Mithouard, Mon–Thu 7.45am–7.45pm, Fri 7.45am–8pm, Sat 8.15–12.30am, 2–8pm, Sun 8.30am–1pm, 3–8.30pm; presbytery garden, 39 Boulevard des Invalides, Thu evenings in summer and during the Fête des Jardins in September

Église Saint-Germain-des-Prés (6th), 3 Place Saint-Germain-des-Prés, Mon–Sat 8am–7.45pm, Sun 9am–8pm

Église Saint-Germain-l'Auxerrois (1st), 2 Place du Louvre, Mon–Sat 8am–7pm, Sun 9am–8pm

Église Saint-Gervais-Saint-Protais (4th), Place Saint-Gervais, Mass Tue–Sat 6.30pm, Sun 11am

Église Sainte-Jeanne-de-Chantal (16th), Place de la Porte de Saint-Cloud, Tue–Fri 8am–8pm, Sat 9am–8.30pm, Sun 8.30am–8.30pm

Église Saint-Jean-de-Montmartre (18th), 19 Rue des Abbesses, Mass Sat 6.30pm, Sun 10.30am

Église Saint-Joseph-des-Carmes (6th), 70 Rue de Vaugirard, church & crypt Sat 3pm

Église Saint-Julien-le-Pauvre (5th), 79 Rue Galande, daily 9.30am–1pm, 3.30–6pm

Église Saint-Leu-Saint-Gilles (2nd), 92 Rue Saint-Denis, Mon–Sat 12am–7.30pm, Sun 9–12am

Église Sainte-Marguerite (11th), 36 Rue Saint-Bernard, Mon–Sat 8–12am, 2–7pm, Sun 9–12am

Église Saint-Médard (5th), 141 Rue Mouffetard, Tue–Sat 8–12.30am, 2.30–7.30pm, Sun 8.30–12.30am, 4–8.30pm

Église Sainte-Odile (17th), 2 Avenue Stéphane-Mallarmé, Mass Sat 6pm, Sun 9am, 11.15am & 7pm

Église Saint-Paul-Saint-Louis (4th), 99 Rue Saint-Antoine, daily 8am–8pm

Église Saint-Pierre-de-Montmartre (18th), 2 Rue du Mont-Cenis, daily 8.45am–7pm; Cimetière du Calvaire, All Saints Day (1st Nov), Journées du Patrimoine & Fête des Jardins

Église Saint-Séraphin-de-Sarov (15th), 91 Rue Lecourbe, Sat vigil 6pm, Sun mass 10am (admission at times of service by pressing main button on the door keypad)

Église Saint-Séverin (5th), Rue des Prêtres-Saint-Séverin, Mon–Sat 11am–7.30pm, Sun 9am–8.30pm

Église Saint-Serge (19th), 93 Rue de Crimée, Mass Sun 10am

Église Saint-Sulpice (6th), Place Saint-Sulpice, daily 7.30am–7.30pm

Église Saint-Thomas-d'Aquin (7th), 3 Place Saint-Thomas-d'Aquin, Mon–Sat 8.30am–7pm, Sun 9am–12am, 4–7pm

Église Saint-Vincent-de-Paul (10th), Place Franz Liszt, Mon 2–7pm, Tue–Sat 8–12am, 2–7pm (Sat 7.30pm), Sun 9.30–12am, 4.30–7.30pm

Elysées Stylos Marbeuf (8th), 40 Rue Marbeuf, Mon–Sat 9.30am–7pm

Eric Kayser (15th), 14 Rue Monge, daily 8am–8pm

Fauchon (8th), 24–26 Place de la Madeleine, Mon–Sat 10am–8.30pm

Finkelsztajn (4th), 27 Rue des Rosiers, Wed–Mon 10am–7pm (closed mid-Jul to mid-Aug)

Fondation Louis Vuitton (16th), 8 Avenue du Mahatma Gandhi, Mon, Wed & Thu noon–7pm, Fri 12am–11pm, Sat & Sun 11am–8pm

Forum des Images (1st), Les Halles, 2 Rue du Cinéma, Tue–Fri 1–9pm, Sat & Sun 2–9pm

François Tamarin (18th), 1 Rue Marcel Sembat, visits by appointment only tel. +33 (0) 1 77 12 66 89

Fromagerie Quatrehomme (7th), 62 Rue de Sèvres, Tue–Sat 9am–7.45pm

Galerie C. T. Loo (8th), 48 Rue de Courcelles, for art sales and events www.pagodaparis.com

Galerie Colbert (2nd), 6 Rue des Petits-Champs, Mon–Sat 8am–8pm

Galerie Véro-Dodat (1st), 19 Rue Jean-Jacques-Rousseau, Mon–Sat 7am–10pm

Galerie Vivienne (2nd), 4 Rue des Petits-Champs, daily 8.30am–8.30pm

Galeries Lafayette (9th), 40 Boulevard Haussmann, Mon–Sat 9.30am–8pm

Gibert Jeune (6th), 4 Place Saint-Michel, Mon–Sat 9.30am–7.30pm

Glacier Berthillon (4th), 29–31 Rue Saint-Louis-en-l'Ile, Wed–Sun 10am–8pm

Gosselin (1st), 123 Rue Saint-Honoré, Mon–Fri 7am–8pm

Goyard (1st), 233 Rue Saint-Honoré, visits by appointment only tel. +33 (0)1 42 60 57 04

Grande Herboristerie Parisienne de la Place Clichy (9th), 87 Rue d'Amsterdam, Mon 11am–1pm, 2–7pm, Tue–Fri 10am-1pm, 2–7pm, Sat 10am–1pm, 2–6pm

Hédiard (8th), 21 Place de la Madeleine, Mon–Sat 9am–8.30pm

Heratchian Frères (9th), 6 Rue Lamartine, Mon 2–7.15pm, Tue–Sat 8.30am–7.15pm

Hermès (6th), 17 Rue de Sèvres, Mon–Sat 10.30am–7pm

Heurtault (12th), 85 Avenue Daumesnil, Tue–Sat 2–7pm

Huîtrerie Régis (6th), 3 Rue de Montfaucon, Tue–Sun 12am–2.30pm, 6.30–10.30pm (closed mid Jul–Aug)

Institut du Monde Arabe (5th), 1 Rue des Fossés-Saint-Bernard, museum Tue–Thu 10am–6pm, Fri 10am–9.30pm, Sat & Sun 10am–7pm, library Tue–Sat 1–8pm

Ishkan (9th), 40 Rue de Trévise, Mon–Sat 10am–5pm

Jardin Atlantique (14th), Gare Montparnasse, Rue des Cinq-Martyrs-du-Lycée-Buffon, daily 8am–8pm

Jardin d'Acclimation (16th), Bois de Boulogne, Apr–Sep daily 10am–7pm, Oct–Mar Mon–Thu 10am–6pm, Fri 10am–10pm, Sat & Sun 10am–7pm

Jardin de la Mission Etrangère de Paris (7th), 28 Rue de Babylone, only open during Journées du Patrimoine on the third weekend in Sep

Jardin de la Vallée Suisse (8th), Avenue Franklin D. Roosevelt/Cours de la Reine, daily 24 hours

Jardin des Plantes (5th), 36 Rue Geoffroy-Sainte-Hilaire, Summer daily 7.30am–8pm; Winter daily 8am–5.30pm; Jardin Alpin Apr–Oct Mon–Fri 8am–4pm, Sat & Sun 1.30–6pm

Jardin du Luxembourg (6th), Boulevard Saint-Michel, daily 7.30am–8.15pm

Jardin Catherine-Labouré (7th), 29 Rue de Babylone, Mon–Fri 8am–9.30pm, Sun 9am–9.30pm

Jardin Naturel (20th), 120 Rue de la Réunion, Mon–Fri 7.30am–dusk, Sat & Sun 9am–dusk

Jardin Saint-Gilles-Grand-Veneur (3rd), Rue des Arquebusiers, Mon–Fri 7.30am–9.30pm, Sat & Sun 9am–9.30pm (Winter 5.30pm)

Jardin Sauvage Saint-Vincent (18th), 17 Rue Saint-Vincent, restricted opening times Apr–Oct, visits

Jim Haynes (14th), 83 Rue de la Tombe Issoire, Atelier A-2, Sun 8–11pm, reservations for Sunday dinner parties in advance only, www.jim-haynes.com

Julien Aurouze (1st), 8 Rue des Halles, Mon–Sat 9–12.30am, 2–6.30pm

Korcarz (4th), 29 Rue des Rosiers, Mon–Thu 8am–8pm, Fri 8am–6pm

L'Adresse – Musée de la Poste (15th), 34 Boulevard de Vaugirard, Mon–Fri 10am–6pm

La Belle Hortense (4th), 31 Rue Vieille-du-Temple, daily 5pm–2am

La Closerie des Lilas (6th), 171 Boulevard du Montparnasse, bar 11am–1.30am; restaurant 12am–2.45pm, 7–11.30pm; brasserie 12am–1am

La Coupole (14th), 102 Boulevard de Montparnasse, daily 8.30am–12pm

La Fermette Marbeuf 1900 (8th), 5 Rue Marbeuf, daily 12am–11.30pm

La Grande Épicerie (7th), 38 Rue de Sèvres, Mon–Sat 8.30am–9pm

La Maison de Baccarat (16th), 11 Place des États-Unis, Mon–Sat 10am–9pm

La Maison du Miel (9th), 24 Rue Vignon, Mon–Sat 9.30am–7pm

La Maison des Millesimes (6th), 137 Boulevard St Germain, Mon–Sat 10am–8pm

La Palette (6th), 43 Rue de Seine, Mon–Sat 9am–2am

La Ravigote (11th), 41 Rue Montreuil, Mon, Tue & Sat 12am–2.30pm, 7–10.30pm, Wed–Fri 12am–10.30pm

La Ruche (15th), 2 Passage de Dantzig (15th), tours available by appointment only www.la-ruche.net

La Sablaisse Poissonerie (7th), 28 Rue Cler, Mon–Sat 8am–8pm

La Tortue Electrique (5th), 7 Rue Frédéric Sauton, visits by appointment only www.tortueelectrique.org

La Tour d'Argent (5th), 15–17 Quai de la Tournelle, Tue–Sat 12am–2pm, 7–10.30pm

Ladurée (8th), 16 Rue Royale, Mon–Thu 8.30am-7.30pm, Fri & Sat 8.30am–8pm, Sun 10am–7pm

Laverdure (12th), 58 Rue Traversiére, Mon–Fri 8.30–12am, 1.30–6pm (Fri 5.30pm), Sat 8.30–12pm

L'Entredgeu (17th), 83 Rue Laugier, Tue–Sat 12am–2pm, 7.30–10.30pm

Le Bistrot d'Henri (6th), 16 Rue Princesse, daily 12am–3pm, 7–11pm (Sun 11.30pm)

Le Grand Colbert (2nd), 2 Rue Vivienne, Wed–Sat 12am–1am, Sun–Tue 12am–12pm

Le Grand Rex (2nd), 1 Boulevard Poissonière, backstage tours by appointment only www.legranderex.com

Le Relais de l'Entrecote (6th), 20 Rue Saint-Benoit, daily 12am–2.30pm, 7–11pm

Le Select (6th), 99 Boulevard du Montparnasse, Mon–Thu & Sun 7am–2am, Fri & Sat 7am–3am

Le Train Bleu (12th), Gare de Lyon, first floor, daily 11.30am–2.45pm, 7–10.45pm

Le Verre à Pied (5th), 118bis Rue Mouffetard, Tue–Sat 9am–9pm, Sun 9.30am–4pm

Les Abeilles (13th), 21 Rue de la

Butte-aux-Cailles, Tue–Sat 11am–7pm

Les Deux Magots (6th), 6 Place Saint-Germain-des-Prés, daily 7.30am–1am

Les Invalides (inc. Le Dôme & Musée de l'Armée) (7th), Place des Invalides, Nov–Mar daily 10am–5pm, Apr–Oct daily 10am–6pm (closed except for Le Dôme first Mon each month) (Le Dôme Jul & Aug 7pm)

Librairie Auguste Blaizot (8th), 164 Rue du Faubourg Saint-Honoré, Tue–Sat 9.30–12.30am, 2–6.30pm

Librairie du Temple (4th), 52 Rue des Rosiers, Sun–Thu 9.30am–7.30pm, Fri 9.30am–4pm

Librairie Jules Verne (5th), 7 Rue Lagrange, occasional opening times only

Librairie Galignani (1st), 224 Rue de Rivoli, Mon–Sat 10am–7pm

Librairie Samuelian (6th), 51 Rue Monsieur-le-Prince, Tue–Fri 11–12.45am, 2–6.30pm, Sat 2–6.30pm

Librairie Ulysse (4th), 26 Rue Saint-Louis-en-l'Île, Tue–Fri 2–8pm; Cargoclub Feb–Dec first Wed in month 6.30pm

Lumière de l'Oeil (5th), 4 Rue Flatters, Tue–Fri 2–7pm, Sat 11am–5pm; Musée des Éclairages Anciens visits by appointment only tel. +33 (0)1 47 07 63 47

Maison d'Auguste Comte (6th), 10 Rue Monsieur-Le-Prince, Wed 2–5pm, Sat 2 & 3.30pm

Maison d'Ourscamp (4th), 44–46 Rue François-Miron, Mon–Sat 11am–6pm, Sun 2–7pm

Maison de Balzac (16th), 47 Rue Raynouard, Tue–Sun 10am–6pm

Maison de Victor Hugo (4th), 6 Place des Vosges, Tue–Sun 10am–6pm

Maison du Fontanier (14th), 42 Avenue de l'Observatoire, only open during the Journées du Patrimoine on the third weekend in Sep

Maison La Roche (16th), 10 Square du Docteur-Blanche, Mon 1.30–6pm, Tue–Sat 10am–6pm

Maison Pou (17th), 16 Avenue des Ternes, Mon–Fri 9.30am–7pm, Sat 9am–7pm

Manufacture des Gobelins (13th), 42 Avenue des Gobelins, guided tours by appointment only Tue–Thu, individuals 1pm, groups 1.15, 2.45 & 3pm www. mobiliernational.culture.gouv.fr

Marché aux Fleurs et aux Oiseaux (4th), Place Louis-Lépine, flower market Mon–Sat 8am–7pm, bird market Sun only 9am–7pm

Marché aux Livres (15th), Rue Brancion, Sat & Sun 9am–6pm

Marché aux Puces de la Porte de Vanves (14th), Avenue Georges Lafenestre, Sat & Sun 7am–7.30pm

Marché aux Puces St-Ouen de Clignancourt (18th), Avenue de la Porte Clignancourt, Mon, Sat & Sun 7am–7.30pm; Chez Louisette Mon, Sat & Sun 8am–6pm

Marché aux Timbres (8th), Cour Marigny, Thu, Sat & Sun 9am–7pm

Marché Bastille (11th), Boulevard Richard Lenoir, Thu 7am–2.30pm, Sun 7am–3pm

Marché Beauvau (12th), Rue d'Aligre, Tue–Fri 7.30am–1.30pm, Sat & Sun 7.30am–2.30pm

Marché de la Création (14th), Boulevard Edgar-Quinet, Sun 9am–7.30pm

Marché des Enfants-Rouges (3rd), 9 Rue de Beauce (3rd), Tue–Sat 8.30am–7.30pm, Sun 8.30am–2pm; Potager des Oiseaux Sat 11am–1pm

Marché Raspail (6th), 4 Boulevard Raspail, Tue & Fri 7am–2.30pm

Marché Rue Dejean (18th), Rue Dejean, Tue–Sun 9–12.30am

Marché Rue Mouffetard (5th), Rue Mouffetard, Tue–Sat 10am–1pm, 4–7pm, Sun 10am–1pm

Marché Saint-Pierre (18th), Place St-Pierre, Mon 2–7pm, Tue–Sat 9am–7pm

Marché Saint-Quentin (10th), 85bis Boulevard de Magenta, Tue–Sat 8am–8pm, Sun 8.30am–1.30pm

Mariage Frères Musée du Thé (4th), 30 Rue du Bourg-Tibourg, daily 10.30am–7.30pm

Martyrium Saint-Denis (18th), 9 Rue Yvonne-le-Tac, Fri 3–6pm (also first Sat & Sun each month or tel. +33 (0)1 42 23 48 94

Massis & Chirag (9th), 40 Rue de Trévise, Mon–Fri 8–12am, 2–6pm

Mémorial du Maréchal Leclerc de Hauteclocque et de la Libération de Paris – Musée Jean Moulin (15th), Jardin Atlantique, 23 Allée de la 2ème Division Blindée, Tue–Sun 10am–6pm

Mémorial de la Shoah (4th), 17 Rue Geoffroy-l'Asnier, Sun–Fri 10am–6pm (Thu 10pm)

M. G. W. Segas (9th), 34 Passage Jouffroy, visits by appointment tel. +33 (0)6 85 55 69 82

Moulin de la Galette (18th), 88 Rue Lepic, daily 12am–11pm

Moulin de la Vierge (14th), 105 Rue Vercingétorix, Tue–Sat 7.30am–8pm

Murciano (4th), 14–15 Rue des Rosiers, daily 8am–8pm

Musée Art Nouveau (8th), 3 Rue Royale, guided tours onlx 2pm (English) & 3pm (French) by appointment www. maxims-de-paris.com

Musée Bourdelle (15th), 16 Rue Antoine-Bourdelle, Tue–Sun 10am–6pm

Musée Carnavalet (3rd), 23 Rue de Sévigné, Tue–Sun 10am–6pm

Musée Cernuschi (8th), 7 Avenue Vélasquez, Tue–Sun 10am–6pm

Musée Clemenceau (16th), 8 Rue Benjamin-Franklin, Tue–Sat 2–5.30pm

Musée Cognacq-Jay (8th), Hôtel Donon, 8 Rue Elzévir, Tue–Sun 10am–6pm

Musée Curie (5th), 1 Rue Pierre-et-Marie-Curie, Wed–Sat 1–5pm

Musée d'Art Dentaire (16th), 22 Rue Emile Ménier, visits by appointment only tel. +33 (0)1 45 53 40 05

Musée d'Art et d'Histoire du Judaisme (3rd), 71 Rue du Temple, Mon–Fri 11am–6pm, Sun 10am–6pm

Musée d'Art Moderne de la Ville de Paris (16th), 11 Avenue du Président Wilson, Tue–Sun 10am–6pm

Musée d'Ennery (16th), 59 Avenue Foch, visits by appointment only tel. +33 (0)1 56 52 53 45

Musée d'Orsay (7th), 1 Rue de la Légion d'Honneur, Tue–Sun 9.30am–6pm (Thu 9.45pm)

Musée de Cluny – Musée National du Moyen Âge (5th), 6 Place Paul Painlevé, Wed–Mon 9.15am–5.45pm

Musée de l'Anatomie Delmas-Orfila-Rouvières (6th), Université Paris Descartes, 45 Rue des Saints-Pères, visits by appointment only tel: +33 (0)1 42 86 20 47

Musée de l'Armée (7th), see Les Invalides

Musée de l'Assistance Publique (5th), 47 Quai de la Tournelle, closed until 2016

Musée de l'Erotisme (18th), 72 Boulevard de Clichy, daily 10am–2am

Musée de l'Éventail (10th), 2 Boulevard de Strasbourg, Mon, Tue & Wed 2–6pm (closed Aug)

Musée de l'Histoire de la Médecine (6th), Université Paris Descartes, 12 Rue de l'École-de-Médecine, summer Mon–Fri 2–5.30pm, winter Mon–Wed, Fri & Sat 2–5.30pm

Musée de l'Orangerie (1st), Jardin des Tuileries, Place de la Concorde, Wed–Mon 9am–6pm

Musée de la Chasse et de la Nature (3rd), 62 Rue des Archives, Tue–Sun 11am–6pm, Wed 9.30pm

Musée de la Cinémathèque Française (12th), 51 Rue de Bercy, Mon–Sat 12am–7pm, Sun 10am–8pm

Musée de la Contrefaçon (16th), 16 Rue de la Faisanderie, Tue–Sun 2–5.30pm

Musée de la Fédération Française de Tennis (16th), 2 Avenue Gordon Bennett, Wed & Thu, Fri–Sun 10am–6pm

Musée de la Franc-Maçonnerie (9th), Grand Orient de France, 16 Rue Cadet, Tue–Fri 10–12.30am, 2–6pm, Sat 10am–1pm, 2–7pm; temple tours Sat 2.30 & 4pm

Musée de la Magie (inc. Musée des Automates) (4th), 11 Rue Saint-Paul, Wed, Sat & Sun 2–7pm

Musée de la Marine (16th), Palais de Chaillot, 17 Place du Trocadéro, Mon–Fri 11am–6pm, Sat & Sun 11am–7pm

Musée de la Monnaie de Paris (6th), 11 Quai de Conti, daily 11am–7pm (Thu 10pm)

Musée de la Musique (19th), Cité de la Musique, 221 Avenue Jean-Jaurès, Tue–Sun 10am–6pm

Musée de la Poupée (3rd), 22 Rue Beaubourg, Impasse Berthaud, Tue–Sat 1–6pm

Musée de la Préfecture de Police (5th), 4 Rue de la Montagne-Sainte-Geneviève, Mon–Fri 9am–5.30pm, 3rd Sat each month 10.30am–5.30pm

Musée de la Vie Romantique (9th), 16 Rue Chaptal, Tue–Sun 10am–6pm

Musée de Matière Médicale (6th), 4 Avenue de l'Observatoire, only open during Journées du Patrimoine on the third weekend in Sep; botanical garden Mon–Fri 9am–7pm

Musée de Minéralogie (6th), 60 Boulevard Saint-Michel, École des Mines de Paris, Tue–Fri 1.30–6pm, Sat 10–12.30am, 2–5pm

Musée de Montmartre (18th), 12 Rue Cortot, daily 10am–6pm

Musée de Picasso (4th), Rue de Thorigny, Tue–Fri 11.30am–6pm, Sat & Sun 9.30am–6pm

Musée des Arts Décoratifs (1st), 107 Rue de Rivoli, Tue–Sun 11am–6pm (Thu 9pm)

Musée des Arts et Métiers (3rd), 60 Rue de Réaumur, Tue–Sun 10am–6pm (Thu 9.30pm)

Musée des Beaux-Arts de la Ville de Paris (8th), Petit Palais, Avenue Winston Churchill, Tue–Sun 10am–6pm

Musée des Compagnons Charpentiers (19th), 161 Avenue Jean-Jaurès, Restaurant Aux Arts et Sciences réunies, open by request from the staff

Musée des Égouts (7th), opposite 93 Quai d'Orsay, May–Sep Mon–Wed, Sat & Sun 11am–5pm, Oct–Apr Mon–Wed, Sat & Sun 11am–4pm

Musée des Moulages (10th), Hôpital Saint-Louis, 1 Avenue Claude-Vellefaux (10th), visits by appointment only Mon–Fri 9am–4.30pm tel. +33 (0)1 42 49 99 15

Musée des Traditions de la Garde Republicaine (4th), 18 Boulevard Henri IV (4th), daily 10am–5pm

Musée du Barreau de Paris (1st), 25 Rue du Jour, visits by appointment only tel. +33 (0)1 47 83 50 03

Musée du Compagnonnage des Paris (6th), 10 Rue Mabillion, Mon–Fri 2–6pm

Musée du Fumeur (11th), 7 Rue Pache, Mon–Sat 11.30am–8pm

Musée du Louvre (1st), Rue de Rivoli, Mon, Thu, Sat & Sun 9am–6pm, Wed & Fri 9am–9.45pm

Musée du Parfum-Fragonard (9th), 9 Rue Scribe, Mon–Sat 9am–6pm, Sun 9am–5pm

Musée du Quai Branly (7th), 37 Quai Branly, Tue, Wed & Sun 11am–7pm, Thu–Sat 11am–9pm

Musée du Service de Santé des Armées (5th), 1 Place Alphonse-Laveran, Tue–Thu, Sat & Sun 12am–6pm

Musée du Vin (16th), 5 Rue des Eaux, Tue–Sun 2–6pm

Musée Dupuytren (6th), 15 Rue de l'École-de-Médecine, Mon–Fri 2–5pm

Musée Édith Piaf (11th), 5 Rue Crespin-du-Gast, visits strictly by appointment only Mon–Wed 1–6pm tel. +33 (0) 43 55 52 72

Musée Édouard-Branly (6th), Institut Catholique de Paris, 21 Rue d'Assas, visits by appointment only tel: +33 (0)1 44 39 52 00

Musée et Mausolée Pasteur (15th), Institut Pasteur, 25 Rue du Docteur-Roux, guided tours only Mon–Fri 2pm, 3pm, 4pm (closed Aug)

Musée Grévin (9th), 10 Boulevard Montmartre, Mon–Fri 10am–6pm, Sat & Sun 9.30am–6pm

Musée Gustave Moreau (9th), 14 Rue de la Rochefoucauld, Mon, Wed & Thu 10am–12.45pm, 2–5.15pm, Fri, Sat & Sun 10am–5.15pm

Musée Jacquemart-André (8th), 158 Boulevard Haussmann, daily 10am–6pm

Musée Marmottan Monet (16th), 2 Rue Louis Boilly, Tue–Sun 10am–6pm (Thu 9pm)

Muséum National d'Histoire Naturelle (inc. Cabinet d'Histoire du Jardin des Plantes) (5th), 57 Rue Cuvier, Wed–Mon 10am–5pm; Cabinet de Curiosités, Bibliothèque Central du Muséum National d'Histoire Naturelle, 38 Rue Geoffroy-Sainte-Hilaire, Mon & Wed–Sat 9.30am–6pm, Tue 1–6pm; Galerie d'Entomologie, 45 Rue Buffon, Wed–Mon visits by appointment only, www.lasef.org; Galerie de Minéralogie et de Géologie, 36 Rue Geoffroy-Sainte-Hilaire, Wed–Mon 10am–5pm; Galerie d'Anatomie Comparée et de Paléontologie, 2 Rue Buffon, Wed–Mon 10am–5pm; Grande Galerie de l'Évolution, 36 Rue Geoffroy-Sainte-Hilaire, Wed–Mon 10am–6pm

Musée National des Arts Asiatiques Guimet (16th), 6 Place d'Iéna, Wed–Mon 10am–6pm; Panthéon Bouddhique, 19 Avenue d'Iéna, Wed–Mon 10am–5.45pm, garden 1–5pm (except when tea ceremonies are in progress); for tea ceremonies telephone +33 (0)1 56 52 53 45

Musée National Eugène Delacroix (6th), 6 Rue de Furstenberg, Wed–Mon 9.30am–5pm

Musée Nissim de Camondo (8th), 63 Rue de Monceau, Wed–Sun 10am–5.30pm

Musée Pierre Cardin (4th), 5 Rue Saint-Merri, Wed–Fri 11am–6pm, Sat & Sun 1–6pm

Musée Rodin (7th), Hôtel Biron, 79 Rue de Varenne, Tue–Sun 10am–5.45pm

Musée Valentin Haüy (7th), 5 Rue Duroc, Tue & Wed 2.30–5pm

Musée Zadkine (6th), 100bis Rue d'Assas, Tue–Sun 10am–6pm

Notre-Dame de Paris (4th), Place du Parvis-Notre-Dame, daily 8am–6.45pm (Sat & Sun 7.15pm); presentation of relics first Fri each month and each Fri in Lent 3pm, Good Friday 10am–5pm; Crypte Archéologique Tue–Sun 10am–6pm; treasury daily

9.30am–6pm; towers Apr–Sep 10am–6.30pm (Jul & Aug Fri & Sat 11pm), Oct–Mar 10am–5.30pm

Observatoire de Paris (14th), 61 Avenue de l'Observatoire, visits by appointment only Tue & Thu 2pm visite.paris@obspm.fr

Opéra Garnier (inc. Bibliothèque-Musée de l'Opéra National de Paris) (9th), Place de l'Opéra, daily 10am–5pm

Pain d'Épices (9th), 29–33 Passage Jouffroy, Mon 12.30am–7pm, Tue–Sat 10am–7pm

Panthéon (5th), Place du Panthéon, Apr–Sep daily 10am–6.30pm, Oct–Mar daily 10am–6pm

Parc des Buttes-Chaumont (19th), Rue Botzaris, Oct–Mar 7am–8pm, Apr 7am–9pm, May–Aug 7am–10pm, Sep 7am–9pm

Parc Georges Brassens (15th), Rue des Morillons, Winter Mon–Fri 8am–5.30pm, Summer 9am–9.30pm

Parc de Monceau (17th), Boulevard de Courcelles, Oct–Mar 7am–7.30pm, Apr 7am–8.30pm, May–Aug 7am–9.30pm, Sep 8am–8.30pm

Parc Montsouris (14th), Boulevard Jourdan, Oct–Mar 7am–7.30pm, Apr 7am–8.30pm, May–Aug 8am–9.30pm, Sep 8am–8.30pm

Passage Brady (10th), 43 Rue du Faubourg-Saint-Martin, Mon–Sat 8.30am–8.30pm

Passage de Choiseul (2nd), 40 Rue des Petits-Champs, Mon–Sat 8am–8pm

Passage des Panoramas (2nd), 10 Rue Saint-Marc, daily 6am–12pm

Passage du Caire (2nd), 2 Place du Caire, Mon–Fri 7.30am–6.30pm

Passage Jouffroy (9th), 10 Boulevard Montmartre, daily 7am–9.30pm

Passage Verdeau (9th), 6 Rue de la Grange Batelière, Mon–Fri 7.30am–9pm, Sat & Sun 7.30am–8.30pm

Patrick Roger (16th), 45 Avenue Victor Hugo, Mon–Sat 10.30am–7.30pm

Pavillons de Bercy (inc. Musée des Arts Forains) (12th), 53 Avenue des Terroirs-de-France, visits by appointment only www.bercy.com, www.arts-forains.com & during Journées du Patrimoine on the third weekend in Sep & during the Festival du Merveilleux in late Dec

Petrossian (8th), 18 Boulevard La Tour-Maubourg, Mon–Sat 9.30am–8pm

Pierre Champion (5th), 110 Rue Mouffetard, Mon–Fri 10am–1pm, 3–7pm, Sat 10am–1pm

Pierre Hermé (6th), 72 Rue Bonaparte, Mon–Wed 10am–7pm, Thu & Fri 10am–7.30pm, Sat 10am–8pm, Sun 10am–7pm

Poilâne (6th), 8 Rue du Cherche-Midi, Mon–Sat 7.15am–8.15pm

Produits des Monastères (4th), 10 Rue des Barres, Tue–Fri 9.30–12am, 2.30–6.30pm, Sat 10–12am, 2–6.30pm, Sun 12.15am–1pm (closed Aug)

Regard de la Lanterne (20th), 213 Rue de Belleville, visits by appointment only tel. +33 0(1) 43 49 36 91, or during Journées du Patrimoine on the third weekend in Sep

Restaurant Cochon à l'Oreille (1st), 15 Rue Montmartre, Mon–Sat 11am–12pm

Restaurant Les Diamantaires (9th), 60 Rue La Fayette, daily 12am–2.30pm, 7.30–11.30pm

Ryst Dupeyron (7th), 79 Rue du Bac, Mon 12.30am–7pm, Tue–Sat 10.30am–7pm

Sainte-Chapelle (1st), 4 Boulevard du Palais, Mar–Oct 9.30am–6pm, Nov–Feb 9am–5pm (mid May–mid Sep Wed 9pm)

Service des Objet Trouvés (15th), 36 Rue des Morillons, Mon–Thu 8.30am–5pm, Fri 8.30am–-.30pm

Shakespeare and Company (5th), 37 Rue de la Bûcherie, daily 10am–11pm, antiquarian sales Tue–Sat 11am–7pm

Sri Manicka Vinayakar Alayam Hindu Temple (18th), 17 Rue Pajol, daily 9.30am–8.30pm; poojas daily 10am, 12am, 7pm, bathing ceremony (Abhishekam) Fri, Sat & Sun

Stohrer (2nd), 51 Rue Montorgeuil, daily 7.30am–8.30pm

Synagogue de la Rue Pavée (4th), 10 Rue Pavée, visits by appointment only Sun–Fri 10.30am–5pm tel. +33 (0)1 42 77 81 51

Synagogue des Tournelles (4th), 21bis Rue des Tournelles, visits by appointment tel. +33 (0)1 42 74 32 80

Tang Frères (13th), 48 Avenue d'Ivry, Tue–Fri 9am–7.30pm, Sat & Sun 8.30am–7.30pm

Temple Antoiniste (13th), 34 Rue Vergniaud, L'Opération Générale Sun–Thu 10am, La Lecture Sun–Fri 7pm

Temple de l'Amicale des Teochews de France (13th), 44 Avenue d'Ivry, daily 9–12am, 2–6pm

Temple de l'Association des Résidents d'Origine Indochinoise (13th), 37 Rue du Disque, daily 9am–6pm

TOMAT's Epicerie Fine (6th), 12 Rue Jacob, Tue–Sat 11am–1.30pm, 2.30–7pm

Tour de Jean Sans Peur (2nd), 20 Rue Etienne Marcel, Nov–Mar Wed, Sat & Sun 1.30–6pm, Apr–Oct Wed & Sun 1.30–6pm

Tour Eiffel (7th), Champ-de-Mars, mid Jun–Aug 9am–12pm, Sep–mid Jun 9.30am–11pm; engine room tours by appointment only www.eiffel-tower.com; Restaurant Le Jules Verne daily 12am–1.30pm, 7–9.30pm

Toute en Peluche (14th), 39 Rue Raymond Losserand, Mon–Fri 10am–8pm, Sat 10am–7pm

UNESCO (7th), 7 Place de Fontenoy, visits by appointment only tel. +33 (0)1 45 68 10 00, visits@unesco.org

Union Bouliste du 15ème (15th), Square Blomet, 43 Rue Blomet, daily 9am–5pm (9pm in summer)

Bibliography

GUIDEBOOKS

Guide des 400 Jardins Publics de Paris (Jacques Barozzi), Éditions Hervas, 1992

The Most Beautiful Walk in the World: A Pedestrian in Paris (John Baxter), Short Books, 2012

Rough Guide to Paris (Ruth Blackmore), Penguin Books, 2012

Paris sacré: 100 Lieux à découvrir (Agnès & Jean-Stéphane Bonneton & Denise Glück), Christine Bonneton 2007

The Definitive Guide to the Da Vinci Code Paris Walks (Peter Caine), Orion Books, 2006

Walking Paris: Thirty Original Walks In and Around Paris (Gilles Desmons), New Holland Publishing, 2008

Paris City Guide (Steve Fallon), Lonely Planet, 2011

The Companion Guide to Paris (Anthony Glynn), Companion Guides, 2000

Paris. Cours et ruelles de charme (Hélène Hatte),Christine Bonneton, 2010

Paris. 300 façades pour les curieux (Hélène Hatte & Frédéric Tran),Christine Bonneton, 2008

Historic Paris Walks (Leo Hollis), Cadogan Guides, 2006

Pariswalks (Sonia, Alison & Rebecca Landes), Owl Books, 2005

Paris: A Literary Companion (Ian Littlewood), John Murray, 2001

Paris Discovered: Explorations in the City of Light (Mary McAuliffe), Princeton Book Company, 2006

Nairn's Paris (Ian Nairn), Penguin Books, 1968

Paris Movie Walks: Ten Guided Tours Through the City of Lights! Camera! Action! (Michael Schurmann), The Intrepid Traveller, 2009

Eyewitness Travel Guide Paris (Alan Tillier), Dorling Kindersley, 2012

Time Out Paris (Various), Time Out Guides, 2012

The Impressionists' Paris: Walking Tours of the Artists' Studios, Homes, and the Sites they Painted (Ellen Williams), The Little Bookroom, 1999

SECRET PARIS

Métiers rares et insolite à Paris (Sybil Canac), Massin Charles, 2008

Un Soir Insolite à Paris (Jean-Laurent Cassely), Editions Jonglez, 2007

Secret Gardens of Paris (Alexandra D'Arnoux & Gilles de Chabaneix), Thames & Hudson, 2001

Paris: 100 Jardins Insolites (Martine Dumond), Christine Bonneton, 2006

Paris, 300 lieux pour curieux (Vincent Formery & Thomas Jonglez), Christine Bonneton, 2009

Secret Paris (Jacques Garance & Maud Ratton), Editions Jonglez, 2012

Curiosités de Paris (Dominique Lesbros), Parigramme, 2012

Découvertes Insolites Autour de Paris (Dominique Lesbros), Parigramme, 2005

Eccentric France (Piers Letcher), Bradt Travel Guides, 2003

Curiosités botaniques à Paris et en Ile-de-France (Anne-Marie Minvielle), Parigramme, 2005

Guide des curiosités funéraires à Paris (Anne-Marie Minvielle), Parigramme, 2008

Quiet Corners of Paris (Jean-Christophe Napais & Christophe Lefébure), The Little Bookroom, 2007

Offbeat Paris – Hidden Tourist Gems of Paris and the Îsle de France (Hugh Oram), Exposure Publishing/Diggory Press, 2006

Paris Secrets et Mystères (Khaitzine Richard), Le Mercure Dauphinois, 2004

Paris Secret et Insolite (Rodolphe Trouilleux), Parigramme, 2012

Guide du Paris Mystérieux (Various), Éditions Sand (2001)

Paris Secret (Various), Gallimard, 2007

Quiet Paris (Siobhan Wall), Frances Lincoln, 2013

HISTORY

Paris After the Liberation 1944-49 (Anthony Beevor & Artemis Cooper), Penguin, 2007

Paris: Histoire d'Hier à Demain (Armand Bindi & Daniel Lefeuvre), Editions Ouest-France, 1990

Is Paris Burning? (Larry Collins & Dominique Lapierre), Little, Brown & Company, 1991

The Invention of Paris: A History in Footsteps (Eric Hazan), Verso Books, 2011

The Days of the French Revolution (Christopher Hibbert), William Morrow, 1999

Paris: Capital of the World (Patrice Higgonet; translated by Arthur Goldhammer), Belknap Press, 2002

The Siege of Paris: The Siege and the Commune 1870-71 (Alastair Horne), Penguin, 2007

Transforming Paris: The Life and Labours of Baron Haussmann (David P. Jordan), The Free Press, 1995

The Sun King (Nancy Mitford), Vintage Classics, 2011

Footprints in Paris – A few streets, a few lives (Gillian Tindall), Chatto & Windus, 2009

The Heroic City: Paris 1945-1958 (Rosemary Wakeman), University of Chicago Press, 2009

ILLUSTRATED BOOKS

Paris by Light (Herve Champollion & Aude de Toqueville), Harry N. Abrams, 2007

Paris – Portrait of a City (Jean-Claude Gautrand), Taschen, 2011

Paris Secrets: Architecture, Interiors, Quartiers, Corners (Janelle McCulloch), Images Publishing Group, 2009

Paris: 500 Photos (Maurice Subervie & Bertrand Delanoe), Flammarions, 2003

ARCHITECTURE AND MUSEUMS

Guides des Cimetières Parisiens (Jacques Barozzi), Éditions Hervas, 1990

Mansions of Paris (Olivier Blanc & Joachim Bonnemaison), Terrail, 1998

Les Cimetières de Paris: Promenade Insolite, Pittoresque et Capricieuse (Michel Dansel), Éditions Denoël, 1987

Les Cimetières Artistiques de Paris, (Josette Jacquin-Philippe), Éditions Léonce Laget, 1993

Little-Known Museums in and Around Paris (Rachel Kaplan), Harry N. Abrams, 1996

Guides des Cimetières de Paris (Marcel le Clère), Hachette, 1990

Musées insolites de Paris (Dominique Lesbros & Sylvain Ageorges), Parigramme, 2011

Guide Pittoresque et Occulte des Cimetières Parisiens (Pierre Mariel), La Table Ronde, 1972

Guide des curiosités funéraires à Paris : Cimetières, églises et lieux de mémoire (Anne-Marie Minvielle), Parigramme, 2008

Royal Châteaux of Paris (Vivian Rowe), Putnam, 1956

SUBTERRANEAN PARIS

Paris Catacombes (Marie-France Arnold), Romillat, 1993

Atlas du Paris Souterrain (Alain Clement & Gilles Thomas), Éditeur, 2001

Paris by Metro: An Underground History (Arnold Delaney), Chastleton Travel, 2006

Les Catacombes de Paris (Delphine Cerf & David Babinet), Éditions Moulenq, 1994

Paris Souterrain (Émile Gérard), DMI, 1991

Histoire Secrète du Paris Souterrain (Simon Lacordaire), Hachette, 1982

Subterranean Cities: The World Beneath Paris and London 1800-1945 (David L. Pike), Cornell University Press, 2005

Paris Sewers and Sewermen (Donald Reid), Harvard University Press, 1993

À la Découverte des Souterrains de Paris (Patrick Saletta), Sidès, 1990

Catacombes et Carrières de Paris: Promenade Sous la Capitale (René Suttel), Éditions du Treuil, 1993

RESTAURANTS, MARKETS AND SHOPS

The Hidden Arcades of Paris (Ann Alter & Alison Harris), Little Bookroom, 2009

Boutiques Anciennes de Paris (Sybil Canac), Massin Charles, 2010

Passages Couverts de Paris (Sybil Canac & Bruno Cabanis), Massin Charles, 2011

Passages Couverts Parisiens (Jean-Claude Delorme), Parigramme, 1996

Secret Bars & Restaurants in Paris (Jacques Garance & Stéphanie Rivoal), Editions Jonglez, 2007

Paris et ses Passages Couverts (Guy Lambert), Éditions du Patrimoine, 2010

Markets of Paris (Dixon and Ruthann Long), The Little Bookroom, 2012

Les Passages Couverts de Paris (Patrice de Moncan), Éditions de Mécène, 2012

Paris – Restaurants and More (Angelika Taschen), Taschen, 2007

Paris – Shops and More (Angelika Taschen), Taschen, 2007

Au vrai zinc parisien (François Thomazeau & Sylvain Ageorges), Parigramme, 2009

The Authentic Bistros of Paris (François Thomazeau), The Little Bookroom, 2005

The Brasseries of Paris (François Thomazeau), The Little Bookroom, 2007

Unusual Shopping in Paris (Jeanne Valère), Editions Jonglez, 2007

Historic Restaurants of Paris (Ellen Williams), The Little Bookroom, 2005

FICTION

Paris Peasant (Louis Aragon), Jonathan Cape, 1971

Les Misérables (Victor Hugo), Signet, 1987

Notre-Dame de Paris (The Hunchback of Notre-Dame) (Victor Hugo), Penguin Classics, 1978

The Phantom of the Opera (Gaston Leroux), Oxford University Press, 2012

WEBSITES

www.parisinfo.com (Official website of the Tourism Office of Paris)

www.paris.fr (City of Paris official portal)

www.ratp.fr (Paris public transport authority)

www.paris-museums.org (The Museums of Paris)

www.paris-walking-tours.com (Private guided walking tours)

www.paris-walks.com (Guided English-language walking tours)

www.parisinconnu.com/promenades (Walks in unknown Paris)

www.parisfacecachee.fr (Tours of rarely-seen locations in Paris)

www.parisisinvisible.blogspot.com (A celebration of Paris off the beaten track)

www.soyouthinkyouknowparis.com (More Paris off the beaten track)

www.journee-du-patrimoine-paris.fr (Annual historic open days in Paris)

www.paris-historique.org (Association pour la Sauvegarde et la Mise en valeur du Paris historique)

www.go-paris.fr (Architectural tours of Paris)

www.secretsofparis.com (The hidden side of the City of Light)

www.meetingthefrench.com (Opportunities to work with artists and artisans in Paris)

www.parisiendunjour.fr (Meet with a Parisian and discover their Paris for a day)

www.creativeparis.com (Creative tourism in Paris)

www.gavroche-pere-et-fils.fr (Locations related to Paris Mondial)

www.lafabriquedeparis.blogspot.com (Industrial sites in Paris)